Essential Computer Applications

 Databases, Spreadsheets, Word Processing
and the Internet

Third Edition

 Gerard Morgan and Séamus O'Neill

Gill & Macmillan

Gill & Macmillan Ltd
Hume Avenue, Park West
Dublin 12
with associated companies throughout the world
www.gillmacmillan.ie

© Gerard Morgan and Séamus O'Neill 2000
© Artwork, Marketing By Design
0 7171 2977 2
Print origination in Ireland by Graham Thew Design

The paper used in this book is made from the wood pulp of managed forests. For every tree felled, at least one tree is planted, thereby renewing natural resources.

The data files mentioned throughout this book can be found at:
www.gillmacmillan.ie/eca

Contents

Acknowledgments

We would like to acknowledge all the people who made this book possible, in particular: Mr Philip Galvin, Principal, Crumlin College of Business and Technical Studies. The staff and students of Crumlin College for their co-operation, especially computer applications classes for their tireless testing of assignments; Mr A. Clifford, Mr D. Cooney, Mr D. Cox and Mr J.T. Smyth for their advice and encouragement; Mr Hubert Mahony and all the staff of Gill & Macmillan.

From G. Morgan, special thanks to Mary, Darragh and Oisín, for their support and encouragement. From S. O'Neill, special thanks to Caroline for her support and encouragement.

Dedicated to our parents

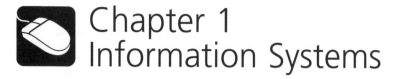

Chapter 1
Information Systems

Before deciding to explore the four application areas outlined in this book, we must have some basic background knowledge of computing. To use a comparison: before beginning to drive a car on the road we need to have some idea of the working of gears and other equipment in the car. We also need to know the rules of the road. Similarly, before using computers we should know about the equipment and procedures we are likely to use.

This chapter will cover the following areas:
1. An introduction to information
2. Hardware
3. Data communications
4. Software
5. Data processing
6. The Information Technology environment

▦ 1. An introduction to information

1.1 Data and information

The distinction between data and information is important.

Data is the term used to describe basic raw facts about activities of a business. These facts are subsequently used to produce useful information. Examples of data would include the hours worked by an individual, the rate of pay and the quantity of goods ordered by a customer.

Information is obtained when data is assembled or processed in a meaningful and useful way. Examples of information would include the average overtime hours in a year, the total payroll expense for the year and a trading profit and loss account.

Data processing to produce information

Manual data processing

Data processing on computer

1.2 Types of information

Information has no value in itself. Its value is derived from its ability to assist and improve decision making. Information is now considered so important that it is regarded as a factor of production in addition to land, labour, enterprise and capital. There are three main reasons why information is needed in organisations.

1. It is necessary to keep a record of events in the company in order to maintain its operational activities. Employees must be paid, invoices must be sent to customers and retained for billing, and statistical information must be kept for the government. This type of information is referred to as **transactional** or **operational information** (see information flows diagram on p. 4).

2. Those responsible for running the organisation need information about what is happening in order to plan and control activities. They need to know the cost of stock, the lead times, machine efficiency and level of sales in order to get an indication of current performance and improve in the future. This information is used by middle management. It is referred to as **tactical information**.

3. Historical information and business environmental information needs to be retained to plan for long term development and forecasts and to maintain competitive advantage. Management need to know summary accounting data, information on competitors and market trends. Using this information long-term decisions can be made, such as how the business should be financed, what business should the organisation be in and how to compete successfully in the market. This type of information is referred to as **strategic information**.

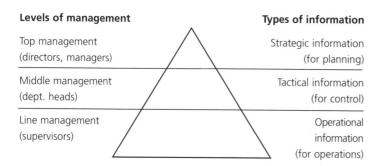

Levels of management

Top management (directors, managers)

Middle management (dept. heads)

Line management (supervisors)

Types of information

Strategic information (for planning)

Tactical information (for control)

Operational information (for operations)

The information pyramid

As you go down the pyramid:
1. More *structured* information is required
2. More *internal* information is required
3. More *detailed* information is required
4. More *historical* information is required
5. More *repetitive* information is required.

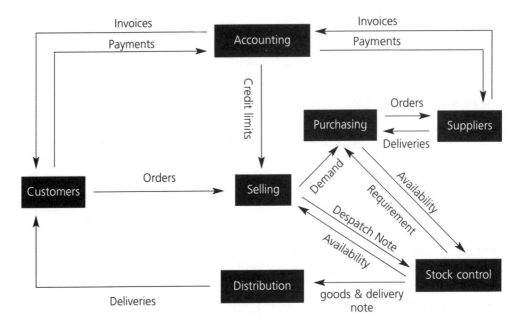

Information flows (simplified) in a non-manufacturing organisation

1.3 Attributes of good information

Good information is that which is used and which creates value. Good information should have the following characteristics.

◣Relevant

The information must be relevant for the purpose. Often information given or produced is irrelevant. This can make understanding more difficult.

◣Concise

The preference is for 'need to know' information rather than 'nice to know information'. The general rule is to give as little information as possible consistent with effective use. This is often called exception reporting, e.g. where only major or important differences between actual figures and budgets are reported.

◣Accurate

The information must be sufficiently accurate for the purpose. The level of accuracy will depend on the decision level involved. Transactional information may need to be very accurate (down to the nearest penny or second). Strategic information does not need such accuracy.

◪Complete
The information must be complete. This requires close liaison with information providers and users.

◪Timing
Good information is that which is communicated in time to be used, otherwise the information will be useless.

◪Clarity
Clarity is improved by the use of different presentation techniques such as graphs, photographs, insert diagrams and three-dimensional models.

◪Cost Effective
The value or benefit to the organisation of obtaining the information should exceed the cost of acquiring it, i.e. cost effective = benefits from information > cost of information.

For information to have value it must result in some benefit e.g. reduced costs, gained competitive advantage, increased sales, prevented fraud. It is often difficult to directly compare costs and benefits as some of the benefits can be intangible (difficult to quantify). However, cost/benefit analysis can be carried out to calculate the net benefit of a new information system. This involves calculating all the costs of the new system and comparing it with the future benefits of the system. The process uses a variety of mathematical techniques such as net present value, payback period calculations, cash flow and internal rates of returns figures.

Examples of typical costs of a new information system may include:
- Equipment costs — hardware
- Software costs
- Installation costs — new buildings, wiring, special conditions
- Development costs — consultancy, systems analysis fees, testing, programmers fees
- Personnel Costs — training, new staff, redundancy, relocation
- Operating costs — consumerables, maintenance, rent, power, backup, data transmission.

Examples of possible benefits of a new system may include:

Tangible benefits
- saving in staff costs
- less wastage
- space saving
- better control over stock

Intangible benefits
- competitive advantage
- quicker response time to customers
- greater customer satisfaction
- improved staff morale
- better decision making.

◼Feedback loop in an Information System

In any system it is very important to make certain that the system is regulated and controlled to ensure it is performing optimally. Standards or goals are often set as guidelines for acceptable performance or output. A control mechanism allows the output of the system to be compared to the standard. Any deviations from the standard are acted upon and fed back into the system. This is referred to as the feedback loop.

System with a feedback loop

Elements of the feedback loop:

1. A standard or goal is set for the system output.
2. A measure of the actual output is made by a sensor.
3. A comparison of the actual output with the standard set is made by the control mechanism.
4. A report of the deviations from the standard is considered.
5. An appropriate action is taken which is then fed back into the system.

◼Exception Reporting

Exception reporting is where management only become involved in an activity when it falls outside the range of acceptable performance standards. In order to manage by exception, reporting upper and lower limits must be set. Output within the limits requires no action from management.

For example a standard production rate of 2000-2200 shirts is set for daily production for a clothing manufacturer. A manager will only follow up on variations outside of this range, below 2000 or above 2200 units.

Advantages of exception reporting:

1. Managers do not waste time monitoring activity that is progressing normally.
2. Fewer decisions need to be made.
3. Attention can be given to both positive and negative deviations.
4. Computer systems are especially suited to exception monitoring.

Disadvantages of exception reporting:

1. Not always easy to set workable standards.
2. This method is not proactive but reactive. Proactivity may be needed to anticipate problems before they happen.

Types of Information Systems

There are many different types of information systems and they can vary in complexity and scope. Here are some examples of such systems.

◼Personal Information System

A personal information system is necessary to carry out everyday activities in our daily lives. Such information may include:

- a diary of appointments and special dates
- names, addresses, phone numbers
- personal accounts
- travel timetables
- work schedules
- recipe book
- manuals
- contents of a filofax
- watch

By using these sources of information we can conduct our normal day to day activities. The information could be highly structured and stored on a PC or diary or it could all be in our memory.

◼Transaction Processing System (TPS)

A TPS is necessary for the day to day running of a *business*. As transactions occur within the organisation the data and information must be immediately recorded and maintained on file. Typically these include all forms of accounting ledger updates, invoicing, credit control and stock control.

Transaction processing systems process high volumes of routine structured data. The information generated from these systems provides information, which is most useful for line managers or supervisors and it forms the basis for all other information systems.

◼Management Information System (MIS)

MIS is a general term used to describe a computer system that converts data from external and internal sources into information, which can be communicated to all levels of managers. This information enables managers to make timely and informed decisions.

Management information systems are the controlling mechanism for the entire organisation. A MIS includes all management information including TPS, Decision Support Systems and Expert Systems.

◪Decision Support Systems (DSS)

The main aim of DSS is to *support* managers when making decisions. Most problems suited to DSS are in a non-structured form (not routinely produced by the system). In order to make decisions managers must construct models or query databases to generate information to aid decision making. Using a variety of tools and procedures the manager can generate this information. These tools include modelling software, spreadsheets, forecasting programs, large interactive database management systems and Expert Systems.

A simple example might include managers using spreadsheet software to develop 'what if' financial models such as evaluating different investment options or calculating the cost benefit calculations for a number of different alternative computer systems.

Applications of DSS:
- Accounting Models — estimating future results using accounting rules e.g. budgeting
- Risk Analysis
- Optimisation Models — calculating optimal results under different constraints e.g. production planning
- Adhoc Data Analysis — unusual/extraordinary queries on a database.

◪Expert Systems (ES)

An Expert System is a computer program, which draws upon the knowledge of human experts captured in a knowledge base to solve problems that normally require human expertise. Unlike DSS, which *supports decisions*, the ES *make decisions*.

Expert Systems contain three elements.

Knowledge base

The base consists of facts, theories, relationships, rules (including subconscious rules) observations, definitions and other types of information gathered from experts, textbooks and manuals. Knowledge engineers gather this information onto common databases.

Inference Engine

This is the computer program, which provides the reasoning capability. These programs use artificial intelligence software systems to make decisions. It allows for searches, reasoning and allows conclusions or inferences to be made from the rules and knowledge base.

User Interface/Justifier

This allows the software to clarify information from the user.

Example: Eye Disease Diagnosis Expert System.

This is a medical diagnosis system for eye related illness. The non-specialist user keys in symptoms of the patient and the system will try to make a diagnosis. The system will use its knowledge base and inference engine and prompt the user for more information regarding symptoms to clarify its diagnosis. This system has been used in place of specialist medical staff in remote locations all around the world.

Applications of Expert Systems:

- Credit card issue systems
- Insurance claims
- Complex fault finding/diagnosis
- Farming advice
- Medical diagnosis.

◩ Qualitative Information (Soft)

Qualitative Information is information that is gathered from direct observation, opinions and case studies. The nature of the information may not always be factually true. The purpose of this type of information is to get an in-depth understanding of something and is exploratory in nature. The information is usually in the form of narrative. This form of information is very difficult to analyse or computerise. However, Expert Systems often use such information in their expert knowledge base.

Example:

In depth interview details from shop floor workers on the problems associated with new work practices, or a list of rules (conscious or subconscious) that an expert uses to find a fault on a machine.

◩ Quantitative Information (Hard)

This form of information is a collection of facts and records of actual happenings. The main purpose for gathering this information is to control activities and inform decisions. Most data capture techniques will record this type of information. In businesses this is the most common form of information.

Example:

Most business transactions generate this form of information.

▦ 2. Hardware

A computer is a programmable electronic device that can store and process data and information and display the results. The term 'hardware' is used to refer to any physical part of a computer system, such as the keyboard, the monitor, the printer, or the disk drive.

2.1 Types of computer systems

Computer systems are usually divided into three main categories according to their processing capabilities.

◢Mainframe computers

Mainframe computers (or 'mainframes') are large, powerful computers that many people can use at the same time. They are also the most expensive systems. They are used for very large processing tasks, and perform many important business and government applications.

◢Minicomputers

These are smaller and more compact systems, and fewer operators can use them compared with a mainframe computer. They are usually found in medium-sized businesses or in divisions within a large organisation, e.g. in government departments.

◢Microcomputers

Microcomputers — also called 'personal computers' (PCs) — are small, self-contained computers that fit on a desk-top and are usually only used by one person. They are the least expensive type, and are widely used in businesses for a variety of tasks, such as word processing, small database management and spreadsheets. They are also used as home computers, for family budgeting and similar tasks, as well as for games.

For the purposes of this book we will be concentrating on microcomputers. However, much of the information here is also applicable to other computer systems. Also, as computers become more powerful and at the same time smaller, this division by size is becoming less useful. In particular, the distinction between mainframe computers and minicomputers is sometimes hard to draw; while at the same time a number of microcomputers joined together or 'networked' can perform many of the functions associated with minicomputers.

2.2 Parts of a typical microcomputer system

The **keyboard** is used to get the information into the computer. The **CPU** is used to process this information, e.g. to do calculations. The **monitor** is used to display the result and the **printer** produces a copy of this display. The **disk drives** make it possible for the information (and programs) to be stored on disks for further use.

2.3 The four-stage model of a computer

In general, then, we can say that a computer has four main components:
- the hardware used to enter data, called **input devices**
- the hardware that produces results from entered data, called the **processor**
- the hardware that display the results, called **output devices**
- the hardware used to store this information for later retrieval, called **auxiliary storage** or **backing storage**.

All the pieces of hardware outside the processor are called **peripherals**.

2.4 Input hardware

◪Keyboard

This is the most common means of entering data. It consists of an array of **keys** or switches, each one producing a particular character on the display when it is pressed. The character keys have a standard layout on all computer keyboards, called the 'QWERTY' layout after the first six letters on the top row; additional keys can include **cursor keys**, **function keys** and editing keys. The 'enter' key is used to implement a command or, in word processing, to mark the end of a paragraph. The 'escape' key is often used to cancel an operation.

◤Mouse

This is a small pointing device connected by a wire to the computer (it vaguely resembles a real mouse!). It is moved about by hand on a flat surface, and the cursor on the screen follows its movements. Buttons on the top of the mouse can also be used to select options. Where used: various 'user-friendly' (easy-to-use) programs, especially graphics.

◤Scanner

Most consumer products now have bar codes on them. A scanner can read these codes by scanning the pattern of lines; this allows the product code to be entered without keyboarding. Scanners are also used for inputting whole pages of text and pictures into a computer. Where used: supermarkets; libraries.

◤Light-pen

This is another pointing device, resembling a pen with a small light on the end. It is used to point to parts of a display to select options. Where used: some 'user-friendly' applications, especially graphics.

◤Magnetic card reader

This is a machine that reads data from the magnetic strip on a plastic card. Where used: cash dispensing machines (ATM); employee access to buildings.

◪Voice data entry (VDE)

Using a microphone connected to the computer, different commands or letters can be called out and then interpreted by special programs. Major advancements have been made in VDE technology for personal computers in recent times. It is now possible for a user to dictate whole documents and commands directly into the computer. Where used: word processing application (text entry) laboratories; computers for the physically handicapped.

◪Optical character recognition (OCR)

This is an input method where a scanner is used to read the text of a document directly into the computer. Special typefaces that the machine recognises can be used, although modern systems can now read ordinary typefaces. Where used: processing of customer bills that have been received with payment; reading of authors' typescripts directly into typesetting systems.

◪Magnetic-ink character recognition (MICR)

Numerals of a special design can be printed with an ink that contains tiny pieces of magnetisable material, and these can then be read into the computer by a special scanner. The numbers along the bottom of a cheque are used by the computer to update a customer's bank account. They include code numbers representing the bank and branch, the customer account number, the number of the cheque (all of which are printed on each page of the cheque book before it is issued to the customer) and the amount (printed on the cheque after it has been presented to the bank). Where used: cheque books and other bank documents.

◩Optical mark recognition (OMR)

With this system a reader connected to the computer can detect the presence or absence of a mark, with the position of the mark determining the value entered. Where used: National Lottery; electricity meter reading; multi-choice examination questions.

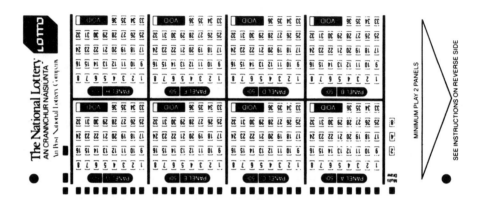

◩Touch-sensitive screen

The screen displays choices and instructions, and the user simply touches the symbol representing the desired choice. Where used: information screens in banks and shopping centres.

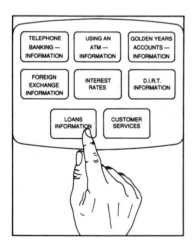

There are many other methods of entering data into a computer for processing. The choice of the most suitable input device depends on the nature of the data to be entered and the environment where the data is generated. A summary of the input devices described above is given on p.15.

	Speed	Volume of input	Advantages	Disadvantages	Where used
			SUMMARY OF INPUT DEVICES		
Keyboard	slow	medium	• standard QWERTY keyboard which people are familiar with	• slow • error prone	• text/data entry
OCR	fast	medium	• no keying required	• scanner and software are expensive • quality of document is important	• archiving • text entry • turnaround documents
OMR	fast	large	• no keying • less errors than keying • easy to complete	• special stationery required	• multi-choice examinations • meter reading • census recording • lotto
MICR	fast	large	• used as standard in world-wide banking • secure as writing over them does not affect the numbers read in	• need to post code cheques	• cheques • giros • travellers cheques
Bar codes	fast	small	• fast • less errors	• expensive hardware and software required	• retail stores • libraries
Light-pen	fast	small	• easy to use	• special screen required • limited use	• graphics
Magnetic card	fast	small	• easy to use • portable • secure	• limited amount of data storage on the card	• ATM card • clock cards
Mouse	fast	small	• easy to use	• limited – pointing device	• GUI-based software
Touch sensitive screens	fast	small	• very user friendly • no keying required	• limited – pointing device	• tourist information • banks
VDE	fast	large	• no keying • can move around while entering data	• expensive software • large memory requirements	• laboratories • word processing • handicapped
Scanner for text/pictures	fast	large	• easy to use • no keying	• large memory requirements	• DTP • word processing • printing

2.5 Processing hardware

◪The central processing unit (CPU)

This is where all calculations and manipulations of the data are carried out: it could be considered the 'brain' of the computer. The CPU is contained on a tiny integrated circuit or 'microchip' that carries a large number of minute electronic circuits. The speed at which the CPU manipulates data is measured in megahertz (MHz) or the number of million cycles per second. For example, a 600 MHz computer has a clock which 'ticks' and 'tocks' 600 million times each second. Each tick-tock is called a cycle. These cycles co-ordinate the movement of data inside the CPU.

There are three main areas in the CPU: the control unit, the arithmetic and logic unit (ALU) and the main storage or 'memory'.

1. The **control unit** takes instructions in a given sequence (rather like a set of traffic lights at a cross-roads) and controls the movement of data inside the computer.
2. The **arithmetic and logic unit (ALU)** performs mathematical functions and logical decisions, such as deciding whether one number is greater than another.
3. The **main storage or 'memory'** allows data to be stored for processing purposes, and holds the results. It also stores programs or sets of instructions. It is similar to our own memory. If you are asked to add three numbers without using pen and paper you would first have to put the numbers into your memory, and then add them. So too with computers. In order to perform any calculations or processes the computer must first have in its memory the data that is required.

A microchip containing the control unit and the ALU is called a **microprocessor**.

◪Computer memory

There are two types of main storage: **read-only memory (ROM)** and **random-access memory (RAM)**.

The read-only memory (ROM) may not be written to by the computer system. The contents of ROM are entered at the time of manufacture and cannot be changed by the user. When the computer is turned off, this information is not lost; this form of storage is referred to as **'non-volatile memory'**. The information normally only takes up a small amount of the total memory of the computer. There are however some variations of ROM chips, namely PROM and EPROM chips. PROM (programmable ROM) is a chip which can be written to once by the user after its manufacture but is fixed once it has been written to. EPROM (erasable PROM) is a special type of PROM which can be erased using ultraviolet light.

The random-access memory (RAM) is memory that may be read from and written to by the programmer or user. It contains information currently being worked on. In our example above, the three numbers to be added would be contained in RAM while the calculation is being performed. Once the calculation has been completed new data can be entered into RAM. RAM could be compared to an erasable note-pad: the user can read the information from this memory and (unlike ROM) can change its contents. When the computer is switched off, however, this memory is completely cleared; this form of storage is known as **'volatile memory'**. Before you turn off you computer, always make sure to save your data if you want it for another day!

◤The representation of data

How is the data inside the computer represented? Computers can only understand the numerals 1 and 0 symbolising the presence (1) or absence (0) of an electrical pulse inside the computer. How, then, can computers deal with other numbers, letters, and words?

Each character (numeral, letter or symbol) on the keyboard has its own unique code number. For example, the capital letter A has a character number 65. (The character numbers are allocated by an international agreement, which was based on an earlier one called the American Standard Code for Information Interchange (ASCII), and they are often still referred to as ASCII code — pronounced 'askey'.) The character numbers do not have to be known by the user: the computer automatically reads them when each key is pressed. The computer converts each character code into this 1 and 0 form, known as a binary number. For the letter A (character 65) this is 01000001. All the data inside the computer is made up of thousands of these pulses or no-pulses of electricity moving in and out of the memory very rapidly.

Each character is thus represented by a binary number, made up of a series of 1s and 0s. Each single 1 or 0 is called a bit, which is the smallest possible element in a computer memory. A group of bits of the size that a particular computer handles — usually eight — is called a byte.

◤Memory capacity

Computer capacity is expressed in terms of the maximum number of bytes or characters the computer can hold in RAM at any time for processing. This capacity is measured in a unit of 1,024 bytes (2^{10}), called a kilobyte (KB) — sometimes also referred to simply as 'K' — or a unit of 1,024 kilobytes, called a megabyte (MB) — approximately 1 million bytes. Thus a computer that has a RAM of 64MB can keep in its memory at any time a maximum of approximately 64,000,000 characters. Personal computers typically have RAM capacities ranging from 64MB to 128MB.

Summary Chart of Memory Capacities

Term	Symbol	Value	Approx value
Bit	b	0 or 1	————
Byte	B	8 bits	————
Kilobyte	KB	1024 bytes (2^{10})	One thousand bytes
Megabyte	MB	1048576 bytes	One million bytes
Gigabyte	GB	1073741824 bytes	One billion bytes
Terabyte	TB	1099511627776 bytes	One thousand billion bytes

Having more RAM available in a computer means that it can manage more data and can also accommodate larger applications programs, thus making it more useful for processing purposes. When buying a computer you should be sure that is has adequate memory capacity for your requirements.

A hardware device is said to be on-line when it is connected to the CPU of the computer and under its control. A device is off-line if it is not under the control of the CPU.

2.6 Output hardware

When information has been entered and processed by the computer, we obviously need to see the result. Output devices allow this data to be viewed.

◪ Monitor

The monitor, also called a **visual display unit (VDU)** or screen, is the most common means of displaying computer information. There are many sizes and types of monitor.

A monochrome screen displays only one colour, often green or amber on black, or black on white, whereas a colour screen can usually display up to 200 different colours. A low-resolution screen, mainly used to display text, has a relatively small number of 'pixels' (the dots that make up an image). A high-resolution screen, often used to display graphics, contains more pixels. Examples of high-resolution displays are those of the VGA (video graphics array) or SVGA (super video graphics array) types.

Instead of the traditional cathode-ray tube (CRT), some screens use a liquid crystal display (LCD), like that on digital watches and calculators. These screens are flat and more compact, and are often used for portable ('note book') computers.

The problem with LCD screens is that they cannot be seen if looked at from an angle. With gas plasma screens the display has a glow, allowing it to be seen from any angle, while also being compact.

◪ Printers

The problem with a display is that it is only temporary: when the computer is switched off, the display is lost! Printers allow the information to be put onto paper, creating a permanent and portable display. The output from a printer on paper is called a print-out or sometimes **'hard copy'**.

There are several types of computer printer. They are sometimes classified as impact printers (those that print characters by striking the paper through an inked ribbon: e.g. dot-matrix printers) and non-impact printers (those where the print head does not make contact with the paper: e.g. laser and ink-jet printers).

Dot-matrix printers use a series of print combs that strike the ribbon to produce a character made up of a pattern of dots. These printers are cheap, but are quite slow, and do not usually produce high quality. The more dots making up the character the better the image;

better dot-matrix printers can produce characters made up of twenty-four or more dots, and this output is described as near-letter-quality (NLQ).

Dot-matrix printing mechanism (moving head)

Ink-jet printers are very popular at present. They work by sending a finely controlled jet of ink onto the paper to produce the required characters. They are very quiet and produce excellent quality print.

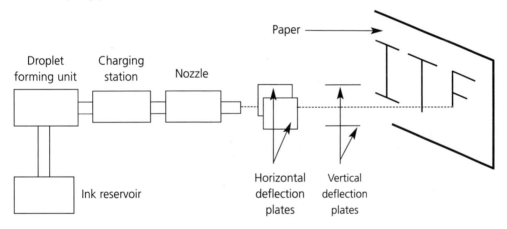

Ink-jet Printer

The mode of operation of **laser** (**l**ight **a**mplification by **s**timulated **e**mission of **r**adiation) printers is similar to that of photocopiers. They produce very high-quality printing and are extremely fast; however, they are expensive to buy and to run.

Drum printers contain characters on a metal drum. The drum hits the ribbon which then produces the image. They are called line printers as the entire character set is repeated 180 times across the drum.

Drum Printer

Chain printers contain characters on a fast revolving metal chain. Again they are impact printers.

Chain Printer

◼Plotters

These are output devices which allow lines to be drawn using different colour pens. There are two basic types: the **flatbed** type where the pen moves up, down, across or to the side along a flat surface and the **drum plotter** where the paper is wrapped around a drum.

The output of low-speed printers is measured by the number of characters they can print per second (cps). The output of high-speed printers is usually measured in lines or pages per minute (lpm or ppm).

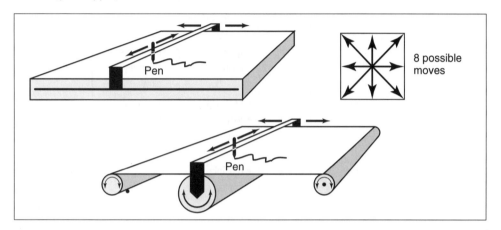

Flatbed plotter (above) and drum plotter

◼Printer paper

Most printers can use two types of paper: fan-fold paper, and sheets.

Fan-fold paper consists of one long sheet perforated at intervals and folded alternately backwards and forwards on the perforations. It is fed into the printer by means of the small holes on the side of the paper (this is called 'tractor feed'). After printing, the sections are pulled apart to form pages of standard (usually A4) size.

Using a 'form feeder', individual sheets of paper, usually A4 size, can be fed into the printer from a tray like that on a photocopier.

◼Computer output on microfiche/film

This is where output is produced on film. This is done by means of a photographic technique where output is projected in a reduced form onto film. The film is not readable by the naked eye and requires a special magnifying reading device.

	Relative speed*	Volume of output	Quality	Advantages	Disadvantages	Where used
					SUMMARY OF OUTPUT DEVICES	
Dot-matrix printer	slow	small	NLQ	• text and graphics output possible • very cheap running cost	• very slow • very noisy • quality can vary	• draft work
Ink-jet printer	slow	medium	LQ	• excellent quality • quiet	• running costs expensive • relatively slow	• low volume/ high quality output
Laser printer	fast	large	LQ (best)	• best quality • very fast • quiet	• running costs expensive	• high volume/ high quality output
Drum printer	fast	large	varies	• multiple copies possible • very fast	• quality can vary	• high volume multiple copy output
Chain printer	fast	large	varies	• multiple copies possible • very fast	• quality can vary	• high volume multiple copy output
Plotters	slow	small	LQ	• attention to detail • different colours and pens	• slow • expensive software and hardware	• graphics • designs
VDU	fast	small	LQ	• no media expense	• temporary display • radiation omissions	• temporary output
COM	fast	large	LQ	• large volume output on small media (space saving/ easier to distribute)	• need special viewing equipment • cannot be edited by hand	• libraries

Slow = 10 CPS to 300 LPM; fast = 300 LPM to 3000 LPM.

2.7 Auxiliary storage

All computer systems can store information for later retrieval. Magnetic disks of various types and sizes are the most common storage medium.

◪Diskettes or 'floppy disks'

Diskettes are small disks made of flexible plastic that is coated with a magnetisable material. These disks are removed from the disk drive when not in use, and can be copied, filed, carried around, or even sent through the post.

The first microcomputer disks had a diameter of 130 mm (5.25 in.) and were enclosed in a strong but flexible plastic envelope (hence the term 'floppy disk'). The modern standard disk has a diameter of 90 mm (3.5 in.) and is completely enclosed in a rigid plastic cartridge.

The information on the disk is stored in the form of spots of magnetisable material, each spot representing one bit (magnetised = 1, unmagnetised = 0). This information is stored on tracks or concentric rings or circles on the disk. There are usually eighty tracks on a 90 mm disk.

Most disks are double-sided (2S), i.e. they have a usable surface on both sides. The amount of information that can be packed onto a disk varies: for example, a 90 mm (3.5in.) 2S-2D disk usually holds about 720KB. A high-density (HD) disk holds approximately 1.5MB.

◪Fixed disks or 'hard disks'

Fixed disks (usually called 'hard disks', in contrast to 'floppy disks') are permanently installed inside the case of the computer. They are made of a hard metal alloy with a magnetisable coating on both sides. These disks can store very large quantities of information of several gigabytes (1 gigabyte (Gb) — 1000 million bytes). They can also access this information much faster than floppy disks.

Hard disk

◨Optical disks

Optical disks are physically similar to the compact disks (CDs) used by the recording industry. They can store up to 650MB of data. The only problem with these disks is that the user can only read information from the disk (read only — CD ROM): it is not possible to record your own information on them. However, there are CDs being developed which can be written to but they are very expensive at present.

◨CD-R disks

It is now possible to get CD-R disks that allow data to be written to the disk. However, once data is written onto the disk it cannot be edited. Also available are CD-RW disks that allow full write and read facilities including editing. However these disks are expensive at present.

◨DVD ROM

A digital versatile disk ROM is an optical, high capacity much improved version of the current CD-ROM technology. Most computer-based DVD drives will allow the playing of DVD video disks as well as data disks and CD-ROM disks.

   The big advantage of DVD disks over CDs is capacity. CD-ROMs have a limited capacity of 650MB of data. Whereas DVDs can store up to 20GB of data. Physically a CD-ROM and a DVD disk are similar. They both store data in the form of tiny pits on the disk surface. These pits are read using a laser beam. The higher capacity of DVD disks is due to smaller pits being used. DVD represents the first coming together of the three technologies, computer, audio, and video into one common format.

   *DVDs have been developed which are recordable, called DVD-R (recordable).

◨Zip Drives

A zip drive is a small, portable disk drive used mainly for backup purposes. The zip disk can hold up to 250MB of information, which is approximately 200 times the capacity of a floppy disk. These disks can be used in the same way as floppy disks and can be written to and changed. Zip disks are becoming very popular because of their portability and capacity. The disks have faster access speeds compared to floppy disks but are slower than hard disks. The main uses of zip disks include:

• storing large files, such as graphics, video clips and audio files
• exchanging large files
• archiving files
• backing up a hard disk.

◼Formatting a disk

A disk is formatted only once — before using it for the first time — and this simply divides the disk into sectors or slices. The procedure is similar to dividing a city into postal districts: the sectors allow data to be stored on specific areas on the disk for easy retrieval. Note: Some floppy discs are pre-formatted when purchased.

Here is an example to illustrate the retrieval method (simplified). When a file or document is stored on the disk it will have to be given a file name. Along with this name the computer will keep a record of where it recorded that file on the disk. For example, the file might be named 'CAR.doc'. When this file is saved the file name will be recorded on the outer track ('file allocation table' ,FAT) of the disk as CAR.doc 712. The number 712 is used to tell the computer where it has stored the file on the disk: 7 means the seventh sector and 12 means the twelfth track. When the computer needs to retrieve this data it will immediately position the read-write head at the twelfth track in the seventh sector.

This method of positioning the read-write head exactly on the spot where the data is stored is called **direct access system (DAS)**. This allows information to be retrieved from disks very rapidly.

◼Care of disks

Magnetic disks must be treated with great care. For this reason, and because of possible loss of data from wear and tear on disks or power failure or hardware problems, you should keep contingency or 'back-up' copies of all data and program files. Back-up disks (which are exact copies of original disks) should be regularly updated, and used only in an emergency.

◼Other storage media

Magnetic tape, similar to that used in tape recorders, can also be used to store computer information. For business use, reel-to-reel tapes and tape streamers are used.

The main disadvantage of tapes is that only serial access is available, compared with the direct access possible with disks. This means that the tape must be wound forward until it reaches the spot where the information is stored, which can take several minutes in certain circumstances.

Magnetic tape is not used very often with business microcomputers, except occasionally for contingency or 'back-up' purposes.

SUMMARY OF BACKING STORAGE DEVICES						
	Floppy disk	**Hard disk**	**Magnetic tape**	**CD-ROM**	**Zip Disk**	**DVD-ROM**
Access speed	slow	fast	varies	fast	fast (slower than hard disk)	fast
Approx. Capacity	1.44MB, 2MB	600MB to 10GB	120MB to 1.25GB	up to 650MB	250MB	4.7GB to 20GB
Method of operation	DAS (direct access system)	DAS	SAS (serial access system)	DAS	DAS	DAS
Where used	microcomputer systems, also to backup	micro, miniframe	mainframe, tape-streamers for backup on micros	micro, mini,	micro backup large files	micro, mini

Hardware Specification Example

Advertisements often display detailed specifications of computers for sale. When considering the choice between one computer and another it is important to understand what the different specifications mean. Here is an example of one such specification and a brief explanation of each item.

PC Specification

700MHZ Pentium 111 processor with MMX technology

128MB SDRAM

17" SVGA screen

20GB hard disk

512K cache memory

8MB 3D AGP x 2 graphics

Internal 56Kbps modem

4 x DVD ROM drive

Windows 2000 preloaded

◪700MHZ Pentium 111 processor with MMX technology
This is the type of Intel CPU chip which uses Multimedia Extensions (MMX) chip enhancements for quicker multimedia communications. The clock speed is 700 million cycles per second. The higher the clock speed of the CPU the quicker the computer can perform tasks.

◪128MB SDRAM
128 million bytes of information can be contained in the memory (Synchronous Dynamic Random Access Memory being the current industry standard). This form of memory RAM has a separate clock signal to the control signals and supports burst access modes.

◪17″ SVGA screen
17″ Super Video Graphics Adapter monitor. This has high resolution capabilities.

◪20GB hard disk
Maximum capacity is 20 billion bytes.

◪512K cache memory
Cache memory is special RAM, which remembers instructions and data that the processor has executed or accessed *previously*. This memory is much faster than SDRAM. This computer has 512KB capacity of this fast memory

◪8MB 3D AGP x 2 graphics
An accelerated graphics port video card is installed. This enables 3D images to access the computer's RAM faster. Graphics and 3D software run faster when this is installed.

◪Internal 56Kbps modem
The modem is contained internally in the casing of the computer. It has a capacity of 56000 bits per second. The modem converts digital signals to analogue and vice versa. This allows the computer to communicate to other computers via the telephone lines. This is essential for e-mail and Internet use.

◪4 x DVD ROM drive
Digital versatile disk 4 times the speed of the original specification of first issue DVDs.

◪Windows 2000 preloaded
Microsoft's graphical user interface operating system is pre-installed.

▦ 3. Data Communications

The basic requirements of any communications systems are:

- a sender of the information
- a receiver of the information
- an encoding system
- a decoding system
- a medium to transmit the message.

Taking the example of two persons communicating over the phone the five requirements or components would be:

- the person making the call
- the person receiving the call
- the language used would be the encoding system
- the decoding system would be the ability of the person receiving the call to comprehend the language
- the medium would be the telephone line.

When communicating via a computer the components would be:

- the sending computer
- the receiving computer
- the **modem** would be the encoding system (the modem converts digital signals from the computer to telephone signals which can be sent over telecommunication lines **(modulation)**
- the decoding would be done by a modem on the other end which converts the telephone signal to digital form to be interpreted by the computer **(demodulation)**
- the medium would be the telephone line.

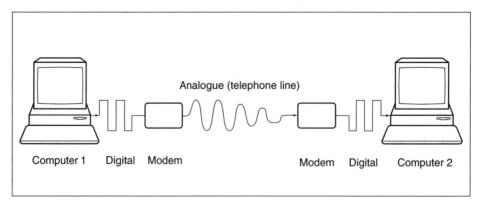

Data transmission and the use of modems

3.1 Communications hardware

◪Modem

A modem (short for modulator/demodulator) is the piece of hardware required to allow two computers to communicate over the normal telecommunication lines. It has a dual function:

- to translate digital information into telephone signals (modulation)
- to translate telephone signals into digital signals (demodulation).

The data transfer rate is the amount of information that can be transmitted along a data channel. The rate is referred to the **baud rate**. The baud rate is the number of bits that can be transmitted per second (bps – beats per second). As a character is normally composed of eight to ten bits a 300 baud line would be capable of transmitting 30 characters per second. Modern modems should have a minimum 28Kbs to 56Kbs baud rate. Modems can be internal (housed in the hard disk), or external.

◪Multiplexor

This is a hardware device which combines data from several sources for transmission down a single line. It can also split data from one line to several other internal communication lines.

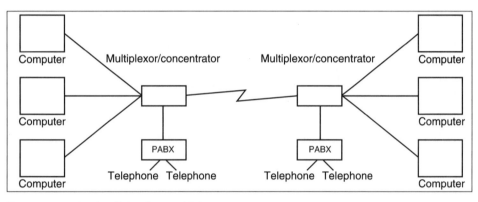

Data communication links via a multiplexor

◪Communication ports

At the back of most computers there are a number of connecting points called ports. These allow the computer to be connected to the keyboard and printer and to other peripheral devices. There are two types of port: serial and parallel.

A **serial port** is a connection point that sends information to or from the CPU one bit after another. This port is usually used to connect the mouse or a modem to the computer.

A **parallel port** is a connection point that sends information one byte at a time, i.e. in groups of eight bits. This port is usually used to connect a printer to the computer.

3.2 Data transmission terms

Simplex link is where communication is possible in one way only (e.g. printer connection).

 Half duplex link is where two-way communication is possible but only in one direction at a time (not simultaneously).

 Full duplex link allows simultaneous two-way communication.

 Synchronous transmission is where bits are sent down the line and this is timed to coincide with the clock pulse of the computer.

 Asynchronous transmission is a high-speed method of transmitting data which is not synchronised by a pulse but requires special start and stop bits.

Serial transmission

0 ◄ 1 ◄ 0 ◄ 0 ◄ 0 ◄ 0 ◄ 0 ◄ 1

Parallel transmission

 ◄ 0
 ◄ 1
 ◄ 0
 ◄ 0
 ◄ 0
 ◄ 0
 ◄ 0
 ◄ 1

Asynchronous transmission

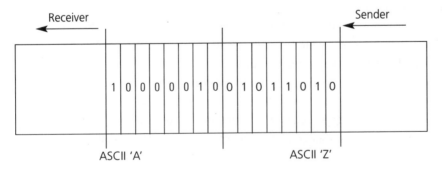

Synchronous transmission

3.3 Networks

A network is a linked set of computer systems capable of sharing computer power and resources. The advantages of networking computers are:

- the ability to share expensive resources such as disks, software, printers and processing power
- the ability to share information, thus avoiding unnecessary duplication
- the ability to communicate directly with others on the network
- the network allows local processing and central control.

◪Types of network

Local area network (LAN)

This is a network which is confined to one local site. External telephone lines are not used. Local cabling such as coaxial or twisted pair cable is used to connect the network.

Wide area network (WAN)

This is a network which is spread over a wide geographical area. It involves the use of telecommunication lines and satellites to connect the computers. These networks are often used to connect external databases or services.

Two methods of transmission are used in WAN communication. **Circuit switching** involves a circuit being made and maintained for the duration of the transmission. Delays often occur when setting up transmission and the line is monopolised for the duration of the transmission. An alternative is to use a method called **packet switching**. This method involves the sending of fixed chunks (packets) of information down the link. It is not necessary to establish a connection with the recipient as the message can be stored forward.

◪Network topologies (configuration)

Star network

The computers are all connected to a central file server through which all messages pass.

Advantages

- Supports dumb terminals
- Central control
- More secure
- Failure of one node will not affect the network

Disadvantages

- Central computer failure means the entire network will be dysfunctional
- Complex software required at hub

Bus Network

Each mode on the network uses a linear communication line (bus) to transmit information. The bus line is not in a loop. It has a terminal box at the end of the bus.

Advantages
- Less cabling required compared with star network
- Fast communication

Disadvantages
- Security problems as data is on the bus all the time (no central control)

Ring network

All nodes are connected together in a ring where none has overall control. Messages are constantly revolving around the loop until they are picked up.

Advantages
- No dependence on central device
- High-speed transmission

Disadvantages
- One-way traffic only
- Repeater to boost the signal often required

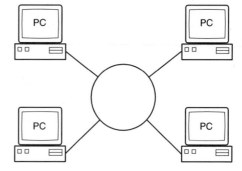

3.4 Modern communication methods

�धTelepHone

Despite the increasing popularity of e-mail the telephone remains the most popular and important method of communications in the office. Telephone technology is also advancing rapidly with such developments as mobile phones, digital phones and PABX exchanges.

▧PABX switchboards

These allow an interface between a group of telephones extensions, teletext devices and computers. They are essentially muliplexors.

Telex

This is a twenty-four-hour communication system. It permits telex users to transmit information to another telex users. All telex messages are received and printed out. Cost is based on an annual rental and a cost per communication.

Advantages
- Printed record of all messages
- Messages may be received when the office is closed
- Legal standing

Disadvantages
- The number of telex users is limited
- Only text can be transmitted

Facsimile transmission (fax)

This is an extremely popular and effective means of communication. Most businesses today have fax machines. These allow pictures, diagrams and text to be transmitted from place to place via the telephone lines. Fax operates in the same way as a photocopier and is often described as a long distance photocopier.

Advantages
- Very fast
- Messages can be received outside office hours
- Text, photos and diagrams can be transmitted
- Very reliable

Disadvantages
- Print quality can vary considerably
- Point-to-point connection must be maintained (no store forward facility)
- The transmission is a copy and hence has no legal standing

Electronic mail (E-mail)

This is the use of computers to transmit information to other computer users. This can be directly to another computer or to a central e-mail box held on a central computer. All e-mail allows for a message to be stored for retrieval at the user's convenience. To send a message the user must have the e-mail address of the receiver. (See chapter 10 for more details.)

Advantages
- Paperless
- Full working documents can be attached
- Fast
- Multiple copies of the same message can be sent to diferent users
- Cheap

Disadvantages
- Computer required by both sender and receiver
- Security

◪Teletext

This is a one-way system where information can be received and displayed on a television screen. A telephone is not required. The information is transmitted across the airways. Examples include CEEFAX, Oracle and Aertel. A teletext adapter must be available in the television but there is no additional charge for the service. The information available on these databases includes weather reports, news, sports reports, subtitles for some programs, jokes and advertising.

Advantages
- No usage fee
- Large databases available without the need for a computer

Disadvantage
- Not interactive, can only receive data

▦4. Software

So far we have discussed the machinery or equipment that makes up a computer system: the 'hardware'. The problem is that if we had all this equipment available to us the computer would still be useless. So what is missing? The answer is programs or 'software'.

The software is the set of instructions that enables the computer to perform its function. A car is useless without instructions to go fast or slow, stop or start. So too a computer is useless without the instructions for performing a particular task. For example, if we want to extract a trial balance from a computer we must first have the accounting program (instructions) in the computer's memory.

4.1 Types of software

There are two types of software that need to be in place before we can use the computer: the **operating system** and **application programs**.

◪The operating system

This is the set of instructions that looks after the internal running of the computer. Its functions include the following:
- providing a user interface to allow the user to give the computer instructions
- managing the memory of the computer as efficiently as possible
- error reporting and error handling

- handling the operation of input, output and backing storage devices
- running application software
- running utilities programs for displaying information on the screen, reading from disks, listing the contents of the disk, formatting disks, copying disks or files and so on.

A common operating system used with IBM microcomputers and other computers based on this design is the Microsoft Disk Operating System (MSDOS — pronounced 'em-ess-doss'). This operating systems has since been transformed to have a graphic user interface where icons (graphic symbols) and pull-down menus are used to select commands. The operating environment is called Microsoft Windows. Other types of microcomputers, such as the Apple Macintosh, have their own operating systems.

These instructions must be in the computer's memory before any other software can function. Programs work by communicating requests to the operating system, which acts as a kind of secretary to the application software.

◪Application programs

Application programs are computer programs that are written to make the computer perform specific tasks, such as:

- word processing
- spreadsheets
- graphics
- database management
- financial accounting
- sales order processing.

Programs that perform specific functions such as these are often called applications (to distinguish them from programs that make the computer itself work more effectively, called the operating system as outlined above). Application programs are written in computer programming languages by large specialist companies, such as Microsoft, Lotus, Claris and Ashton-Tate, and these programs can then be bought 'off the shelf' from computer suppliers. Alternatively, computer programs can be specially written (or customised) for a particular company's needs: this kind of program can be very expensive.

◪Easy-to-use (user friendly) programs

Greater emphasis is placed nowadays on programs that are easy to learn and to use, or 'user-friendly' programs. Some or all of the following features may be found with such programs.

Sound: Sound may be used to signal to the user that a mistake has been made. Sound may also indicate that a task is complete or that the computer is awaiting more data.

Colour or contrast: Colour can highlight displays and improve the presentation of information. With a monochrome monitor changes in contrast can be used instead to highlight various options.

Help facility: The user can give a special command to request help if needed. With some programs, if an error occurs the computer will automatically give the required explanation and offer ways to remedy the mistake. This is called 'on-line help'.

Icons: These are small symbols displayed on the screen to represent commands or options, and are usually selected by using a mouse. This means that complex commands do not have to be remembered.

Menus: The use of menus means that the user is guided through the application.

Program prompts: At no stage during the operation of a program should the user be left not knowing what to do next or in what form the information should be entered. Program prompts are messages telling the user the next action to take or offering choices, such as 'Press any key to continue' or 'Do you want to exit the system (Y/N)?' or 'Do you want to save before exiting?'.

On the other hand poor choice of sound, graphics or colour may not enhance the ease of use of a particular program. Frequent beeps may be a source of irritation to the user, and may distract others working in the same room. The graphics and colour chosen may only serve to cause eye discomfort.

4.2 Programming languages

As a computer can only interpret binary code it is necessary for all programs to be broken down or translated into this form (called the **object program**). All software is generated using programming languages (referred to as the **source code**). There are four generations of programming language, as shown in the table on p.37.

GENERATIONS OF PROGRAMMING LANGUAGES				
Generation	**First**	**Second**	**Third**	**Fourth**
Known as	machine code	assembler language	procedural languages	non-procedural
Description	a machine understandable code which is expressed in 1s and 0s	symbolic language which largely corresponds to machine code	common language based code	menu and command based languages designed to speed up software development (code is automatically produced)
Level	low	low	high	high
Translated by	none required	assembler software	compiler software (or interpreter software for small PCs)	compiler software
Where used	• where speed and strict control of hardware is important, e.g. control of machine controls	• computer games • as for machine code	• most application software • training	• rapid development of software • development of prototypes • non-specialist uses
Examples	10101011010	ADD, SUB, MULT	BASIC, COBOL, PASCAL, C	DBASE, LOTUS123 EXCEL, Program Generator, Visual Basic
Advantages	• fastest running time (as no translation time) • very detailed control over the hardware	• fast running time • detail control • easier to understand than machine code	• easy to learn and understand • machine independent language • detailed knowledge of hardware not required	• very quick development time • user friendly • non-procedural
Disadvantages	• error prone • difficult to understand and learn • machine dependent • detailed knowledge of hardware required	• translation required which slows down execution • machine dependent • detailed knowledge of hardware required	• less control over hardware • slow execution time	• often inefficient programs produced

▦ 5. Data-processing concepts

5.1 Elements of a computer file

A **file** is a collection of records.

A **record** is made up of a collection of related fields.

A **field** consists of a number of characters.

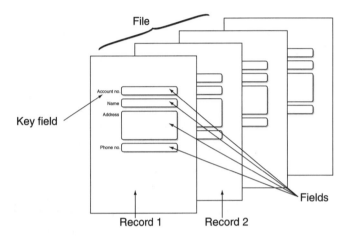

The elements of a file

◣ Key field

The key field is a field within a record that uniquely identifies the record, e.g. a bank account number.

5.2 Types of record

◣ Fixed length records

Every record of this type in the file will have the same fixed number of fields, and characters. The maximum size of the fields is always specified. The main advantage of this type of record is that it is easier for programmers to use. The main disadvantage is that some space allocation may be wasted.

◣ Variable length records

With this type of record not all records in the file are the same size. The number of fields may vary or the amount of characters in a particular field may vary. The main advantage of this type of record is that it is a better use of space. The main disadvantage is that programming can be difficult.

5.3 Types of file

◤Transaction file

This consists of records that relate to individual transactions that occur from day to day, e.g. sales invoices, orders.

◤Reference file

This contains reference data that is normally altered or updated infrequently, e.g. price lists, company regulations. It does not contain any transaction data.

◤Master file

This consists of reference data and transaction data that is built up over time, e.g. the payroll master file would contain reference data such as PRSI numbers and cumulative totals of pay and tax to date.

5.4 File Organisation

File organisation refers to the way records are held on file. Usually a key field, e.g. student number or account code, is used to identify each record.The various types of file organisation are outlined below.

◤Serial

The key fields are stored one after the other but not in any logical order. This method is usually used for recording transaction data initially.

◤Sequential

Records are ordered by the the key field. Often transaction files are ordered sequentially before master files are updated.

◤Index sequential

Records are held sequentially but are accessed by means of an index.

◤Random

Records are not stored in any particular order. They are stored in addressable locations which are calculated based on the key field.

5.5 Updating disk files

Individual records on a disk are addressable directly (DAS). It is possible to write back to and update a record to the same place from which it was read. This involves overwriting the existing information with the new information. This is often referred to as **updating by overlay** or in **place**.

Updating consists of the following sequence:

- The transaction file data and master file data are are read into main memory.
- The transaction data and master file data are matched and updated in the memory and transferred to the same place on the master disk.

5.6 Stages of data collection

◼1. Data collection

Data may be collected on manually prepared source documents, e.g. invoices, orders etc., or the data could be captured in a machine sensible form at source, e.g. bar codes.

◼2. Data transmission

This involves sending source documents to a central location by post, telephone, electronic mail or fax for processing.

◼3. Data preparation

This can involve transcription of data from the source documents to a machine sensible form if there is no direct data capture and verification. **Data verification** is the process of checking that the original source information has been correctly transcribed. It is essentially a process of checking that the data input is identical to the source documents.

A common method of verification is to have the data rekeyed by another person and compared with the first entry. Misspelling and transposition errors can be detected. Tranposition errors are those where characters are mixed up, e.g. code 2343 is keyed in as 2334.

◼4. Input

The verified data is then subject to validation checks before processing. **Data validation** is a process which checks verified data before processing. Common validation checks are outlined below.

Range check: checks whether the input data is within specific allowable ranges, e.g. accounts code are only allowed between 0000 and 9999

Limit check: certain numbers are not allowed to be above or below a certain level, e.g. 24 hours in a day

Existence check: data is checked to ensure that all necessary fields are present.

Format check: data is checked to ensure that it contains only characters of the correct type, e.g. there should only be numbers in numeric fields.

Reasonablesness check: checks that numbers are not unusually high or low. There have been cases of householders getting electricity bills for thousands of pounds due to a meter reading error.

Check digits: these are used to check codes for validity. The computer calculates a check which is added to each code for validation purposes. For example: calculation of the check digit using 11 as the division factor. Original code: 9564

Multiply each digit by a weight starting one greater than the number of digits: 5432.

Product $9 * 5 = 45$

$5 * 4 = 20$

$6 * 3 = 18$

$4 * 2 = 8$

Sum the product = 91

Divide by 11 = 8 and remainder of 3

Subtract the remainder from 11 = 8 (11–3)

8 is the check digit

When the new code number is input to the computer a weighting system is used. One is used for the right most digit and two for the next and so on. The product is calculated and summed. It is then divided by eleven and the remainder should be zero. If the remainder is not zero the code is not valid.

New code: 95648

Product $9 * 5 = 45$

$5 * 4 = 20$

$6 * 3 = 18$

$4 * 2 = 8$

$8 * 1 = 8$

Sum = 99

Divide by 11 =9 and remainder 0

Thus this code would pass the validition test.

Note: an original code giving rise to check digit of '10' is normally discarded.

5.7 Methods of data processing

◪Batch processing

This involves individual source documents being grouped or batched manually or on computer and processed at a predetermined interval of time. For example, in an accounting system all the invoices for a week could be entered into the computer but not processed (updating the accounts) until the end of the week. At the end of the week all accounts relating to the batch would be processed in one run.

Advantages

• Better control

• More efficient use of processing time

- Large tasks can be broken down into small batches
- Access to the computer not always required

Disadvantages
- Random enquiries not possible as files are not constantly up-to-date
- Causes peaks and lows in computer use
- Only applicable to certain applications

Applications suited to batch processing
- Payroll
- Accounting updates
- Sales statistics

◼On-line transaction processing

This involves processing of transactions as they occur. An example would be an airline booking system. As bookings are received they are immediately reserved on the system.

Advantages
- Files always up-to-date
- No data preparation necessary
- Random enquiries possible

Disadvantages
- Computer power must always be available
- Back-up systems vital

Applications suited to on-line processing
- Airline booking system
- Electronic point of sale systems using bar code readers
- ATMS

5.8 Data-processing department

The data-processing department is like any other department in any business in that it usually has a structure where diffferent people have specific tasks to perform. The typical structures for two sizes of data-processing departments are given on p. 43. The number and nature of the tasks performed by these staff will vary with the size and nature of the business. A list of the common tasks performed by data-processing staff is also outlined.

A small data-processing department

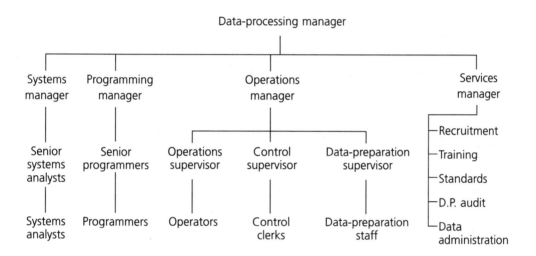

A large data-processing department

◤The data-processing manager/IT manager

ROLE

- In charge of the DP department
- Leadership and motivation of systems and programming and operations work

QUALITIES REQUIRED

- Leadership skills and experience
- Up-to-date knowledge of current computer technology
- Probably experience in all areas of the department

◪ Systems analyst

ROLE

- Designing new information processing systems
- Improving existing systems
- Liaison with programmers and computer users

QUALITIES REQUIRED

- Good business experience
- Programming and computer knowledge and experience
- Interpersonal skills

◪ Programmer

ROLE

- Writing programs according to specifications
- Testing programs
- Assisting the systems analyst
- Documenting all programs

QUALITIES REQUIRED

- Programming qualifications or knowledge
- Logical mind and attention to detail

◪ Operations manager

ROLE

- Responsible for the smooth running or operation of the computer systems

QUALITIES REQUIRED

- In depth knowledge of computers
- Leadership qualities

◪ Operator

ROLE

- Data entry
- Maintaining backups

QUALITIES REQUIRED

- Accuracy
- Speed
- Ability to work to deadlines
- Computer application knowledge

◩ Computer librarian

ROLE
- Responsible for all program disks
- Responsible for all data disks
- Responsible for all back-up disks
- Filing and labeling disks
- Issuing disks when required
- Physical security of all magnetic media

◩ Database administrator

ROLE
- Design and maintenance of a large database and integration of new applications into the database
- Documentation of the database
- Back-up procedures for the database
- Monitoring performance

▥ 6. The information technology environment

The aim of this section is to describe ways to minimise risks to the information technology environment.

6.1 Definitions

The **security** of computer systems 'is the establishment and application of safeguards to protect data, software and computer hardware from accidental or malicious modification, destruction or disclosure' (The British Computer Society).

The **privacy** of computer systems is a part of overall security and involves methods of protection against unauthorised access or disclosure.

6.2 Risks to computer systems

1. INPUT FRAUD

This involves entering false or misleading information into a computer system. This is the most common method of fraud because the majority of users have input access.

Examples are:
- use of 'ghost' or fictitious employees on a payroll system
- creation of fictitious suppliers

- positive falsification, i.e. inserting additional data which is false
- negative falsification, i.e. where data is suppressed (not shown).

2. ALTERATION OF PROGRAMS

This is less common as very technical skills are required to alter commercial programs. The most common form of alteration is where a small slice or portion of an account is redirected into a secret account. This is called salami programming.

3. OUTPUT FRAUD

This is where computer output is suppressed, stolen or altered. Slow output devices mean that data is sometimes exposed to fraudulent attempts in a data queue.

4. UNAUTHORISED ACCESS

5. COMPUTER VIRUSES

These are computer programs, designed as a prank or to damage data, which can copy themselves by attaching to other programs.

6. PHYSICAL DAMAGE FROM FIRE, FLOOD AND BREAK-INS

7. ENVIRONMENTAL FACTORS SUCH AS DUST, DAMPNESS AND HEAT

8. POWER SUPPLY CUT-OFF

9. LOSS OF DATA AND PROGRAMS

10. POOR PERSONNEL PROCEDURES

6.3 Methods of minimising the risks to the information technology environment

There are three main types of method:
- physical
- logical
- procedural.

◪Physical methods
- Air conditioned rooms, especially for mainframe computers
- Dust-free rooms
- Controlled temperature systems
- Back-up power supply (generator)
- Surge controller, to control any variations in power going into computer systems
- High-security locks on computer room doors
- Limited access to keys
- Locks on computer equipment

◼Logical methods

These involve the use of computer programs to minimise risks.

- Use of non-display passwords for access to programs or data.
- The use of passwords to limit what the user can do on the system, e.g. the system manager's password will normally allow access to all areas whereas the computer operator may be resticted to data entry only.
- Built-in user monitor programs. These are programs which monitor the activities of every user of the system. Information such as log-on time, update activities, files read, menus visited, log-off time etc. is stored for future reference. Printed summaries of this information are taken at regular intervals.
- Virus protection programs prevent viruses from infecting the computer. An alarm is usually sounded when a virus is present. These programs must be updated regularly to keep up with the many new viruses.
- Virus destruction software enables the user to delete or remove certain viruses if detected on a disk.
- Screen blank programs. These programs are time activated. After a set period of time of non-activity the screen will blank off. To reactivate the screen the password must be given.

◼Procedural methods

Good personnel procedures are very important for minimising risks to computer systems

- Back-up copies of data should be regularly made. These back-up copies (on disk or tape) should be stored in separate locations in fire-proof safes.
- Proper log-out procedure should be adhered to. The computer should not be switched off before logging out.
- Audit trials should be carried out randomly (once or twice yearly) and at regular intervals (twice a year). The audit trial will perform a full check on the working of the system and is particularly useful for detecting input fraud, program alterations and output fraud.
- Computer output should be shredded if not required or if confidential.
- Personnel should sign for important documentation.
- Proper care of floppy disks:
    — store away from electrical devices
    — store in disk boxes
    — never insert a disk in the disk drive before switching on the computer
    — always take the disk out before turning off the computer
    — never take a disk out when the drive is active
    — do not touch the surface of the disk
    — disks should be labelled clearly.
- Digruntled staff should be closely monitored.

- No employee should be put into a situation where there is a 'conflict of interest', e.g. a bank employee updating his/her own account.
- Personnel must follow legislation regarding data storage, e.g. The Data Protection Act 1988.

◼The Data Protection Act 1988

The eight principles of The Data Protection Act 1988 are as follows:

1. Personal data should be obtained and processed fairly and lawfully.
2. Personal data should only be held for a lawful purpose.
3. Personal data should not be disclosed.
4. Personal data should be adequate, relevant and not excessive.
5. Personal data should be accurate and kept up-to-date.
6. Personal data should not be kept longer than deemed necessary.
7. An individual is entitled at reasonable intervals and without undue delay to find out
   — whether information is held about that individual
   — what the content of the information is
   and where appropriate, the individual can have the data edited or erased.
8. Appropriate measures should be used to limit access to personal data or for the destruction of personal data.

To ensure adherence to this Act the following procedures should be adopted:
- Store only essential information.
- Improve the security of data using methods outlined above.
- Identify data elements which are sensitive, in particular, personal details and monetary data.
- Adopt a policy of regularly updating information.
- Anticipate change — when designing or purchasing new software ensure that it takes into account future anticipated changes or that it is flexible.

◼The Freedom of Information Act 1997

The Freedom of Information Act 1997 established three new statutory rights. These are:
- A legal right for each person to access information held by public bodies.
- A legal right for each person to have official information relating to him/herself amended when it is incomplete or misleading.
- A legal right to obtain reasons for decisions affecting oneself.

6.4 Improving the Information Technology Environment for Users — Ergonomics

Ergonomics is the study of work environments with a view to improving employee comfort and in turn employee productivity.

Ergonomic considerations were thought of as luxuries in the past. Today ergonomic considerations are now a management responsibility, enforceable by law. This is especially true with the passing of the EC directive (90/270/EC) on Display Screen Equipment which came into force on 1st January 1993.

The regulations have six major requirements.

◪1. Analysis of workstations

Every employer must perform a suitable and sufficient analysis of user workstations to assess the risks which they may pose for the health and safety of users. Any risks identified must be reduced.

Common risks are:
- eyes (strain and glare)
- musculo-skeletal (posture)
- mental stress
- space problems.

An ergonomics checklist can be very useful for analysing the workstations.

◪2. Requirements for workstations

These include:
- equipment should be adjustable
- glare-free working conditions
- software suitable for the task.

◪3. Daily routine for users

Users should where possible have a mix of screen based and non-screen based work or, if this is not possible, the provision of breaks in work routine is essential.

◪4. Eyes and eyesight

Users have the right to request an eyesight test at their employers expense. If it is found that corrective appliances are required for display screen work, then the employer is liable for the cost.

◪5. Provision of training

All users of work stations must be provided with adequate training in the areas of software use and health and safety issues.

◪6. Provision of information

All employers are required to ensure that all relevant information available is provided to users of work stations.

The diagram below shows a workstation that is ergonomically designed.

user should be provided with adequate training

user should have a mix of screen-based tasks and non-screen-based tasks or regular breaks

user should be informed of all regulations and work practices dealing with health and safety

local illumination provided where required

700mm max (viewing range to screen)

document holder should be arranged to minimise frequent head and eye movements

windows should be fitted with adjustable coverings to avoid reflection and glare

monitors should be as adjustable as possible to suit individual operator

anti-glare and anti-radiation or low-radiation visors or screens should be used

'user friendly' software or software appropriate to the task should be provided

angle to be in range of 70° to 90°

chair should have fully adjustable seat and backrest

knee and thigh clearance essential

keyboard should be detachable so as to avoid strain of hands and arms

footrest should be provided if required by individual operator

An ergonomically sound work station

▦ Questions

Multi-choice questions

1. Which of the following is the smallest computer system?
    (a) megacomputer
    (b) minicomputer
    (c) mainframe
    (d) microcomputer

2. A monitor is —
    (a) an output device
    (b) an input device
    (c) a peripheral device
    (d) an item of hardware
    (e) all of the above

3. The CPU consists of —
    (a) control unit, ALU and main storage
    (b) ROM, RAM and ALU
    (c) main storage
    (d) chips

4. ROM is —
    (a) non-volatile
    (b) storage
    (c) permanently required
    (d) all of the above

5. Typically, how many bits are there in one byte?
    (a) 4
    (b) 2
    (c) 65
    (d) 8

6. Which of the following disks holds most information?
    (a) DVD-ROM
    (b) 90 mm (3.5 in.) disk
    (c) fixed (hard) disk
    (d) CD-ROM

7. Formatting a disk is usually done —
    (a) once before using a new disk
    (b) every time something is saved on the disk
    (c) every time the disk is full
    (d) to make a back-up copy of a file

8. The instructions that enable a computer to function are called —
    (a) hardware
    (b) applications
    (c) software
    (d) instructions

9. Which one of the following printers **cannot** produce letter-quality printing?
    (a) laser printer
    (b) ink-jet printer
    (c) dot-matrix printer

10. Which pair are the most commonly used input and output devices?
    (a) mouse, printer
    (b) keyboard, printer
    (c) VDE, monitor
    (d) keyboard, monitor

11. The information needed for long-term planning is called —
    (a) tactical
    (b) transactional
    (c) operational
    (d) strategic

12. Which of the following is not a utility?
    (a) copy file
    (b) format a disk
    (c) directory of contents of a disk
    (d) memory management

13. Where records are stored in order of their key fields the file organisation method is called —
    (a) index sequential
    (b) serial
    (c) sequential
    (d) random

14. Which of the following generations of languages requires the most detailed knowledge of computer hardware?
    (a) first generation
    (b) second generation
    (c) third generation
    (d) fourth generation

15. The software used to translate second generation languages to binary form is called —
    (a) assembler
    (b) compiler
    (c) interpreter
    (d) translator

16. The person who is responsible for the design of new computer systems is known as —
    (a) systems programmer
    (b) data processing manager
    (c) systems analyst
    (d) database administrator

17. Aertel is an example of —
    (a) teletex
    (b) teletext
    (c) telex
    (d) viewdata

18. A PABX is a form of —
    (a) telephone
    (b) modem
    (c) multiplexor
    (d) file server

19. The check digit for the code 4214 using division by 11 is —
    (a) 6
    (b) 5
    (c) 1
    (d) 39

20. Which of the following would not be used to combat input fraud?
    (a) passwords
    (b) monitoring disgruntled employees
    (c) virus protection
    (d) monitoring programs

Short-answer questions

1. Name three types of computer system, and give an example of where each system is normally used.
2. What is an input device? Name six different input devices.
3. How is data inside the computer's memory represented?
4. What unit is computer capacity measured in?
5. What is a port?
6. What type of paper can a printer use?
7. List conditions likely to damage disks.
8. What is the function of the operating system, and how does it differ from application software?
9. What do the terms 'on-line' and 'off-line' mean? Give examples of on-line and off-line devices.
10. Explain the functions of ROM and RAM, and how they differ.

Structured questions

1. Information in an organisation is often classified as strategic, tactical and operational.
   (a) Take an organisation with which you are familiar (e.g. a company or college) and explain the nature of the strategic, tactical and operational information giving examples.
   (b) When communicating information to management, give five rules that should be observed so as to ensure that management will be satisfied with the information.
2. What method of data capture would you recommend as input to computer systems in each of the following situations:
   • time recording for employees in a company
   • multi-choice examination answers
   • sales orders in a mail order business.
   (a) Describe the main features of each method you would recommend for the applications given above.
   (b) Give possible advantages and disadvantages of each method described.
3. Describe the main features of any three output devices (other than printers) and indicate the most suitable application for each device.
4. (a) Explain what you understand by the term the 'modern electronic office' and explain the principal hardware features of such an office.
   (b) List the possible benefits of the modern electronic office.
5. Owing to a combination of errors including an electrical fault and an error made by an inexperienced operator the master file containing details of 10,000 insurance policy holders was destroyed.
   (a) Describe how this situation could be rectified if the master file was (i) on tape and (ii) on disk.

(b) Describe what precautions should have been taken so that the above situation could have been avoided.

6. 'Computer networks are becoming extremely popular in business organisations today'.

   (a) List the main reasons why companies set up computer networks.

   (b) Describe, using diagrams, three network topologies.

   (c) Discuss the relative merits and demeritsof each topology.

Sample structured questions (NCVA)

1. (a) Distinguish clearly between data and information. (2 marks)

   (b) Describe the importance of the following in relation to information flows:

   comparison

   exception reporting

   feedback (3 marks)

   (c) Describe the following information systems, and give   example of each.

   Transaction processing system (TPS)

   Decision support system (DSS) (5 marks)

2. The range of software available for computers is growing at a phenomenal rate.

   (a) Define the term 'software'. (1 mark)

   (b) Distinguish between 'systems software' and 'applications software' and give an example of each. (3 marks)

   (c) Describe the difference between 'off the shelf software' and 'custom software' and state the advantages of each type. (3 marks)

   (d) Describe three major functions performed by an operating system. (3 marks)

Sample Assignments (NCVA)

Assignment 1 — Information Processing

Select an organisation of your choice and investigate the organisation under any five of the following headings:

   i. Identify items of technology utilised in the organisation. Give their specification and outline their uses.

   ii. Describe the tasks performed by information processing personnel in the organisation.

   iii. Identify examples of the following in the organisation:
   - operational information
   - tactical information
   - strategical information.

   iv. Describe the flow of information for one process or operation in the organisation and identify the data and information at each stage.

   v. Describe one information process, in the organisation, in terms of efficiency and cost effectiveness.

vi. Describe the layout of technological equipment in ergonomic terms.

vii. Describe how the organisation deals with threats to data integrity and suggestions for improvements.

viii. List the applications software in use in the organisation and comment on their suitability.

ix. Another appropriate task.

Assignment 2 — Internet and E-mail

(a) Select a specific topic in the module Information and Communications Systems and carry out the following tasks:

i. Use at least two search engines on the Internet to access information on the selected topic. Print one relevant search results page from each search engine.

ii. Select a page containing relevant information on the topic and print at least one page of relevant information.

iii. List the addresses of at least five sites visited in your search for information on the topic.

(b) Use e-mail to carry out the following tasks:

i. Compose an e-mail message and send it to multiple recipients, with an attachment.

ii. Create an e-mail address book for at least two individuals and two groups containing at least two addresses in each group.

Assignment 3 — Data Capture Form

You are employed in the marketing department of McNulty Shoes Ltd. You have been asked to create a data capture form to gather information on the firm's customers and their shopping habits. The form should contain the following:

i. have a minimum of ten fields

ii. have appropriate field names or questions

iii. have at least one text, numeric, logical, date and currency field

iv. field formats should be indicated or stated separately

v. field lengths should be indicated or stated separately

vi. fields should be grouped in an appropriate manner.

Sample short answer questions (NCVA)

1. List **four** attributes of Information. (1 mark)

(i) _____   (ii) _____

(iii) _____   (iv) _____

2. List **four** advantages of using computers for information processing. (1 mark)

(i) _____ (ii) _____

(iii) _____ (iv) _____

3. State an appropriate input device for the following applications. (1 mark)

(i) Keying in text _____

(ii) Activating a card-phone _____

(iii) Selecting an item displayed on a computer screen _____

(iv) Producing a digital image from a photograph _____

4. List **two** types of error that could be caught by means of data verification. (1 mark)

(i) _____ (ii) _____

5. List **four** essential items required in order to connect to the Internet. (1 mark)

(i) _____ (ii) _____

(iii) _____ (iv) _____

▦ Glossary of computer terms

access time: the amount of time to retrieve data from a storage device, measured from the instant of executing the command to retrieve data to the moment when the data is stored in a specified location.

ALU (arithmetic and logic unit): the part of the CPU that performs mathematical functions and logical decisions, such as deciding whether one number is greater than another.

application software: programs to perform specific tasks, such as word processing or database management, as distinct from system software (operating system), which maintains and organises the computer system.

ASCII (American Standard Code for Information Interchange): a term sometimes used to describe the system of allocating code numbers to different characters.

assembler: software that translates low level languages to binary code.

auxiliary ('backing') storage device: hardware used to store information for later retrieval.

bar code: a distinctive pattern of lines printed on a product or label, usually containing a code for the product number and capable of being entered into the computer by means of a suitable scanner.

binary number: a number system using only the digits 1 and 0, and therefore capable of being represented inside a computer by means of the presence (1) or absence (0) of an electrical current or magnetic charge.

bit: one digit in a binary number, either 1 or 0; the minimum unit of information in a computer system.

block: a group of records or words treated as a logical unit of data.

byte: a collection of bits, usually eight, to represent a single character.

cache memory: fast RAM memory which remembers instructions and information that the processor has executed or accessed *previously*.

catalogue: a listing of details of the files stored on a disk.

character: any of the signs used in creating text, whether a letter, a numeral or a symbol.

compiler: software that translates high level languages to binary code.

computer: a machine that processes data and supplies results.

contingency ('back-up') copy: a duplicate of data or program files kept in case of loss of this information; should be up-dated regularly and only used in an emergency.

control unit: the part of the CPU that takes instructions in a given sequence and controls the movement of data inside the computer.

corruption: the accidental alteration of data stored on any storage medium.

CPU (central processing unit): the part of the computer that decodes instructions and controls the hardware used to execute them; it consists of the control unit, arithmetic unit, and main storage (memory).

cursor: a movable mark on the screen that shows where the next character will be displayed.

cursor keys: a group of keys that move the cursor left, right, up or down the display.

data: unprocessed source material.

default: an automatic option or value in a program that is used unless an alternative is specified (this term should not be confused with a fault of any kind).

direct access: a type of access used when reading information from a disk; the read–write head goes directly to the place on the disk where the data is stored.

directory: another term for 'catalogue'.

disk drive: an auxiliary storage device that enables data and programs to be stored and retrieved.

diskette/'floppy disk': a flexible plastic disk coated with a magnetisable material and enclosed in a plastic envelope or case.

dot-matrix printer: a printer that produces characters made up of patterns of dots.

dumb terminal: a VDU and keyboard link to a network. It has no local processing capability.

DVD: Digital Versatile Disk or Digital Video Disk. These optical disks (similar to CD-ROMs) can store large quantities of video, audio and computer data. Storage capacities for DVD are considerably higher than CD-ROMs.

editing keys: a group of keys that perform specialised functions such as page up, page down, go to end of file, etc.

electronic mail (e-mail): facility to send messages directly from one computer to another or to a specific 'mail box'.

EPROM: erasable PROM (see below).

ergonomics: the study of the environment of work in order to improve efficiency.

file server: a computer which controls the sharing of resources in a network.

fixed (hard) disk: a rigid, non-removable disk coated in a magnetisable material.

formatting: the procedure used to prepare a blank disk before use for a particular computer; it divides the disk into sectors so that information can be stored and retrieved.

function keys: a group of keys that can be programmed to execute commands or to choose options.

gigabyte: a unit of 1000 million bytes

GUI: Graphical User Interface. Software where icons and graphics are used

hardware: the physical components of a computer system.

hit rate: the percentage of master file records that are updated in an update run.

information: processed data.

input device: any hardware device that enables data to be transmitted from the source into the computer.

intelligent terminal: a VDU, CPU, keyboard link to a network. It has local processing capability.

inter block gap: a blank space between blocks of information on a magnetic tape.

interpreter: a line by line translator of high level languages to binary code (used mainly on small microcomputers).

keyboard: an input device with a systematic arrangement of keys, used for entering instructions and data.

kilobyte (KB): a unit of 1,024 bytes (sometimes rounded to 1,000).

laser printer: a high-quality printer that uses a method of reproduction similar to a photocopier and prints whole pages at a time.

light pen: an input device used in conjunction with a screen to choose commands or data.

local area network (LAN): a network confined to one local site.

mainframe computer: the largest type of computer, capable of being used by many people at the same time.

megabyte (MB): a unit of 1,0048,576 bytes (sometimes rounded to 1 million).

menu: a list of the options available at any stage in the execution of a program.

MICR (magnetic-ink character recognition): an input system that allows magnetic characters (usually found on cheques) to be read into a computer.

microcomputer: a self-contained desk-top computer built around a microprocessor and that can be used by only one person at a time; sometimes called a 'personal computer' (PC).

microprocessor: an integrated circuit or 'microchip' that contains the ALU and control unit of a computer.

minicomputer: a medium-sized computer system, usually used by one department or a medium-sized company.

modem (modulator/demodulator): hardware required to convert a digital signal to a telephone signal and vice versa.

monitor: an output device like a television set that shows the stages in the operation of a program and displays the results; sometimes called a 'visual display unit' (VDU).

mouse: an input device housed in a palm-sized case used for pointing to commands or icons on the screen; the movement of the mouse on the desk-top corresponds to the movement of the cursor on the display, and one or more buttons on the mouse can be used to select options or execute commands.

multiplexor: hardware used to split and connect different communication lines.

network: a group of computers linked together to communicate or share resources.

NLQ (near-letter-quality): a simulation of high-quality printing on a dot-matrix printer.

OCR (optical character recognition): an input system that reads printed or typewritten characters.

off-line: not under the direct control of the CPU.

OMR (optical mark recognition): an input device that can recognise the presence or absence of a mark.

on-line: under the control of the CPU.

operating system: all the software used to operate and maintain the computer system and utilities.

operational information: information required for day-to-day operations.

optical disk: an auxiliary storage device similar to a compact disk.

output device: any hardware device that enables computer data to be displayed, transmitted or printed.

parallel port: a communications port that allows information to be received or transmitted in groups of bits.

parity bit: a bit appended to a byte. The state of the bit is such as to ensure that the parity is consistently either even or odd.

port/communications port: an external socket allowing peripheral devices to be connected to a computer.

printer: an output device that produces printed text or graphics on paper.

PROM: programmable ROM (see below).

RAM (random-access memory): an area of electronic storage inside the computer used to hold current data and programs; information is constantly read from and written to this memory area.

ROM (read-only memory): an area of electronic storage used to hold instructions essential to the running of the computer; it is not possible to write to this area.

scanner: a method of access used with magnetic tape, where files are stored one after another and information is retrieved by rapid winding or rewinding until the required files are found.

sector: a storage area on a disk.

seek time: the amount of time taken by a disk drive to move its head from one track to another.

serial port: a communications port that allows bits of data to be received or transmitted one after the other.

software: another name for programs.

strategic information: information required for long-term planning.

tactical information: information required to plan for the medium term.

teletext: one-way information service using the television airways.

track: one of the concentric rings of data on a magnetic disk.

utility program: part of operating software which allows the user to carry out standard procedures such as formatting, copying files etc.

validation: a procedure carried out by a computer to check if the data is complete and reasonable.

VDE (voice data entry): an input system that responds to the human voice.

VDU (visual display unit): another name for a monitor.

verification: a method of checking that the original data has been correctly entered. It often involves re-keying data.

viewdata: interactive information service via telephone connection.

wide area network (WAN): a network which spans over a wide area and is connected using telephone lines and other communication links.

WYSISWYG (What You See Is What You Get): this means that the image on the screen is very close to how it will appear when printed.

Chapter 2
Introduction to Databases

When is the next available flight to New York? What is the current exchange rate for the Canadian dollar? Are there any rooms available at a certain hotel?

To answer these questions we may have to consult a travel agent, a bank clerk, and the hotel receptionist, respectively. It is unlikely, however, that they will know these answers immediately. They may have to consult their respective databases.

◩ What is a database?

A database is an organised collection of related information. It usually consists of one or more files that may be related to one another.

◩ What is a file?

A file is a collection of similar records.

An employment agency, Bestmatch Recruitment, holds a personnel file on people looking for suitable employment. For simplicity, we will assume that there are only six people on the agency's file at present:

The information on each of the people seeking employment is arranged under these headings:

NAME	ADDRESS	PHONE_NO	SEX	JOB	YEARS
Murphy P	6 Greenore Pk	4449234	M	Secretary	2
Hopkirk L	16 Kilkenny Rd	8349042	F	Secretary	3
Maher K	56 Main St	8899593	M	Chef	0
Greene A	55 Wicklow Rd	5231772	F	Accountant	10
Burns J	57 Hazel Rd	7783924	M	Chef	2
Owens M	56 Ashe St	4931448	F	Pharmacist	4

NAME: the person's name (surname and initial);
ADDRESS: the person's home address;
PHONE_NO: the person's home telephone number;
SEX: the person's sex;
JOB: the job sought;
YEARS: the number of years' experience the person has of this work.

(Note that there is an underline character rather than a space in 'PHONE_NO': this is because some database programs need the parts of a heading to be joined together so that the computer can treat them as one word, and this character is the one usually used.)

◢ What is a record?

A record is a complete unit of related data items organised in named fields. In our example, the information held on each person seeking a job is stored in a separate record. The third record in our file holds information on Kevin Maher.

◢ What is a field?

A field is a space for a specified item of information in a record. In our example, 7783924 (a specific item of information) is held in the PHONE_NO field of the fifth record of the file. The content of a field is often referred to as a data item.

◢ Why is information now stored in computer databases?

Information, stored in a computer database, can be:

(a) found extremely quickly, e.g. the number of three-bedroom houses in a certain area can be extracted from an estate agent's file;

(b) sorted and re-sorted quickly and efficiently, e.g. a personnel file can be sorted in chronological order of the date that each employee joined a company;

(c) kept up-to-date very easily, e.g. adding new member and erasing lapsed member details on a golf club membership file;

(d) used by other applications, e.g. the names and addresses of customers in a customer file can be extracted and used in producing mailshots by a word processor.

In summary, a database may consist of one or more files. Each file consists of a number of records, and each record comprises a number of fields.

▦ Holding a database on computer

In order to hold a database on computer, we need a database program or **database management system (DBMS)**. On a microcomputer, this is a program that allows us to store information in a database, as well as to edit, organise or retrieve that information.

The database program is like our own private librarian, who looks after our database and carries out any editing, organising or retrieval requests from us.

We now examine how to set up a database on a computer and how we can carry out various activities on the file, under the following headings:

1. Defining the data entry form
2. Entering data into the file
3. Editing the file
4. Searching the file

5. Displaying selected fields
6. Sorting the file
7. Indexing the file
8. Changing the record structure
9. Performing mathematical operations
10. Creating reports

1. Defining the data capture form

Before we enter a new file into our computer database, we must define the data entry form.

A data entry form is a screen layout resembling a form that displays only one data record at a time, which makes it easier to enter and edit data.

We must decide the following:

(a) the heading of each field within the record structure, e.g. NAME, ADDRESS;

(b) the maximum width of each field. The longest address is 16 KILKENNY RD, so we must define a field width of 14 for the ADDRESS field to accommodate this address;

(c) the data type: **alphabetic** (letters only), **numeric** (numbers only), or **alphanumeric** (a combination of letters and numbers) **date** (dd/mm/yy), currency, logical (y/n). In our example the NAME field is alphabetic, the YEARS field is numeric and the ADDRESS field is alphanumeric.

We would now give our database program the following information about our personnel file:

FIELD	FIELD NAME	FIELD WIDTH	DATA TYPE
1	NAME	9	Alphabetic
2	ADDRESS	15	Alphanumeric
3	PHONE_NO	7	Numeric
4	SEX	1	Alphabetic
5	JOB	10	Alphabetic
6	YEARS	2	Numeric

This is the record structure for the file. The corresponding data entry screen is displayed below:

NAME
ADDRESS
PHONE_NO
SEX
JOB
YEARS

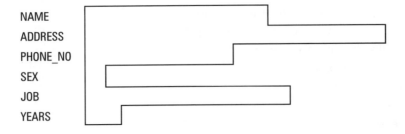

2. Entering data into the file

Once we have defined our data entry form, we must now enter data into the file. It is usually entered without punctuation.

It is important that data be entered consistently: in the YEARS field you must not enter '2' in one record and 'two' in the next. This can cause problems when you wish to search or sort the file later. You must take care at this stage, as incorrect data can be entered accidentally.

When you have entered all the data, the file can be displayed on the screen, or printed, and should appear as follows:

NAME	ADDRESS	PHONE_NO	SEX	JOB	YEARS
MURPHY P	6 GREENORE PK	4449234	M	SECRETARY	2
HOPKIRK L	16 KILKENNY RD	8349042	F	SECRETARY	3
MAHER K	56 MAIN ST	8899593	M	CHEF	0
GREENE A	55 WICKLOW RD	5231772	F	ACCOUNTANT	10
BURNS J	57 HAZEL RD	7783924	M	CHEF	2
OWENS M	56 ASHE ST	4931448	F	PHARMACIST	4

3. Editing the file

Once we have set up our file on computer, we can add new records or delete unwanted records. We can also change the contents of individual records in the file.

◪ Adding and deleting records

Let us assume that we have just received the following information about a person who is looking for a job:

Name	Address	Phone	Sex	Job	Years
McCann A	32 Shannon Park	8568264	M	Mechanic	7

We can select the command or option in our database program to add a new record to the file. A data entry form appears on the screen, and we simply enter the appropriate details. Let us also say that Kevin Maher finds a suitable job and no longer requires the agency's services. We can delete his record from the file by using the command or option to delete a record in our database program.

The file will now appear as follows:

NAME	ADDRESS	PHONE_NO	SEX	JOB	YEARS
MURPHY P	6 GREENORE PK	4449234	M	SECRETARY	2
HOPKIRK L	16 KILKENNY RD	8349042	F	SECRETARY	3
GREENE A	55 WICKLOW RD	5231772	F	ACCOUNTANT	10
BURNS J	57 HAZEL RD	7783924	M	CHEF	2
OWENS M	56 ASHE ST	4931448	F	PHARMACIST	4
MCCANN A	32 SHANNON PK	8568264	M	MECHANIC	7

◧ Changing the contents of records

Using the appropriate command or option, we can display a record and then delete or insert various items of information.

Let us say that Aisling Greene has moved to 68 Shannon Park, and her new telephone number is 8568234. Also, a mistake was made in the name field of the second record: the name should be Hopkins, not Hopkirk.

When we have made these changes, the file will appear as follows:

NAME	ADDRESS	PHONE_NO	SEX	JOB	YEARS
MURPHY P	6 GREENORE PK	4449234	M	SECRETARY	2
HOPKINS L	16 KILKENNY RD	8349042	F	SECRETARY	3
GREENE A	68 SHANNON PK	8568234	F	ACCOUNTANT	10
BURNS J	57 HAZEL RD	7783924	M	CHEF	2
OWENS M	56 ASHE ST	4931448	F	PHARMACIST	4
MCCANN A	32 SHANNON PK	8568264	M	MECHANIC	7

4. Searching the file

One of the really useful features of having files stored on a computer database is the ease and speed with which we can search for information. As records are numbered according to their position in a file, we can cause a particular record to be displayed. We can also display or print all those records that meet a certain condition or set of conditions.

◧ Searching for records by their position in the file

We can select the appropriate command or option to display record 3 in the personnel file:

RECORD NO.	NAME	ADDRESS	PHONE_NO	SEX	JOB	YEARS
3	GREENE A	68 SHANNON PK	8568234	F	ACCOUNTANT	10

◪ Searching for records using one condition

Let us say that Bestmatch Recruitment get a telephone call from a company's personnel officer looking for a secretary. We can search the file for the records containing details of secretaries. We follow these steps:

(a) select the option or command for searching the file;

(b) choose the correct field for our search: the JOB field;

(c) enter the job we are searching for: SECRETARY;

(d) some programs may then require the user to give an 'execute' command to start the search.

The results of this search may appear as follows:

NAME	ADDRESS	PHONE_NO	SEX	JOB	YEARS
MURPHY P	6 GREENORE PK	4449234	M	SECRETARY	2
HOPKINS L	16 KILKENNY RD	8349042	F	SECRETARY	3

◪ Searching for records using more than one condition

We can obtain details of those people on our file who are female and who have more than three years' experience in their chosen career, by carrying out the following steps:

(a) select the option or command for searching the file;

(b) choose the field for our first search condition: the SEX field;

(c) enter the sex for which we are searching: FEMALE;

(d) choose the field for our second search condition: the YEARS field;

(e) select the greater-than operand (>) and enter 3;

(f) some programs may then require the user to give an 'execute' command to start the search.

Once the request has been carried out, the results may appear as follows:

NAME	ADDRESS	PHONE_NO	SEX	JOB	YEARS
GREENE A	68 SHANNON PK	8568234	F	ACCOUNTANT	10
OWENS M	56 ASHE ST	4931448	F	PHARMACIST	4

◪ Searching for records using variable symbols

Sometimes we may have to search a file without knowing the precise conditions under which we are performing the search. This can be done by using **variable symbols** (sometimes called 'wild cards'). These are characters (for example ? or *) that the program interprets as 'any character'.

Let us say that someone whose details are on the personnel file has just phoned the agency. The receptionist takes the caller's telephone number and assures her that the manager will return the call within the hour. The manager, however, loses the telephone number, but remembers the first three digits: 834. The database program will allow him to search the file for the details of any person whose telephone number starts with 834.

The steps taken to carry out this type of search on most database programs are as follows:

(a) select the option or command for searching the file;

(b) choose the correct field for the search: the PHONE_NO field;

(c) enter the portion of the data entry that we know: 834;

(d) fill the remainder of the field with the variable symbol: ****;

(e) some programs may then require the user to give an 'execute' command to start the search.

The result of this search on th personnel file will be displayed as follows:

```
HOPKINS L    16 KILKENNY RD     8349042    F   SECRETARY        3
```

5. Displaying selected fields

Another feature of a database program is its ability to display only a certain number of fields. This is useful when our records contain a large number of fields.

We may wish to display only the NAME, JOB and YEARS fields of all the records in the file. These are the steps we take:

(a) select the option or command that enables us to select the fields that we want displayed;

(b) select the fields in the order in which we would like them displayed;

(c) then select the command or option to execute the 'display selected fields' facility.

The result should appear as follows:

NAME	JOB	YEARS
MURPHY P	SECRETARY	2
HOPKINS L	SECRETARY	3
GREENE A	ACCOUNTANT	10
BURNS J	CHEF	2
OWENS M	PHARMACIST	4
MCCANN A	MECHANIC	7

It is possible to combine the 'display selected fields' and search facilities.

We may wish to display the NAME, ADDRESS and JOB fields of all those records belonging to the males on file. In order to carry this out we must:

(a) select the fields to be displayed: NAME, ADDRESS and JOB;

(b) select the option or command for searching the file;

(c) choose the field for the search condition: the SEX field;

(d) enter the sex for which we are searching: MALE;

(e) some programs may then require the user to give an 'execute' command to start the search. The result should appear as follows:

NAME	ADDRESS	JOB
MURPHY P	6 GREENORE PK	SECRETARY
BURNS J	57 HAZEL RD	CHEF
MCCANN A	32 SHANNON PK	MECHANIC

6. Sorting the file

Another useful feature of our computer database is the ease with which we can sort the records. In this section we examine the following methods:
• alphabetic sorting
• numeric sorting
• reverse sorting
• multi-level sorting
• group sorting.

Most database programs would normally allow us to sort a file in the following way:

(a) select the option or command for sorting;

(b) select the key field (this is a field chosen by the user on which sorting will be carried out);

(c) use the option or command to choose whether we wish to sort the records in ascending order (with text this is the same as alphabetical order) or descending order. The default setting in most database programs is in ascending order.

◪Alphabetical sorting

Let us assume that we wish to sort the records by name, in alphabetical order. The NAME field will thus be the key field. The results of this sort may be displayed as:

NAME	ADDRESS	PHONE_NO	SEX	JOB	YEARS
BURNS J	57 HAZEL RD	7783924	M	CHEF	2
GREENE A	68 SHANNON PK	8568234	F	ACCOUNTANT	10
HOPKINS L	16 KILKENNY RD	8349042	F	SECRETARY	3
MCCANN A	32 SHANNON PK	8568264	M	MECHANIC	7
MURPHY P	6 GREENORE PK	4449234	M	SECRETARY	2
OWENS M	56 ASHE ST	4931448	F	PHARMACIST	4

◪Numeric sorting

We can sort the file by number of years' job experience of each person. The YEARS field will be chosen as the key field. The sorted file will then appear as follows:

NAME	ADDRESS	PHONE_NO	SEX	JOB	YEARS
MURPHY P	6 GREENORE PK	4449234	M	SECRETARY	2
BURNS J	57 HAZEL RD	7783924	M	CHEF	2
HOPKINS L	16 KILKENNY RD	8349042	F	SECRETARY	3
OWENS M	56 ASHE ST	4931448	F	PHARMACIST	4
MCCANN A	32 SHANNON PK	8568264	M	MECHANIC	7
GREENE A	68 SHANNON PK	8568234	F	ACCOUNTANT	10

◪Reverse sorting

The file, as it appears above, is sorted in ascending order of number of years' job experience of each person. We can also sort the file in descending order, again using the YEARS field as the key field. The sorted file will now appear as:

NAME	ADDRESS	PHONE_NO	SEX	JOB	YEARS
GREENE A	68 SHANNON PK	8568234	F	ACCOUNTANT	10
MCCANN A	32 SHANNON PK	8568264	M	MECHANIC	7
OWENS M	56 ASHE ST	4931448	F	PHARMACIST	4
HOPKINS L	16 KILKENNY RD	8349042	F	SECRETARY	3
MURPHY P	6 GREENORE PK	4449234	M	SECRETARY	2
BURNS J	57 HAZEL RD	7783924	M	CHEF	2

◪Multi-level sorting

In our examples we have been sorting on one field: either the NAME field or the YEARS field. It is possible, however, to sort on a number of fields at the same time.

If we are sorting on two fields, the first field we select is the **primary sort field** and second is the **secondary sort field**. We can now sort our file using the SEX field as the primary key field and the NAME field as the secondary key field. The result would be as follows:

NAME	ADDRESS	PHONE_NO	SEX	JOB	YEARS
GREENE A	68 SHANNON PK	8568234	F	ACCOUNTANT	10
HOPKINS L	16 KILKENNY RD	8349042	F	SECRETARY	3
OWENS M	56 ASHE ST	4931448	F	PHARMACIST	4
BURNS J	57 HAZEL RD	7783924	M	CHEF	2
MCCANN A	32 SHANNON PK	8568264	M	MECHANIC	7
MURPHY P	6 GREENORE PK	4449234	M	SECRETARY	2

As F comes before M in the alphabet, all the female entries are listed first, in alphabetical order, then the male entries in alphabetical order.

◤Group sorting

We can select a particular group of records from the file and display this group sorted on one or more fields. We may wish to have all records of those people who have more than two years' experience sorted alphabetically by name, and then displayed.

Some database programs may allow us to sort the file using the NAME field as the key field and then search the sorted file for all those people with more than two years' experience. Other programs may allow us to extract the records of those people with more than two years' experience and then sort these records into alphabetical order. The result, in either case, should appear as follows:

NAME	ADDRESS	PHONE_NO	SEX	JOB	YEARS
GREENE A	68 SHANNON PK	8568234	F	ACCOUNTANT	10
HOPKINS L	16 KILKENNY RD	8349042	F	SECRETARY	3
MCCANN A	32 SHANNON PK	8568264	M	MECHANIC	7
OWENS M	56 ASHE ST	4931448	F	PHARMACIST	4

7. Indexing the file

When we sort a database file, the records are physically sorted by the computer into the order required. We have seen, in an earlier example, that the records are numbered according to their position in the file.

NAME	ADDRESS	PHONE_NO	SEX	JOB	YEARS
BURNS J	57 HAZEL RD	7783924	M	CHEF	2
GREENE A	68 SHANNON PK	8568234	F	ACCOUNTANT	10
HOPKINS L	16 KILKENNY RD	8349042	F	SECRETARY	3
MCCANN A	32 SHANNON PK	8568264	M	MECHANIC	7
MURPHY P	6 GREENORE PK	4449234	M	SECRETARY	2
OWENS M	56 ASHE ST	4931448	F	PHARMACIST	4

We can get a print-out of the file sorted on the NAME field:

Many computer database programs offer an alternative to sorting, namely **indexing**. We can get a computer print-out of our unsorted file:

RECORD NO	NAME	ADDRESS	PHONE_NO	SEX	JOB	YEARS
1	MURPHY P	6 GREENORE PK	4449234	M	SECRETARY	2
2	HOPKINS L	16 KILKENNY RD	8349042	F	SECRETARY	3
3	GREENE A	68 SHANNON PK	8568234	F	ACCOUNTANT	10
4	BURNS J	57 HAZEL RD	7783924	M	CHEF	2
5	OWENS M	56 ASHE ST	4931448	F	PHARMACIST	4
6	MCCANN A	32 SHANNON PK	8568264	M	MECHANIC	7

If we index our file using the NAME field, the records themselves are not ordered. Instead, the numbers of the records are ordered in a small file called an 'index file'. As BURNS would head the list in alphabetical order, the first number in the index file would be 4, because this person's record is the fourth record in the file. The index file in this case would contain the following list of numbers: 4, 3, 2, 1, 6, 5.

When we activate this index file and then request a print-out, we would obtain the following:

RECORD NO	NAME	ADDRESS	PHONE_NO	SEX	JOB	YEARS
4	BURNS J	57 HAZEL RD	7783924	M	CHEF	2
3	GREENE A	68 SHANNON PK	8568234	F	ACCOUNTANT	10
2	HOPKINS L	16 KILKENNY RD	8349042	F	SECRETARY	3
6	MCCANN A	32 SHANNON PK	8568264	M	MECHANIC	7
1	MURPHY P	6 GREENORE PK	4449234	M	SECRETARY	2
5	OWENS M	56 ASHE ST	4931448	F	PHARMACIST	4

The records are printed according to the order of the numbers in the index file. Frequent database users rarely use sorting and prefer indexing, as index files can be activated very quickly. Sorting a large file can take some time.

Another advantage of using indexing rather than the sorting facility is that some database programs, when sorting a file, set up a completely new file, and copy the records across to this new file in sorted order. We would then have two files containing exactly the same information stored on our disk — one sorted and one unsorted. In this case indexing is obviously preferable to sorting, as index files will take up a much smaller amount of disk space than sort files. The indexing facility is not available on all database programs.

8. Changing the record structure

Sometimes, after we have defined the record structure of a file and entered information into it, we may wish to change the record structure. This could be for one or more of the following purposes:
- adding a new field
- deleting an existing field
- changing the order of fields
- widening fields
- changing field names.

The commands and techniques to change the record structure vary, depending on the database program you are using. As you proceed through this section you should check the appropriate command or technique to undertake a particular change to the record structure.

◼Changing the field width

The field width of the NAME field in our example was set at 9 in order to accommodate the longest name, which was HOPKINS L. The field is not wide enough, however, to allow us to include the first names. If we include the first name instead of the initial, Aisling Greene has the longest name: we need a field width of 14 to accommodate this name.

When we have redefined the field width of the NAME field to 14 and edited the file to include the first names, it will appear as follows:

NAME	ADDRESS	PHONE_NO	SEX	JOB	YEARS
BURNS JOHN	57 HAZEL RD	7783924	M	CHEF	2
GREENE AISLING	68 SHANNON PK	8568234	F	ACCOUNTANT	10
HOPKINS LIZ	16 KILKENNY RD	8349042	F	SECRETARY	3
MCCANN AIDAN	32 SHANNON PK	8568264	M	MECHANIC	7
MURPHY DANIEL	6 GREENORE PK	4449234	M	SECRETARY	2
OWENS MARY	56 ASHE ST	4931448	F	PHARMACIST	4

◼Deleting a field from the record structure

As we have the telephone number of each person on file, there is little need for a field that includes the address. We will use the commands specific to our database program to delete this field from the record structure. The file would then appear as follows:

NAME	PHONE_NO	SEX	JOB	YEARS
BURNS JOHN	7783924	M	CHEF	2
GREENE AISLING	8568234	F	ACCOUNTANT	10
HOPKINS LIZ	8349042	F	SECRETARY	3
MCCANN AIDAN	8568264	M	MECHANIC	7
MURPHY DANIEL	4449234	M	SECRETARY	2
OWENS MARY	4931448	F	PHARMACIST	4

◣Adding a new field to the record structure

As companies often phone the agency from various towns looking for staff in their own area, we might include a TOWN field for the home town of each person on file. When we have set up this new field and included the appropriate details, our file would appear as follows:

NAME	TOWN	PHONE_NO	SEX	JOB	YEARS
BURNS JOHN	TRIM	7783924	M	CHEF	2
GREENE AISLING	NAVAN	8568234	F	ACCOUNTANT	10
HOPKINS LIZ	DROICHEAD NUA	8349042	F	SECRETARY	3
MCCANN AIDAN	MONAGHAN	8568264	M	MECHANIC	7
MURPHY DANIEL	CAVAN	4449234	M	SECRETARY	2
OWENS MARY	TRALEE	4931448	F	PHARMACIST	4

Changing a field name

We can change the name of the field that includes each person's occupation from JOB to CAREER.

Changing the order of fields

We may wish to move the YEARS field so that it appears second in the record structure. When we have made these final two changes to our record structure, our personnel file will now appear as follows:

NAME	YEARS	TOWN	PHONE_NO	SEX	CAREER
BURNS JOHN	2	TRIM	7783924	M	CHEF
GREENE AISLING	10	NAVAN	8568234	F	ACCOUNTANT
HOPKINS LIZ	3	DROICHEAD NUA	8349042	F	SECRETARY
MCCANN AIDAN	7	MONAGHAN	8568264	M	MECHANIC
MURPHY DANIEL	2	CAVAN	4449234	M	SECRETARY
OWENS MARY	4	TRALEE	4931448	F	PHARMACIST

Careful planning

The facilities for changing a record's structure are very useful but should be used sparingly. A prudent database user will always plan the record structure of a new file on paper before defining it on computer. A little early planning with field names and field widths will save a lot of alterations to the record structure later.

9. Performing mathematical operations

Two useful facilities offered by most database programs are:

(a) the ability to perform one of the four basic mathematical operations (add, subtract, multiply or divide) on the data items of two or more numeric fields and to place the result in another field;

(b) the summation function.

Performing mathematical operations on data items

Set up the following file on your computer. It contains details of goods that are for sale at Jim's Electrical Superstore. The file consists of five records, and each record has four fields:

ITEM: the name of the electrical item;
COST: its cost price;
QUANTITY: the number in stock;
RETAIL: its retail price.
The file's contents are as follows:

ITEM	COST	QUANTITY	RETAIL
WASHING MACHINE	250.00	7	318.00
REFRIGERATOR	400.00	3	625.00
VIDEO RECORDER	290.00	8	428.00
TELEVISION	350.00	4	520.00
VACUUM CLEANER	180.00	2	245.00

We can quite easily change the record structure to include two new fields:

PROFIT: the data item in this field will be the profit obtained on the sale of one item, and can be obtained by the simple formula 'retail minus cost', which subtracts the contents of the COST field from the contents of the RETAIL field for each of the five records;

VALUATION: the data item in this field will be the total value of all items of a particular type, for example the total value of all television sets. The valuation is obtained by a formula, 'cost multiplied by quantity', which multiplies the contents of the COST field by the contents of the QUANTITY field for each of the five records.

When you have set up the file containing the two fields, it should look like this:

ITEM	COST	QUANTITY	RETAIL	PROFIT	VALUATION
WASHING MACHINE	250.00	7	318.00	68.00	1750.00
REFRIGERATOR	400.00	3	625.00	225.00	1200.00
VIDEO RECORDER	290.00	8	428.00	138.00	2320.00
TELEVISION	350.00	4	520.00	170.00	1400.00
VACUUM CLEANER	180.00	2	245.00	65.00	360.00

◼The summation function

Most database programs have a summation function, which allows us to sum fields. Let us say that someone wishes to buy all five of the items listed in the file. We can use the summation function to obtain the total value of the data items in the RETAIL fields of the five records. We get:

> 5 records summed on the RETAIL field
> Total = £2,136.00

As we will see in the next section, the summation of fields can be carried out automatically when we generate reports.

10. Creating reports

A report is any meaningful information retrieved from a database and displayed or printed. Strictly speaking, all the output from the two files outlined in this chapter are reports. Most database programs, however, are equipped with a **report generator**. This is a facility that allows us to design the presentation of the output from a database file. The report generator can also total columns of numeric data automatically.

The following is a print-out of a report generated on the electrical shop file:

JIM'S ELECTRICAL SUPERSTORE VALUATION REPORT					
ITEM	COST	QUANTITY	RETAIL	PROFIT	VALUATION
WASHING MACHINE	250.00	7	318.00	68.00	1750.00
REFRIGERATOR	400.00	3	625.00	225.00	1200.00
VIDEO RECORDER	290.00	8	428.00	138.00	2320.00
TELEVISION	350.00	4	520.00	170.00	1400.00
VACUUM CLEANER	180.00	2	245.00	65.00	360.00
TOTAL		24			7030.00

░Summary

In this chapter we have examined the main facilities of a database program. Most of these facilities should be available on your program.

We have dealt with the simplest type of database, the **flat-file** database. This is one where all the files are treated individually by the program and are not linked in any way.

░Glossary of database terms

batch processing: the technique of updating a file at one time with all the transactions that have occurred in a given period.

database: a collection of related information about a subject, organised in a way that provides the means for retrieving and sorting the information, drawing conclusions and making decisions.

database management system (DBMS): a computer program used for creating databases and that provides the tools for inserting, retrieving, modifying and deleting information and for producing relevant reports from the database.

data entry form: a form layout on the screen that facilitates the entering of information into a database file. Only one record is displayed at a time, and the fields within each record are usually listed vertically.

field: a space for a specified piece of information in a record.

file: a collection of similar records.

fixed-length field: a field that is capable of holding a predetermined maximum number of characters.

fixed-length record: a record that is capable of holding a predetermined number of fixed-length fields.

flat-file database: a database in which all the files are treated individually by the program and are not linked in any way.

flat-file database program: a program that stores, organises and retrieves information from one file at a time.

index: a small file containing 'pointers' or information about the physical location of records in a database file. When searching or sorting, the database program uses the index rather than the full database.

microfiche: a form of microfilm in which documents are photographically reduced and copied onto small sheets of film.

microfilm: an information storage system in which documents are photographically reduced and copied onto 16 mm film strip.

multi-level sort: a sort that uses two fields, a primary sort field and a secondary sort field, to determine the order in which records are arranged.

multi-user system: a system that allows more than one person to have access to the database program and files at the same time.

programmable database: a database system that has its own programming language, allowing the user to structure files and reports according to specific needs.

random access: a method that allows the system to retrieve information by going directly to a specific part of a disk rather than having to go through all the preceding tracks and sectors.

real-time processing: the technique of updating a file when the operator is 'on-line' to the CPU and the updating is carried out immediately by the computer.

relational database: a database system that can link two or more files together through at least one common field. Such a program allows the user to update two or more linked files simultaneously in the same operation.

sequential file: a file in which the records are arranged in a particular order, usually ascending or descending order of key field.

serial file: a method in which the records in a file are not physically arranged in any particular order on a disk or tape.

sort: an operation that arranges data in a particular order.

variable-length field: a field whose length varies according to the contents of the field at a particular time.

variable-length record: a record in which the number of fields may vary from that of other records in the same file. Variable-length records usually consist of variable-length fields.

Chapter 3
Practical Database
Assignments

These assignments are graded, and we advise that you work through them in the order in which they are given. **Note: you may enter the data given for each assignment into a new database table or file or you can download the database file containing the tables for each assignment (Microsoft Access 97 format) from the Gill & Macmillan website at www.gillmacmillan.ie/eca.**

▦ Guidelines for students

Unless the actual assignment specifies otherwise, the following guidelines apply.

1. The data entry screen

A properly formatted data entry screen must be created for each assignment.

- All fields must have suitable field names.
- There should be two fields per line on the data input screen. (In the case of an odd number of fields, the last field will obviously stand alone.)
- The input screen should have a centred title at the top.
- There is no need for borders or other effects.

2. Entering data

Care must be taken when entering data into a file and the following rules apply:

- Commas in numbers must not be entered, e.g. enter 10300 instead of 10,300.
- Currency amounts must be entered as values in numeric fields, e.g. enter 2.85 instead of £2.85.
- Where field names consist of two separate words these should be joined by an underscore, e.g. Age Profile should appear as Age_Profile.

3. Creating reports

Assignment 12 onwards specifies the production of report formats.

- The field names used on data entry screens will suffice as column headings in reports.
- Do not, unless specifically asked, perform any mathematical calculations on any numeric fields (e.g. averaging or totalling).

4. Using Microsoft access

If you are using Microsoft Access, make a copy of the table and carry out the required edits on this copy

◪Functions and commands required

As you progress through these assignments you will need to check the commands, functions, icons and pull-down menus specific to your database program. You will also be practising commands and techniques learned in earlier assignments. (Note: if you do not have access to a printer, you can display the result of the task instead.)

The new work involved in each assignment is as follows:

ASSIGNMENT 1
- Creating a file
- Designing the data entry form
- Entering data
- Editing the contents of individual records
- Adding a new record
- Deleting an existing record
- Saving the file

ASSIGNMENT 2
- Consolidation assignment

ASSIGNMENT 3
- Consolidation assignment

ASSIGNMENT 4
- Searching on one condition

ASSIGNMENT 5
- Searching on two conditions

ASSIGNMENT 6
- Searching on three conditions
- Displaying selected fields for all records

ASSIGNMENT 7
- Combining the 'displaying selected fields' facility with a one-condition search

ASSIGNMENT 8
- Combining the 'displaying selected fields' facility with a two-condition search
- Sorting a file in alphabetical order on one field

ASSIGNMENT 9
- Sorting a file in ascending numerical order on one field
- Using the global replace facility

ASSIGNMENT 10
- Searching on four fields
- Sorting a file in descending numerical order on one field
- Organising a file on one field using the indexing facility (if possible)

ASSIGNMENT 11
- Deleting a field
- Inserting a new field
- Creating and saving a subset of a file

ASSIGNMENT 12
- Producing a report format

ASSIGNMENT 13
- Sorting a file chronologically
- Developing mailing labels

ASSIGNMENT 14
- Sorting on primary and secondary fields

ASSIGNMENT 15
- Producing a grouped report format

ASSIGNMENT 16
- Consolidation assignment

ASSIGNMENT 17
- Consolidation assignment

ASSIGNMENT 18
- NCVA Database Methods Paper I

ASSIGNMENT 19
- NCVA Database Methods Paper II

ASSIGNMENT 20
- NCVA Database Methods Paper III

Assignment 1

You are required to set up a file containing information on eight students. The information on each student falls under the following six headings: name, age, sex, telephone number, area and class.

In database language you must set up a file of eight records, each record consisting of six fields. When defining the record structure, the field name and width for each field are as follows:

FIELD	FIELD NAME	WIDTH
1	Name	10
2	Age	2
3	Sex	1
4	Phone	7
5	Area	11
6	Class	3

Once you have set up your record structure **and** designed a suitable data entry screen with the heading 'Student Record', you should enter the following information into the file:

NAME	AGE	SEX	PHONE	AREA	CLASS
Maher R	17	M	5612431	Ballyfermot	LW1
Andrews K	16	F	2977116	Dundrum	AC2
Stephens G	18	F	8346002	Beaumont	LW1
O'Brien P	17	F	4977701	Rathgar	ST1
Byrne S	18	M	7679061	Sutton	CM1
Williams M	19	M	4511782	Kimmage	AC2
Conway C	16	F	8360890	Glasnevin	ST1
Doyle E	18	M	4566102	Crumlin	CM1

◼Carry out the following tasks:

Save:

1. all the details to a file called STUDENT1.

Make the following alterations to the relevant records:

2. Andrews is male and lives in Rathmines.

3. Conway is 17 years old.

4. E Doyle is a student in ST1 and not CM1.

Delete:

5. P O'Brien's record from the file.

Add:

6. the following information on a new student who has just joined the school: D Ryan, 16, male, 8453222, Cabra, LW1.

Save:

7. this edited version of the file as STUDENT2.

Assignment 2

The following is a list of information on eight films that are available for rental from Leisure Video Ltd:

TITLE	CATEGORY	LEAD	LENGTH	CERT	PRICE
Jurassic Park	Thriller	Sam Neill	120	15	£2.00
Pretty Woman	Comedy	Julia Roberts	115	12	£1.50
Schindler's List	Drama	Ben Kingsley	187	18	£2.50
Speed	Action	Keanu Reeves	111	15	£2.00
The Lion King	Cartoon	Simba	101	12	£1.50
Unforgiven	Western	Clint Eastwood	125	15	£2.50
Forrest Gump	Comedy	Tom Hanks	136	12	£2.50
Circle of Friends	Drama	Minnie Driver	115	15	£2.00

The information on each film includes its title, category, leading actor or actress, running time, suitability certificate and rental cost. You are required to transfer this information to a database file on your computer. The record structure for the file is as follows:

FIELD	FIELD NAME	WIDTH
1	Title	17
2	Category	9
3	Lead	14
4	Length	3
5	Cert	2
6	Price	5

Carry out the following tasks:

Save:

1. the file to disk as FILM1.

Make the following alterations to the relevant records:

2. *Jurassic Park* is best described as an adventure film.

3. The leading role in *Schindler's List* was played by Liam Neeson.

4. The running time for *The Lion King* is only 87 minutes.

5. The cost of renting *Forrest Gump* is only £2.00.

6. Leisure Video Ltd have withdrawn *Unforgiven*. Erase the record on this film from the file.

Add:

7. the following information on two more films:

TITLE	CATEGORY	LEAD	LENGTH	CERT	PRICE
The Flintstones	Comedy	John Goodman	87	12	£2.50
Wyatt Earp	Western	Kevin Costner	183	15	£2.00

Save:

8. this edited version of the file as FILM2.

Assignment 3

Getaway Travel Ltd, specialists in sun holidays, have just given you the following details on available bookings:

COUNTRY	RESORT	PRICE	DAY	TIME	FLIGHT	PLACES
Turkey	Kusadasi	445	Thursday	08:00	TK63	19
Portugal	Faro	610	Sunday	15:00	PO71	6
Spain	Marbella	390	Friday	00:30	SP16	0
Greece	Kos	575	Tuesday	06:30	GR95	3
Malta	Valetta	525	Friday	11:00	MA52	8
Spain	Salou	435	Sunday	18:00	SP23	12
Cyprus	Limassol	480	Saturday	09:30	CY48	2
Morocco	Agadir	415	Sunday	14:30	MO91	15

You are required to transfer this information to a database file on your computer.

Carry out the following tasks:

Save:

1. the file to disk as HOLIDAY1.

Make the following alterations to the relevant records:

2. The departure time for the Portuguese holiday should be 19:00.

3. The price of the holiday in Malta should only be £385.

4. There are only 8 places left on the Spanish holiday in Salou.

5. The holiday in Cyprus should be in Paphos and not Limassol.

6. The departure day for the Moroccan holiday should be Friday.

7. As the holiday in Marbella, Spain is fully booked, delete this record from the file.

8. Information on two other holidays must be added to the file. The details are as follows:

COUNTRY	RESORT	PRICE	DAY	TIME	FLIGHT	PLACES
Greece	Corfu	460	Thursday	21:00	GR97	23
Portugal	Penina	585	Saturday	17:30	PO73	18

Save:

9. this edited version of the file to disk as HOLIDAY2.

Assignment 4

Express Couriers Ltd, based in Dublin, delivers items nationwide. Articles are classified as high (H), medium (M) or low (L) priority and are billed accordingly. Sandra Cosgrave, the managing director of the company, wishes to hold delivery details on a computer database file. You are requested to create the file and enter the following details:

ITEM	SENDER	LOCATION	RECIPIENT	COST	PRIORITY
Garden shed	Davy's DIY	Galway	P O'Dea	£42.00	M
Books	Reader's Heaven	Birr	T Dooley	£16.00	L
Wedding dress	Zoe's Boutique	Sligo	A Walsh	£50.00	H
Computer	Bits & Bytes Ltd	Galway	S O'Sullivan	£55.00	H
Dog kennel	Pet Mansions Ltd	Cork	G Dillon	£28.00	L
Satellite dish	DS Electrical Ltd	Dundalk	D McDonnell	£22.00	L
Contact lenses	Vision Care Ltd	Tralee	L Sheehy	£30.00	H
Cello	Endless Chords	Limerick	R Patterson	£36.00	M
Sunbed	Body Tones	Cork	O Hayes	£25.00	L
Safe	MD Security Ltd	Cavan	M O'Reilly	£45.00	H

Carry out the following tasks:

Save:

1. the file as COURIER1.

Make the following alterations to the relevant records:

2. Padraig O'Dea ordered a lawnmower and not a garden shed.

3. The charge for the delivery to Birr should be £19.00.

4. The satellite dish is a high priority delivery and the charge should be £42.00.

5. The Cello is to be collected from Waltons.

6. The sunbed should be delivered to O Hynes in Tuam.

7. The computer delivery has been cancelled. Remove this record from the file.

Add:

8. the following details on a new delivery to the file:

ITEM	SENDER	LOCATION	RECIPIENT	COST	PRIORITY
Water cooler	Oasis Coolers	Galway	P Brogan	£65.00	H

Save:

9. this edited version of the file as COURIER2.

Display all the details of those deliveries:

10. which are high priority.

11. which go to Galway.

12. where the cost is less than £30.00.

Assignment 5

A hotelier who specialises in angling holidays has compiled information for her guests on all the lakes within 12 km of her hotel. She can give the name of any lake, its distance from the hotel, the presence of trout in the lake, the year it was last restocked with young fish, its floor type, its depth and the availability of boats.

The information available is as follows:

LAKE	DISTANCE	TROUT	RESTOCKED	LAKE FLOOR	DEPTH	BOAT HIRE
Tully	4.0	N	1996	Sand	10.2	N
Gulladoo	3.7	Y	1995	Sand	13.5	Y
Carrigallen	0.5	N	1996	Mud	8.5	N
Garadice	11.3	Y	1994	Sand	15.4	Y
Woodford	4.6	Y	1996	Mud	11.9	N
Glasshouse	2.6	Y	1995	Mud	10.3	Y
Keeldra	6.4	N	1994	Sand	9.6	N
Errew	13.8	Y	1996	Sand	13.0	Y
Killegar	3.2	N	1996	Mud	8.8	N
Cullies	4.4	N	1994	Mud	11.3	N

You are required to set up a database file on your computer containing the above information, using the headings given above as field names.

◪Carry out the following tasks:

Save:

1. the file as LAKES1.

Make the following alterations to the relevant records:

2. The distance to Tully lake, as given in the file, is by an old unapproved road. The actual distance from the hotel to this lake by the new road is 5.5 km, and this distance should be given in the file.

3. Trout are not present in Woodford lake but are present in Cullies lake.

4. Keeldra lake was last restocked with young fish in 1996.

5. The maximum depth of Garadice lake has been measured incorrectly. Members of a visiting sub-aqua club have discovered an underwater channel with a depth of 24.3 m, and this must now be reflected in the file as the maximum depth of this lake.

6. Errew lake is more than 12 km from the hotel and should not be listed. Erase this record from the file.

7. The hotelier, when compiling the information, overlooked an excellent trout lake that is only 7.2 km from the hotel. You must include its details in the file. The information is as follows:

LAKE	DISTANCE	TROUT	RESTOCKED	LAKE FLOOR	DEPTH	BOAT HIRE
Calloughs	7.2	Y	1996	Sand	14.1	Y

Save:

8. this edited version of the file as LAKES2.

Display all the details of those lakes:

9. where trout are present.

10. that have a lake floor of sand.

11. that are less than 4 km from the hotel and have boat hire.

12. that are more than 10 m deep and have a lake floor of mud.

Assignment 6

The marathon, a race over 26 miles, is held each year in a certain city. To aid efficient running of the event the organisers hold the following information on each entrant: the athlete's name, vest number, age, sex, club, wheelchair user (Y/N), number of previous marathons run and the athlete's personal best time in a marathon.

You are requested to set up a database file on computer containing the following details on ten marathon entrants using the headings given as field names:

ATHLETE	NUMBER	AGE	SEX	CLUB	WHEELCHAIR	MARATHONS	TIME
P Brady	6783	19	M	Cavan	N	1	3.2
O Murphy	2910	24	F	Wexford	N	5	2.8
K Nugent	3420	37	M	Portlaoise	Y	6	3.1
R O'Brien	8003	21	F	Santry	N	8	3.0
C Murtagh	4430	29	F	Trim	N	2	3.9
H Greene	7821	36	M	Drimnagh	N	11	2.7
S Daly	9926	44	M	Longford	N	6	3.3
R McCann	3418	18	F	Tuam	Y	4	2.9
F Lynch	1099	32	M	Santry	N	7	3.5
M Quinn	6225	23	F	Thurles	N	9	3.1

◪**Carry out the following tasks:**

Save:

1. the file as MARATHON.

Display all the details of the entrant(s) who:

2. has vest number 4430.
3. are from the Santry club.
4. are more than 30 years of age.
5. have personal best times of less than 3 hours.
6. is male **and** is a wheelchair user.
7. is more than 30 years of age **and** has a personal best time of less than 3 hours.
8. are female **and** have run more than five marathons.
9. are under 25 years of age **and** are not wheelchair entrants **and** who have run more than one marathon to date.
10. Display the Athlete, Age and Club fields **only** for all the entrants in the file.

Assignment 7

Noeleen's Newsagents stock a wide range of magazines. Noeleen Mooney, the owner of the shop, holds the following information on each magazine in stock:

- the magazine name
- its category and price
- its frequency (weekly or monthly)
- quantity on order
- day of issue
- the number of copies which must be reserved
- whether the magazine is imported or not.

Noeleen wishes to hold the magazine details in a computer database file. You are employed to set up this file containing the information given below. You can use the headings given as field names.

MAGAZINE	CATEGORY	PRICE	FREQUENCY	QUANTITY	DAY	RESERVED	IMPORT
RTE Guide	TV	£0.85	W	80	Wed	15	N
Vogue	Women's	£4.96	M	45	Wed	12	Y
Runner's World	Sport	£2.87	M	10	Mon	5	Y
PC Direct	Computing	£2.93	M	30	Tue	8	Y
TV Times	TV	£0.69	W	25	Sat	0	Y
Touchdown	Sport	£3.00	M	20	Mon	6	Y
U	Women's	£1.65	M	35	Wed	11	N
Carsport	Sport	£2.35	M	8	Fri	0	N
PC Plus	Computing	£4.56	M	50	Mon	25	Y
Garden Answers	Gardening	£2.18	M	25	Fri	3	Y
Irish Cycling	Sport	£1.50	M	5	Thu	0	N
Best	Women's	£0.68	W	20	Tue	5	Y

◥Carry out the following tasks:

Save:

1. the file as MAGAZINE.

Display all the details of the magazine(s) that:

2. are issued on a Wednesday.

3. are produced in Ireland.

4. are women's magazines **and** cost more than £1.00.

5. are issued weekly **and** are imported.

6. cost less than £1.00 **or** more than £3.00.

7. is issued on a Monday **and** costs less than £3.00 **and** is in the sport category.

Display:

8. the magazine name, category and price of all the magazines in the file.

9. the magazine name, category, price and quantity details of all the computing magazines in the file.

10. the magazine name, frequency, quantity, day and number of details of all the magazines that are reserved .

Assignment 8

Leinster Coach Hire Ltd, established in 1995, offers carefree and cost effective access to any part of the country. Each booking is recorded, at present, in the company's day log book. The following table shows the details of 12 separate bookings:

TO	PURPOSE	ORGANISER	DATE	GROUP	AGE PROFILE	COST	PREVIOUS USE?
Cork	Holiday	Greene P	04/10/96	22	1	£190.00	N
Knock	Pilgrimage	O' Connor K	15/09/96	83	5	£520.00	Y
Mosney	School tour	Daly T	14/06/96	38	3	£140.00	Y
Roscommon	Wedding	Cox D	18/08/96	14	2	£115.00	N
Killarney	Holiday	Cooney D	10/07/96	8	2	£85.00	Y
Blarney	Holiday	Mahon D	03/06/96	20	4	£175.00	N
Lough Derg	Pilgrimage	Galvin P	23/08/96	51	2	£330.00	N
Cavan	Fishing trip	Brennan M	25/07/96	12	2	£72.00	N
Belfast	School tour	Smyth J	28/06/96	60	3	£365.00	Y
Knock	Pilgrimage	Jones R	07/08/96	90	5	£600.00	N
Doolin	Field trip	Elsdon H	18/09/96	27	4	£280.00	Y
Galway	Holiday	Dunne C	18/08/96	9	1	£110.00	Y

Each booking shows:
- destination
- purpose of the coach hire
- organiser
- date of proposed trip
- number in the group
- age profile of the passengers
- cost of the booking
- whether a previous booking has been made by the organiser.

The age profile is recorded using a 1–5 code system: 1 — old age pensioners, 2 — adults, 3 — children, 4 — students and 5 — mixed. You are required to set up a database file on your computer containing the information in the table above. You should use the headings given in the table as field names.

◪ Carry out the following tasks:

Save:
1. the file as COACH.

Display all the details of the booking(s):
2. where there are more than 10 in the group **and** the age profile of the intending passengers is adult.
3. that were made for August.
4. that are either pilgrimages **or** holidays.
5. that are neither pilgrimages **nor** holidays.
6. where there are more than 50 intending passengers in the group **and** the cost is less than £500.00 **and** where previous bookings have been made.
7. made for a group of old age pensioners in October.

Display:

8. the destination, organiser, date and group details for any wedding bookings.

9. the destination, date and cost details for any bookings where the age profile of the group is either adult **or** mixed.

Sort:

10. the entire file in alphabetical order of the organiser's name.

Save:

11. this sorted file as COACH2.

Assignment 9

A maternity hospital holds the following information on new mothers:

- mother's name
- ward
- mother's age
- date of the birth
- sex of the baby
- weight of the baby in kilograms
- the number of children born to the mother
- VHI membership (Y or N)
- attending doctor.

Set up a database file on your computer holding the details on the ten mothers listed below. You can use the headings given as field names.

MOTHER	WARD	AGE	DATE	SEX	WEIGHT	CHILD	VHI	DOCTOR
Mills D	St Peter's	22	3/9/96	F	2.9	1	Y	Dr Wilcox
O'Dea F	St Clare's	34	6/9/96	F	3.2	4	Y	Dr Evans
Willis P	St Anne's	29	6/9/96	M	3.0	1	N	Dr Evans
O' Hare Y	St Anne's	30	2/9/96	F	3.6	2	Y	Dr Kent
Sammon M	St. Anne's	41	3/9/96	M	2.9	5	Y	Dr Wilcox
O' Neill A	St Clare's	25	5/9/96	M	4.2	2	Y	Dr Kent
Molloy K	St Peter's	19	1/9/96	F	2.5	1	N	Dr Evans
Byrne L	St Anne's	33	5/9/96	M	3.7	1	Y	Dr Kent
Conway T	St Peter's	24	4/9/96	M	3.4	2	Y	Dr Kent
Quinn A	St Peter's	27	6/9/96	F	4.0	3	N	Dr Wilcox

◣Carry out the following tasks:

Save:

1. the file as BABY1.

Replace:

2. the ward name *St Peter's* with *St Mark's* in the file by using the global replace facility of your database program

Display all the details of the mother(s) who:

3. had baby girls and are in St Mark's ward.
4. are 30 years old or more **and** are being attended by Dr Kent.
5. had a baby girl weighing less than 4 kilograms on 6 September.

Sort:

6. the file into alphabetical order of mothers' names.

Save:

7. the sorted file as BABY2.

Display from the BABY2 file:

8. the name, age and attending doctor of those mothers who are not members of the VHI.

Sort:

9. the BABY2 file into ascending order of babies' weights.

Save:

10. this file as BABY3.

Display from the BABY3 file:

11. the name, ward, sex, weight and child details of those mothers whose new baby weighed 4 kilograms or less **and** who have more than one child.

Assignment 10

The Denver Pizza Company, established in 1996, supplies succulent American-style pizzas to homes all over Dublin. Nine items of information are held on each order received. Rick Baker, the owner of the company, wishes to transfer these order details to a computer database file. The information held on each order is as follows:

- customer's name and address
- the exact time that the order was placed
- the pizza type
- the pizza size — large (L), medium (M) or small (S)
- the base type — deep pan (DP) or light and crispy (LC)
- the number of toppings (Tpns) requested
- the price of the pizza

- whether or not the pizza was delivered.

Set up the database file on your computer containing the details in the table below. The headings in the table can be used as field names.

CUSTOMER	ADDRESS	TIME	PIZZA	SIZE	BASE	TPNS	PRICE	DELIVERY
O' Brien G	4 Seacliff Rd	18:33	Hawaiian	L	DP	8	£10.15	Y
White M	51 Idrone Dr	17:51	Hot & Spicy	L	DP	3	£8.55	Y
McCann F	3 Elkwood St	18:55	Mighty Meaty	S	LC	5	£2.85	N
Wilson H	15 Wood Ct	18:03	Full House	L	LC	4	£6.20	Y
Brady A	9 Hill Gdns	18:24	BLT	M	LC	7	£4.25	Y
McHugh M	121 Myrtle St	17:46	Veggie's Delight	M	DP	3	£5.80	N
O'Reilly P	67 Russell Ave	18:15	Hawaiian	S	LC	8	£4.05	Y
Foley K	19 Kincora Rd	16:40	Original	L	DP	5	£8.80	Y
Cummins B	4 Church Ave	17:05	Bombay Double	S	DP	4	£5.20	N
Dowd P	22 Ludford Pk	18:37	Sicilian	S	LC	3	£2.05	Y
Maher R	156 Barry Rd	17:30	Mighty Meaty	L	DP	6	£8.90	N
Colgan E	10 Hilltop St	16:51	Original	M	DP	5	£6.55	Y

◪Carry out the following tasks:

Save:

1. the entire file as PIZZA1.

Display all the details of the order(s) for any:

2. medium original pizza.
3. large pizzas with five toppings or less.
4. small pizzas delivered after 18:00.
5. large deep pan pizzas that were delivered and cost less than £9.00.

Sort:

6. the file into chronometric (time) order.

Save:

7. the sorted file as PIZZA2.

Display:

8. the customer's name and address, the pizza type and the order time for all light and crispy pizzas that were delivered.

Sort:

9. the file into descending order of pizza prices.

Save:

10. this sorted file as PIZZA3.

11. the customer's name, the pizza type, size and price for all orders listed except those for Hawaiian **and** Original pizzas.
12. Produce, using the indexing facility of your program (if possible), a display of the entire file organised in alphabetical order of customer names.

Assignment 11

You are required to set up a database file containing information on the twelve countries listed below. The information on each country includes:

- the name of the country
- its population
- its area (in square kilometres)
- the capital city
- the principal language
- its unit of currency
- the highest point above sea level in metres (HP)
- the type of government (Govt)
- the main religion (Rel).

In the table, abbreviations have been used for the government types and main religions. The abbreviations for government types are as follows:

- constitutional monarchy — Cm
- federal republic — Fr
- constitutional republic — Cr
- Islamic republic — Ir
- multiparty republic — Mr

The abbreviations for the religions are:

- Christianity — Ch
- Islam — Is
- Judaism — Ju.

You can use the headings in the table as field names.

COUNTRY	POPULATION	AREA	CAPITAL	LANGUAGE	CURRENCY	HP	GOVT	REL
Ireland	3,509,000	70,284	Dublin	English	Punt	1,041	Cr	Ch
UK	57,376,000	244,100	London	English	Pound	1,343	Cm	Ch
Germany	77,754,000	356,755	Berlin	German	Mark	2,963	Cr	Ch
USA	250,941,000	9,372,614	Washington	English	US dollar	6,194	Fr	Ch
Pakistan	122,666,000	796,095	Islamabad	Urdu	Rupee	8,611	Ir	Is
Brazil	150,368,000	8,511,965	Brasilia	Portuguese	Cruzeiro	3,014	Mr	Ch
Israel	4,616,000	20,770	Jerusalem	Hebrew	Shekel	1,208	Mr	Ju
Argentina	32,880,000	2,766,889	Buenos Aires	Spanish	Austral	6,960	Fr	Ch
Iran	56,923,000	1,648,000	Tehran	Farsi	Rial	5,604	Ir	Is
Peru	22,332,000	1,285,216	Lima	Spanish	Inti	6,768	Mr	Ch
Morocco	25,228,000	458,730	Rabat	Arabic	Dirham	4,165	Cm	Is
Sweden	8,523,000	449,964	Stockholm	Swedish	Krona	2,111	Cm	Ch

◪ Carry out the following tasks:

Save:

1. the file as COUNTRY1.

Display all the details of any:

2. non-English speaking countries where Christianity is the main religion.
3. countries that are either constitutional or multiparty republics with populations of less than 50 million people.

Delete:

4. the field containing the details for the highest point above sea level from the file.

Insert:

5. a new field between the Currency and Govt fields to hold the per capita gross national product details for each country. The latter is expressed in US dollars. Use GNP as the field name.

Enter:

6. the following per capita GNP details for each country into the new field in each record:
Ireland — $8,500, UK — $14,570, Germany — $20,750, USA — $21,100,
Pakistan — $370, Brazil — $2,550, Israel — $9,750, Argentina — $2,160, Iran — $4,500,
Peru — $1,090, Morocco — $900, Sweden — $21,170.

Sort:

7. the file into descending order of per capita GNP.

Save:

8. the sorted file as COUNTRY2.

Extract:

9. from the COUNTRY2 file all the details of countries whose per capita GNP is less than $US 10,000.

Save:

10. this subset to a new file called COUNTRY3.

Recall:

11. the original COUNTRY1 file to the screen.

Sort:

12. this file into alphabetical order of country names.

Save:

13. this sorted file as COUNTRY4.

Print:

14. the entire COUNTRY4 file.

Assignment 12

MountainView Business Park is home to twelve different companies. Pat Cash, the manager of the park, holds the following details on each company:

Company — the company's name

Business — its line of business

Owner — the owner of the company

Established — the year that the company was set up

Type — whether it is a service (S) or manufacturing (M) company

Employees — the number of staff

Premises — whether the company's premises are owned (O) or rented (R)

Export — whether the company exports its products (Y or N).

You must enter the details in the table below into a database file using the italicised words above as field names.

Absel Drilling	Concrete drilling	Stone D	1992	S	12	R	N
HomeWorld	Kitchens	Brady P	1996	M	7	O	N
Curtex Blinds	Window blinds	Curtain R	1994	M	21	O	Y
Moo-moo Foods	Dairy Products	O' Grady K	1992	M	43	O	Y
Elegant Rooms	Interior design	Ashley A	1996	S	5	R	N
P Murtagh & Co.	Architects	Murtagh P	1990	S	9	O	N
GA Ices	Ice cream	O' Grady K	1995	M	18	O	N
Cans and all	Recycling	Tidy D	1993	M	26	R	N
Which Way?	Brass signs	Knowles S	1995	M	8	R	N
Little Ones	Children's clothes	McEniff B	1994	M	35	O	Y
EasyClean	Carpet cleaning	Waters B	1996	S	4	R	N
Jetwash	Pressure washers	Richards M	1996	M	15	R	Y

◪Carry out the following tasks:

Save:

1. the file as COMPANY1.

Display:

2. the company names and owners for all companies set up prior to 1996.

Insert:

3. a new *telephone* field after the owner field.

Enter:

4. the telephone number of each company: Absel Drilling — 21988, HomeWorld — 32751, Curtex Blinds — 30887, Moo-moo Foods — 21997, Elegant Rooms — 32880, P Murtagh & Co. — 20017, GA Ices — 31634, Cans and all — 24119, Which Way? — 31772, Little Ones — 30955, EasyClean — 32859, Jetwash — 30910.

Sort:

5. the file into descending order of the number of staff employed.

Save:

6. the sorted file as COMPANY2.

Extract:

7. from the COMPANY2 file all the details of the non-exporting companies who own their own premises.

Save:

8. this subset to a new file called COMPANY3.

Print:

9. the COMPANY3 file.

Recall:

10. the original COMPANY1 file to the screen.

Sort:

11. the file into alphabetical order of company name.

Save:

12. this sorted file as COMPANY4.

Create:

13. a report format, using the COMPANY4 file, that has the heading 'MountainView Business Park' and shows the company names, respective owners and respective numbers of employees.

Assign:

14. the name BUSPARK to the report.

Print:

15. the report.

Assignment 13

Ticketron Ltd take bookings for various entertainment events. Details of each booking are held on a record card. A blank record card looks like this:

```
                    TICKETRON LTD

    NAME ................    ROAD......................
    AREA ................    COUNTY ...................
    EVENT ................   VENUE ....................
    TYPE ................    PRICE ......................
    DATE ................    TICKETS ...................
    CREDIT CARD ........
```

The type field shows whether the event is a concert (C), a play (P) or a sporting (S) occasion. The credit card field shows whether the booking was made by credit card (Y/N). Set up a database file on your computer and enter the following details of eight separate bookings:

Nolan P	22 Clogher Rd
Crumlin	Dublin 12
The Mai	Peacock
P	£10.00
26/08/96	2
Y	

Hoey A	9 Muirhevna Rd
Dundalk	Co Louth
R.E.M	Slane
C	£25.00
21/07/96	1
Y	

Cahill F	12 Farnham St
Cavan	Co Cavan
Wrestlemania	Point
S	£20.00
29/08/96	1
N	

Keran P	High St
Ballinamore	Co Leitrim
Elton John	RDS
C	£22.00
08/09/96	4
Y	

Daly S	65 Greenlea Rd
Terenure	Dublin 6
The Cranberries	Millstreet
C	£15.00
07/07/96	2
Y	

Murphy M	85 Glanmire Rd
Cork	Co Cork
Big Maggie	Gaeity
P	£8.00
25/06/96	3
Y	

Quinn J	8 Main St		Fox P	34 Ennis Rd
Clifden	Co Galway		Limerick	Co Limerick
Feile	Pairc Ui Caoimh		Sive	Abbey
C	£45.00		P	£12.00
21/07/96	2		19/07/96	2
N			Y	

◩ Carry out the following tasks:

Save:

1. the file as TICKET1.

Organise (using the sort or indexing facilities):

2. the file into chronological (date) order.

Save:

3. the index or sort file as TICKET2.

Extract:

4. from the organised file all the details of those bookings made by credit card for events in July.

Save:

5. this subset to a new file called VISA.

Print:

6. the VISA file.

Recall:

7. the original TICKET1 file to the screen.

Sort:

8. the file into ascending order of event type (primary key) and alphabetical order of name (secondary key).

Save:

9. this sorted file as TICKET3.

Create:

10. a report format, using the TICKET3 file, that has the heading 'Ticketron Ticket Sales' and shows only the name, road, area, county, event and number of tickets. Do not total the number of tickets in the report.

Save:

11. this report as TICKETRP.

Re-sort:

12. the TICKET3 file into reverse chronological order.

Save:

13. this new sorted file as TICKET4.

Develop:

14. suitable mailing labels (name, road, area and county) from the TICKET4 file with two labels across the page.

Save:

15. the mailing labels to a file called LABELS.

Print:

16. the mailing labels.

Assignment 14

Autoline Insure Direct PLC, based in Cork, provides car insurance for drivers of all ages. Details of each insured driver are currently held in paper files. A blank insurance card from the files would appear as follows:

```
┌─────────────────────────────────────────────────┐
│          AUTOLINE INSURE DIRECT PLC              │
│            DRIVER INSURANCE CARD                 │
│                                                  │
│   NAME ................   POLICY NO. ............ │
│   CAR ......................   MODEL .................... │
│   REG. NO. ............   EXPIRY DATE .......... │
│   PREMIUM ............   CATEGORY .............. │
│   CLAIM ................   FULL LICENCE .......... │
└─────────────────────────────────────────────────┘
```

Two fields on this card require explanation:

- **Category** — the type of insurance bought. This may be fully comprehensive (Co), third party, fire and theft (Tt) or third party (Tp).
- **Claim** — whether the driver has claimed on a policy during the past five years (Y/N).

You are given the following details on eight different drivers that are insured with the company:

Hughes Mary	MP0987
Nissan	Almera
96-CN-559	12/09/97
£722	Co
N	Y

Silke Sean	MO1009
Volkswagen	Vento
94-LS-6712	31/10/97
£458	Tt
N	Y

Murphy Noel MP7812 Toyota Carina 96-D-4599 02/09/97 £1,239 Co Y Y	Nugent Kathy SK2388 Renault Clio 96-WX-1008 19/04/97 £355 Tp N Y
Larkin Brenda MO7661 Toyota Starlet 95-MO-812 25/09/97 £640 Tt N N	Moore Owen RD4556 Volkswagen Passat 96-LM-88 15/08/97 £550 Co N Y
Keegan James SK9948 Ford Mondeo 95-C-9120 30/09/97 £1,085 Tt N N	Evans Sandra MP8110 Nissan Micra 94-KE-226 28/06/97 £970 Co Y Y

Set up a database file on your computer and enter the details given. Your data entry screen should look identical to the record card shown on p. 100 (the border is optional).

◼Carry out the following tasks:

Save:

1. the file as POLICY1.

Extract:

2. a subset of records from the file that consists of all policies that expire during September **and** October 1997.

Save:

3. this subset to a new file called SOPOLICY.

Sort:

4. the POLICY1 file into alphabetical order of category (primary key) **and** descending order of premium (secondary key).

Save:

5. the sorted file as POLICY2.

Extract:

6. a subset of records from the POLICY2 file that consists of all the details for drivers who have bought either third party **or** third party, fire and theft policies.

Save:

7. this subset to a new file called POLICY3.

Produce:

8. a report format from the POLICY3 file showing all the fields with the heading 'Non Fully Comprehensive Policies'.

Save:

9. this report as POLRPT1.

Retrieve:

10. the POLICY1 file.

Sort:

11. this file into reverse alphabetical order of driver name.

Save:

12. this sorted file as POLICY4.

Extract:

13. from the POLICY4 file all the details of policies on cars that were registered before 1996.

Save:

14. this subset to a new file called PRE96.

Produce:

15. a report format from the PRE96 file that has the heading 'Old Car Policies' and shows the driver's name, car, model, expiry date and premium only. This report should also show the average premium for the listed policies.

Save:

16. this report as OLDERCAR.

Print:

17. this latter report.

Assignment 15

Irish Estates Ltd provides details of farms for sale throughout Ireland. The following details are held on each farm:

• Auctioneer — handling the sale

- County — where the farm is located
- Code — each farm has a unique code
- Acres — number for sale
- Type — Beef, dairy, mixed or tillage farm
- Price — seller's reserve price
- Lots — the farm may be divided into several lots
- Frontage — along the roadside (Fr)
- Dwelling house — on the land (Dw).

Set up a database file containing the details in the table below. The data input screen should have the centred title 'Irish Estates Ltd' and there should be three fields per line. Choose appropriate field names.

AUCTIONEER	COUNTY	CODE	ACRES	TYPE	PRICE	LOTS	FR	DW
Trim Agri-sales Ltd	Meath	M244	8	Beef	£25,000	1	N	N
O'Shea Properties	Cork	D397	212	Dairy	£750,000	1	Y	Y
Cody & Daughter	Kilkenny	T098	103	Tillage	£315,000	2	Y	Y
Mahon Estates	Louth	M249	27	Beef	£65,000	1	Y	N
Brady & Co	Cavan	J884	77	Dairy	£190,000	1	Y	N
McHale & Co	Mayo	C452	67	Mixed	£132,000	2	Y	Y
O'Shea Properties	Kerry	D391	45	Mixed	£110,000	3	Y	Y
Mahon Estates	Meath	M230	12	Beef	£45,000	1	N	N
Wilson & Sons	Wexford	H348	52	Tillage	£150,000	2	Y	N
Brady & Co	Cavan	J763	32	Beef	£80,000	1	Y	N
Green Acres Ltd	Tipperary	K019	150	Dairy	£410,000	1	Y	Y
Mahon Estates	Meath	M238	80	Dairy	£225,000	3	N	Y

◪Carry out the following tasks:

Save:

1. the file as FARM1.

Extract:

2. from the file the county, acres, price and auctioneer fields **only** for any dairy farm listed.

Save:

3. this subset to a new file called MILKFARM.

Print:

4. the MILKFARM file.

Extract:

5. from the original FARM1 file the county, acres, lots, dwelling house and price fields (in that order) for all non-dairy farms costing £150,000 or less.

Save:

6. this subset to a new file called NONMILK1

Sort:

7. the NONMILK1 file into descending order of farm size (acres).

Save:

8. this sorted file as NONMILK2.

Produce:

9. a report format from this file showing the acres and price fields. The report should have the centred heading 'Non-Dairy Farms'. The report should also highlight the price of the cheapest farm listed.

Save:

10. this report as FARMREP1.

Modify:

11. the report to include the dwelling house field.

Save:

12. this modified report as FARMREP2.

Recall:

13. the original FARM1 file to the screen.

Sort:

14. the file into alphabetical order of type (primary key) and descending order of price (secondary key)

Save:

15. this sorted file as FARM2.

Produce:

16. a *grouped* report format based on the type field from the file showing the auctioneer, county, type, price, acres and lots fields (in that order) **only** for each farm listed. The report should have the centred heading 'Farms for Sale'. The report should also include the average size (acres) of each farm type listed.

Save:

17. this report as FARMREP3.

Print:

18. this latter report.

Assignment 16

Mayfield College provides a range of evening classes during the winter months. Elizabeth Gormley, the head of the evening school at Mayfield College, must hold the following details on each course:

- *Course*
- *Code*
- *Day*
- *Time*
- *Weeks* — duration of the course
- *Size* — number in class
- *Teacher*
- *Exam* — Y/N
- *Cost*
- *Room*.

Using the italicised words as field names, enter the details outlined in the following table into a database file:

Spreadsheets	Wp	Wed	19:00–21:00	10	15	Flynn T	Y	£80	C31
Accounting	Ac	Thu	19:00–20:30	20	25	Cox D	Y	£150	A15
Typing	Ty	Mon	19:00–20:30	10	18	Cahill A	Y	£70	S12
Psychology	At	Mon	20:00–21:00	6	25	Watson B	N	£40	S19
Yoga	Yo	Tue	20:00–22:00	12	10	Wilson M	N	£90	Gym
Economics	Ec	Thu	19:30–21:00	20	20	Moore D	Y	£150	A17
Spanish	Sp	Wed	19:00–21:00	15	15	O'Reilly K	N	£100	L04
Cookery	Co	Mon	19:00–21:00	8	12	Murtagh C	Y	£80	H10
Aerobics	Ae	Thu	20:30–22:00	12	15	Wilson M	N	£80	Gym
databases	Dp	Mon	19:00–21:00	10	18	Flynn T	Y	£90	C31

◣Carry out the following tasks:

Save:

1. the file as EVENING1.

Make the following alterations to the relevant records:

2. Desmond Cox takes his Accounting class in room A09.
3. Denise Moore's Economics class starts at 19:00 on Wednesday evenings.
4. Caroline Murtagh's Cookery class costs £115.
5. Michael Wilson's Aerobics class has been cancelled. Delete this record from the file.

Enter:

6. the following details on two new courses:

GERMAN	GE	THU	20:00–22:00	15	20	KALTZ M	Y	£100	L05
LAW	LA	MON	19:00–21:00	18	25	SMYTH J	Y	£180	A17

Erase:

7. the Code field from the file.

Enter:

8. a new field called *Dept* to show the department running the course and insert the following details for the relevant records:

COURSE	DEPT
Spreadsheets	Computer
Accounting	Business
Typing	Secretarial
Psychology	Fitness
Yoga	Fitness
Economics	Business
Spanish	Language
Cookery	Catering
Aerobics	Fitness
databases	Computer
German	Language
Law	Business

Save:

9. this edited file as EVENING2.

Extract:

10. all the records for courses that are run on Monday evenings **and** cost less than £100.

Save:

11. this subset to a new file called MONCLASS.

Sort:

12. the EVENING2 file into alphabetic order of department (primary key) and descending order of cost (secondary key).

Save:

13. this sorted file as EVENING3.

Produce:

14. a report format using the EVENING3 file that has the heading 'Mayfield College — Evening Classes' and shows only the course, time, day, weeks and cost fields. The duration and cost fields must not be totalled on the report.

Save:

15. this report as CLASSRPT.

Print:

16. the report.

Assignment 17

The *Evening Echo*, Ireland's fastest growing evening newpaper, carries twelve pages of classified advertisements. Mary McCarthy, the editor, holds nine different items of information on each classified advertisement in the paper:

- *Section* — under which the advertisement is placed
- *Description* — of item or service
- *Words* — number of words in the advertisement
- *Evenings* — number for which the advertisement is carried
- *Date* — of first printing
- *Name* — of person who placed the advertisement
- *Cost* — of placing the advertisement
- *Box no.* — reply (Y/N)
- *Payment* — credit card (Cc), cheque (Ch) or Cash (Ca).

  Using the italicised words above as field names, produce a database file containing the details in the table below:

Section	Description	Words	Evenings	Date	Name	Cost	Box	Payment
Jobs	Secretary	20	2	12/09/96	Logan R	£13.00	Y	Cc
Holidays	Kerry B & B	12	5	14/09/96	Keegan M	£22.00	N	Ch
Pets	Pony	17	4	17/09/96	Byrne A	£25.50	Y	Cc
Lost & Found	Wallet	8	2	10/09/96	Lawlor K	£7.50	Y	Ch
Holidays	Sligo Hotel	30	3	18/09/96	Silke D	£31.75	N	Cc
Equipment	Piano	25	2	13/09/96	Evans H	£16.50	Y	Ca
Pets	Dog	18	2	16/09/96	Joyce C	£12.50	N	Ca
Jobs	Accountant	14	2	14/09/96	Logan R	£10.75	Y	Cc
Equipment	Gas Cooker	22	3	18/09/96	Brogan A	£24.00	N	Cc
Pets	Budgie	14	4	15/09/96	Conway T	£20.00	Y	Ch
Pets	Cat	12	4	12/09/96	O' Dea J	£16.00	Y	Ca
Jobs	Chef	27	2	16/09/96	Foley S	£17.00	Y	Cc
Equipment	Bicycle	20	3	16/09/96	Lynch B	£21.50	N	Ch
Holidays	Cavan Chalet	18	5	11/09/96	O'Reilly P	£30.00	Y	Cc

⬛Carry out the following tasks:

Save:

1. the file as ADVERT1.

Make the following alterations to the relevant records:

2. the cost of advertising for the wallet in the *Lost & Found* section was only £5.00.
3. the piano was advertised in the *Music* section.
4. Susan Foley's advertisement was carried for three evenings, cost £24.00 and was paid for in cash.

Delete:

5. the record containing the details of an advertisement of a cat.

Save:

6. this edited version of the file as ADVERT2.

Extract:

7. all records of those advertisements that cost more than £20.00 and were paid for by credit card.

Save:

8. this subset to a new file called CCPAY.

Sort:

9. the ADVERT2 file into chronological order.

Save:

10. the sorted file as ADVERT3.

Produce:

11. a report format from the file using all the fields with the heading 'Evening Echo — Classifieds'. The cost field **only** must be totalled.

Save:

12. this report as ECHORPT1.

Sort:

13. the ADVERT3 file in ascending order of the number of *evenings* (primary key) and ascending order of *cost* (secondary key).

Save: .

14. this sorted file as ADVERT4.

Produce:

15. a *grouped* report format from the file showing the section, description, words, cost and name fields. The report should have the centred heading 'Customer Enquiries'. The report should also include averages for the words **and** cost fields for 2, 3, 4 and 5 evening advertisements.

108

16. this report as ECHORPT2.

17. this latter report.

Assignment 18
NCVA Database Methods Sample Paper I

◤Task 1

Set up a database structure from supplied structure data (see Figure 1), choosing appropriate data types, print the structure, and save as 'CUSTOMER'.

Note: You may make changes to the suggested field names, if necessitated by your data-base software, provided they accurately describe the contents of the field.

NAME OF FIELD	TYPE	WIDTH
Account No.	?	4
Customer Name	?	12
Address 1	?	17
Address 2	?	10
Equipment	?	20
Price	?	5
Invoiced?	?	1
Paid?	?	1

Figure 1

◤Task 2

Enter the data supplied in Figure 3 accurately, using a formatted Data Entry Screen, (see Figure 2), and save again as 'CUSTOMER'.

WIZZARD COMPUTER SALES TRACKING SYSTEM

Customer Account Code: Customer Name:

Customer Address:

Type of Equipment: Price:

Have the Goods Been Invoiced?:   Has Payment Been Received?:

Figure 2

Notes on the Data Entry Screen Format (see Figure 2 for suggested format):

a) The screen format should have a centred heading, 'Wizzard Computer Sales Tracking System'.

b) There should be at least two input fields and suitable field labels on each line of the data entry screen.

A/C NO.	CUSTOMER	ADD1	ADD2	EQUIPMENT	PRICE	INVOICED	PAID
2378	VCR Supplies	21, Fade St	Dublin 1	33 Mhz 386SX 100MB HD	1289	Y	N
2376	Gone West	123, Lagan St	Dundalk	66 Mhz 486DX 350MB HD	1974	Y	N
2337	Murphy Ltd	80, Cork St	Dublin 12	66 Mhz 486DX 85MB HD	1243	Y	N
2347	Alma Stores	9 Dublin Road	Carlow	33 Mhz 386SX 85MB HD	1243	Y	N
2357	Shea Travel	9, Bray Ind Est	Wicklow	33 Mhz 386SX 185MB HD	1378	Y	N
2356	People Power	41, Clare St	Cork	66 Mhz 486DX 85MB HD	1243	Y	N
2358	Sports Wear	76, Church St	Arklow	33 Mhz 386SX 100MB HD	1289	Y	N
2334	Dutch Import	10, Lesson St	Dublin 4	66 Mhz 486DX 170MB HD	1624	Y	N
2322	Willy Porter	Main St	Wicklow	66 Mhz 486DX 85MB HD	1428	Y	N
2393	ABC Cars Ltd	Hill House	Portrush	33 Mhz 386SX 85MB HD	1243	Y	N
2374	Car Valets	91, Pearse St	Dublin 2	33 Mhz 386SX 200MB HD	1579	Y	N
2372	New Age Tours	14, Market Square	Kildare	33 Mhz 386SX 120MB HD	1320	Y	N

Figure 3

◼Task 3

a) Change the contents of the PAID field to 'Y' for those customers with the following account numbers: 2337, 2356, 2357, 2322, 2376 and 2374.

b) Print the resulting database using a full report format, choosing an appropriate report title, and appropriate column titles for each field, as well as totalling the price field.

a) Create a subset of this file, extracting those records where invoices have not been paid, and save the resulting file as 'NOTPAID'.

b) Organise the new file 'NOTPAID' in DESCENDING order of price (primary key field) and customer name (secondary key field), and save as 'NOTPAID2'.

c) Develop and print mailing labels for the customer records in the file 'NOTPAID2' (at least two labels across the printed page).

■Task 5

a) Using the original file 'CUSTOMER', make the following alterations:

   I. change the address of Murphy Ltd from '89, Cork St' to '10, JFK Ind Est'.

   II. change the equipment for Shea Travel to a 66 Mhz 486DX, leaving the hard disk as is, and altering the price to 1768.

   III. delete the record for Willy Porter.

b) Using the updated file, 'CUSTOMER', and an appropriate search string, select only those records for customers who purchased an 85MB Hard Disk, and print them.

c) Print the contents of the fields Account No., Customer Name, Address 1, and equipment from the updated file, 'CUSTOMER'.

Assignment 19
NCVA Database Methods Paper II
■Introduction

Ardara Crafts Distribution Centre collects articles, both handmade and machine-made, from craftspeople throughout a wide area, for sending on to buyers both overseas and within the country. Some of the articles sent in to the Centre are sent on as they are, because they are made for a single order; while other articles are divided up between a number of buyers. Michael Herrity, the manager of the Centre, requires a database to be set up in order to facilitate the handling of the articles and to ensure that the correct articles go to make up the correct orders.

■Task 1 (6 marks)

From the database structure provided in Figure 1, create a database to store the data provided in Figure 2, using appropriate field names and data types. Write out this structure, and save the resulting database as **'CRAFTS'**.

NAME OF FIELD	DATA TYPE	WIDTH
Name of Worker	?	15
Address	?	25
Method by which Article was Made	?	8
Category of Article	?	11
Size	?	6
Colour of Article(s)	?	12
Quantity	?	3
Are Goods Part of Single Order ?	?	1

Figure 1

NAME	ADDRESS	HOW_MADE	CATEGORY	SIZE	COLOUR	QTY	SINGLE ORDER
Cashin Alma	Ardamin House, Sligo	Handmade	Pullover	M/L	Brown/Blue	12	Y
O'Neill Ian	24, Rock Road, Ardara	Machine	Shawl	M/L	Black/Brown	4	N
Clarke Anne	Glebe House, Carigoe	Handmade	Scarves	M/L	Red/Green	11	N
Buitlear Sean	Carraig Dubh, Ath an Ri	Handmade	Pullover	S/M/L	Grey/Green	8	Y
Fleming Sandra	Barton House, Ardara	Machine	Rug	M	Red/White	3	Y
Walsh Catriona	Rose Cottage, Beltra	Machine	Tablecloth	M/L	White	2	Y
Kinnear Martha	45, Carnlough Rd, Ardara	Machine	Bedspread	L	Red/Blue	3	N
O'Hare Enda	Clonagoe, Sligo	Handmade	Pullover	S/M	Red/Blue	9	N
Kernaghan Sean	Hill Farm, Killybegs	Machine	Socks	S/M	Blue/Grey	14	Y
O'Shea Aine	12, Tymon Way, Ardara	Handmade	Rug	M	Blue/Red	1	Y
Tormey Alan	Craft Shop, Portnoo	Handmade	Pullover	M/L	Brown/Black	7	N
O'Fiach Maire	Dronamore, Donegal	Handmade	Scarves	S/M/L	White/Brown	8	N

Figure 2

◪Task 2 (13 marks)

Using a suitable data input format screen, enter and save the data in Figure 2 into the database 'CRAFTS'.

Notes on data input format screen:

I. Where possible, there should be at least two fields and suitable field labels on each line of the data entry screen.

II. The entry screen should have a suitable centred heading.

III. No extra marks will be given for borders, highlighting etc.

Task 3 (14 marks)

Mr Herrity requires labels for those deliveries from his suppliers which are **not** part of a single order, in order that he may identify who made the articles, using what method, to what category they belong, in what colour(s) they are provided, and how many there are in each consignment.

a) Extract a suitable subset of the master file for this purpose, saving it to a new file, NOTSING.

b) Organise the file 'NOTSING' in ascending order of colour (primary key field) and descending method of manufacturing (secondary key field), and save this organised file or index as 'NOTSING2' for printing now or later.

c) Develop suitable labels from the file 'NOTSING', for the purpose specified in the introduction to this task, placing at least two labels across the page, for printing now or later.

Task 4 (6 marks)

Using the original database 'CRAFTS', develop a report format, containing all fields and all records, which will include a suitable report title, suitable column titles, and a total for the quantities of articles, for printing now or later.

Task 5 (11 marks)

a) Make the following alterations to the database 'CRAFTS':

   I. Delete the records for Ian O'Neill and Martha Kinnear.

   II. Change the colour of Anne Clarke's scarves from red/green to red/grey.

   III. Change the pullover from Enda O'Hare to a bedspread, and the quantity to 3 (three).

b) Using the altered file 'CRAFTS' from 5(a), select only those records for suppliers who can provide articles in small sizes, using an appropriate search string, and saving the results as 'CRAFTS2', for printing now or later.

c) Select the fields containing the name of the suppliers, the manner in which the articles are made, the type of articles, the sizes supplied and the colours, from all the records in the altered file 'CRAFTS' from 5(a), and save as 'CRAFTS3' for printing now or later.

Assignment 20
NCVA Database Methods Paper III

◣Introduction

The Casualty Department of St Paul's Hospital receives over 200 patients on a busy day. Patients will be present for a variety of reasons ranging from road traffic accidents (RTA) through to suspected heart attacks. As each patient arrives he/she is assigned to one of the consultants working in the Casualty Department. Upon examination the consultant will record the initial diagnosis and decide what further action should be taken. This action will be one of the following:

• admit the patient to one of the hospital's wards

• refer the patient to the X-ray department

• discharge the patient.

For the purpose of maintaining accounts the hospital also needs to establish whether or not the patient is a member of VHI and to keep records of the charge for the consultation. This charge will be recorded as follows:

1. When the patient presents him/herself the charge is £10.

2. When the patient is taken to hospital by ambulance the charge is £50.

The patient may, of course, decide to pay all or part of the payment at the time he/she arrives. The amount recorded in the charge field is therefore the balance owed.

The Casualty Department wants to maintain these details on a database.

◣Task 1 (4 marks)

From the database field layout provided in Figure 1, create a structure appropriate to the database package you are working *with (for example, a database file structure in dBase or Table in Microsoft Access), to store the data provided in Figure 2, using appropriate field names and data types. Write out this structure on the form provided and save the structure with the name 'CASUALTY'.

NAME OF FIELD	DATA TYPE	WIDTH

Figure 1

◥Task 2 (8 marks)

Design and create a data input screen (FORM) and then use the data input screen to enter the sample data shown in Figure 2 into the database structure 'CASUALTY' created in task 1.

With regard to the data input screen you should follow these guidelines:

a) All fields must have suitable field labels.

b) The input screen should have a title on top and be centred.

c) There is no need for borders or other effects.

Your invigilator will award marks to your screen design during the examination.

RECORD NUMBER	DATE	PATIENT'S NAME	ADDRESS	CONSULTANT	INITIAL DIAGNOSIS	VHI	CHARGE	ACTION TAKEN
00001	23/11/95	Bob Dunne	W'Ford	Dr Davies	RTA	Y	50.00	X-RAY
00002	23/11/95	Steve Smith	Dublin	Dr Martin	Heart Cond.	Y	10.00	ADMIT
00003	23/11/95	Jane Dawe	Dublin	Dr Byrne	Scalding	N	0.00	DISCHARGE
00004	24/11/95	Mark Roe	Galway	Dr Davies	RTA	Y	50.00	ADMIT
00005	24/11/95	Mary Murray	Sligo	Dr Martin	RTA	N	10.00	DISCHARGE
00006	24/11/95	Michelle Black	Dublin	Dr Martin	Heart Cond.	Y	50.00	ADMIT
00007	25/11/95	Jenny Smith	W'Ford	Dr Davies	RTA	Y	10.00	X-RAY
00008	25/11/95	Ruth Byrne	Cork	Dr Byrne	Heart Cond.	N	10.00	ADMIT
00009	26/11/95	Martin Keane	Cork	Dr Davies	Unknown	N	50.00	ADMIT
00010	26/11/95	Pat Smith	Ballina	Dr Martin	Heart Cond.	N	10.00	DISCHARGE

Figure 2

Note: in the case of the VHI Field you may substitute Yes for Y and No for N if this is appropriate for the package that you are using.

Print the data set either now or at the end of the examination.

◥Task 3 (12 marks)

The accounts officer in St Paul's wishes to send invoices *only to those patients who have either been admitted to one of the hospital's wards or sent for X-ray*. You are asked to produce these mailing labels. For logistical reasons the accounts officer requests that the labels be printed in a particular sequence:

1. Ascending order on the consultant field (primary sort field).

2. Descending order on the charge field (secondary sort field).

Each label should show the date as well as the patient's name, address and record number.

The actual printing of the labels can take place at the end of the examination if you so wish.

◪Task 4 (13 marks)

Before attempting tasks 4(a) through 4(d) below, make a copy of your original data set (entered at task 2) with the name 'CAQUERY'. Then, using this data set:

(a) Find and print (now or later) all records for patients who are members of the VHI. **Write the query condition you used on the listing.**

(b) Substitute all occurrences of the value £50.00 in the charge field with the value £30.00.

(c) Find and print (now or later) all records for patients who owe more than £20. **Write the query condition you used on the listing.**

(d) Delete all records for patients who have been discharged.
    Print the resulting database now or later.

◪Task 5 (13 marks)

Using the original database created in tasks 1 and 2, design and print a report that shows for all records the following fields (and in the order listed)

• Patient's name
• Patient's address
• Consultant in attendance
• Diagnosis
• Action taken
• Charge

The report should be headed 'St Paul's CASUALTY Report' and should show the print date. Choose suitable titles for each field above. The Charge column should be totalled.

Database Structure Entry Form

Name: _____

Examination Number: _____

Date: _____

Chapter 4
Introduction to Spreadsheets

◣What is a spreadsheet?

A spreadsheet is a screen image of a form or matrix made up of rows and columns in which automatic and interconnected calculations are made.

In 1978 an American business student named Dan Bricklin got very tired of adding columns of numbers and then adding them again and again when only a few changes had been made. He approached a programming friend for help in solving his problem, and they came up with a program called Visicalc, written for the Apple II computer. There are now many other spreadsheets available, such as Microsoft Excel, Lotus 1-2-3 and Quattro Pro. Most of these programs contain many new features.

◣What does a spreadsheet look like?

	A	B	C	D	E	F
1		CELL B1				
2						
3						
4						CELL F4
5						
6	CELL A6					
7						
8						
9				CELL D9		
10						
11						
12						
13						
14						
15						
16						
17						
18						
19						
20					CELL E20	

Each **column** in a spreadsheet is usually labelled with a letter, and each **row** with a number. The panel where a column and a row cross each other is a **cell**. Where column A and row 6 meet is cell A6; where column B and row 1 meet is cell B1.

A small spreadsheet might contain 200 rows and 60 columns; this means that it would have 12,000 cells. The size of a computer screen would not allow all these cells to be seen together: usually a screen can show about 6 columns and 20 rows at a time. Any movement outside or below the edge of the screen will mean losing the display of some information from the previous screen.

In fact the display can be considered as a movable window that can view only one 'page' or screen of the spreadsheet at any time.

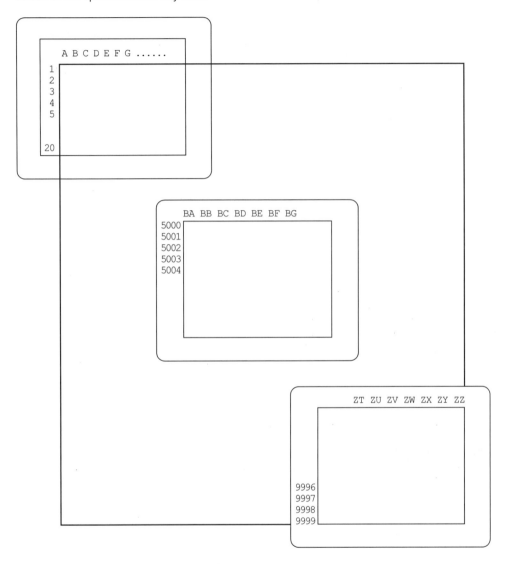

◪What can be put into a spreadsheet?

Any of three types of data can be entered in a cell: a value, a label, or a formula.

A **value** (or 'numeric') is any number on which calculations can be performed. This excludes dates and times, numbers followed by units of measurement and numbers at the beginning of headings. Also, large numbers must be entered without the traditional comma (or, in modern practice, the space) used as the 'thousand marker', as this would prevent calculations being carried out on them; most spreadsheets, however, can add such markers to the results.

A **label** is any non-numeric data. Normally it is text used as headings, such as the labels INCOME, EXPENSES and PROFIT in the example below, but can also include numbers that are not used for calculation purposes, e.g. year headings.

A **formula** is any algebraic expression used for performing calculations on different cells. In cell C8 in the illustration below, +C5-C6 is a formula that subtracts the contents of cell C6 from the contents of cell C5. When a formula is typed into a cell, the result of the calculation is displayed in that cell, not the formula.

Remember to use the asterisk (*) as the multiplication sign, the stroke (/) for division, and the circumflex (^) for 'to the power of', and to leave no spaces between numbers and signs.

	A	B	C	D	E	F
1	PROFIT STATEMENT, 1994 TO 1996					
2						
3			1994	1995	1996	
4						
5	INCOME		10000	20000	40000	
6	EXPENSES		5000	8000	17000	
7						
8	PROFIT		+C5-C6	+D5-D6	+E5-E6	
9						
10						

▦ Example 1

◪ Personal budget

The following topics will be discussed using example 1 below:

1. Setting up the spreadsheet
2. Entering formulae
3. The summation function
4. Improving the appearance of the spreadsheet
5. Replication
6. Editing the spreadsheet
7. Considering 'what if?' situations
8. The 'logical if' function
9. Other facilities

◪ Explanation

This example contains a record of personal income and weekly expenditure of a family for four weeks.

◨ Data entry

The only items entered directly are the wages and the various expenses during the week. All other totals and figures are worked out automatically.

	A	B	C	D	E	F
		WEEK 1	WEEK 2	WEEK 3	WEEK 4	TOTAL
1	PERSONAL BUDGET	WEEK 1	WEEK 2	WEEK 3	WEEK 4	TOTAL
2						
3						
4	OPENING BALANCE	0	12.14	9.82	3.28	
5	WAGES	170	155	150	182	657
6						
7	TOTAL MONEY	170	167.14	159.82	185.28	
8						
9	EXPENSES					
10						
11	CAR EXPENSES	22.45	22	11	18.33	73.78
12	FOOD	40.86	43.77	51.67	35.45	171.75
13	BILLS	13	23	26	33	95
14	ENTERTAINMENT	18	10	5.32	29.55	62.87
15	BANK SAVINGS	8	8	8	8	32
16	MORTGAGE	50.55	50.55	50.55	50.55	202.2
17	MISC.	5	0	4	10	19
18						
19						
20	TOTAL EXPENSES	157.86	157.32	156.54	184.88	656.6
21	CLOSING BAL.	12.14	9.82	3.28	0.4	
22						
23						
24						
25						

1. Setting up the spreadsheet

In this example, column A contains labels that explain the contents of rows 4 to 21. The labels WEEK 1 etc. are column headings that identify which week the figures in the columns relate to.

The width of column A will have to be changed to accommodate the labels in it. This is done by giving the appropriate command. Here the width is changed from the default setting of 9 characters to 18 characters wide. On most spreadsheets it is possible to change all or just one column width.

The labels in the example would be typed into the blank sheet first. Formulas will be used to calculate totals and closing and opening balances. The information on income and expenses would then be typed in each week.

The opening balance in week 1 is any spare money we have. For the other weeks it is the difference between the total we receive in a week and the total expenses, i.e. the previous week's closing balance.

2. Entering formulae

The TOTAL MONEY is the opening balance plus net wages (wages after tax). The formula in B7 would therefore be +B4+B5. (Remember that when a formula is entered in a cell it is the result that is displayed, not the formula.)

To total the expenses we must again use a formula in B20. This would be +B11+B12+B13+B14+B15+B16+B17.

The CLOSING BAL. is the difference between total income and total expenses this week. The formula to be typed in B21 therefore is +B7-B20.

The opening balance for week 2 will be the closing balance for week 1. So in C4 we enter the formula +B21.

For the next three weeks the formulae will be repeated, except for cell references. The formulae for week 2 are:

Cell C4: + B21
Cell C7: + C4 + C5
Cell C20: + C11 + C12 + C13 + C14 + C15 + C16 + C17
Cell C21: + C7 - C20

Similarly the formulae for week 3 will be:

Cell D4: + C21
Cell D7: + D4 + D5
Cell D20: + D11 + D12 + D13 + D14 + D15 + D16 + D17
Cell D21: . . .

Try working out the formulae for week 4 yourself.

Cell E4: . . .
Cell E7: . . .
Cell E20: . . .
Cell E21: . . .

Finally, the totals for the month are entered. The formula for total wages is B5+C5+D5+E5. This will be entered in cell F5. Similarly the formula for total car expenses will be +B11+C11+D11+E11. This would be entered in cell F11. Try working out the formulae for the following cells:

Cell F12: . . .
Cell F13: . . .
Cell F14: . . .
Cell F15: . . .
Cell F17: . . .
Cell F20: . . .

3. The summation function

You may have noticed that the formulae in cells B20, C20, D20 and E20 are very long. They would be even longer if we had any more expenses.

We can use the summation or total function to add up whole columns or rows of numbers. Instead of typing all the parts of the formula we only have to type in the first and last cell references. Using Microsoft Excel the formula in cell B20 would be =SUM(B11:B17); in Lotus 1-2-3 it would be @SUM(B11..B17). Similarly the formula in F5(+B5+C5+D5+E5) would be replaced with SUM(B5,E5) or @SUM(B5..E5). Check your own spreadsheet program for the formula for this function. Write down on a page all the shorter summation formulae required to add up the rows and columns in this example.

Other mathematical functions are available on most spreadsheets, e.g. the 'average' function, which will find the mean of a range of numbers. Other mathematical functions available include sin, cos, tan, etc. More advanced financial and statistical functions are available on some spreadsheets.

4. Improving the appearance of the spreadsheet

◣Changing the format of numbers

You will notice that the money amounts in our example are very untidy in appearance. This is because all the numbers do not have the same number of decimal places. For money amounts of course this is usually two. If possible also the pound sign should be displayed in front of the amounts. A special command can be given to change the required range or group of numbers to this style, called 'cash format'.

◣Aligning the labels

You will notice also that the week labels are not exactly in line with the amounts below them. This is because numbers are automatically displayed **flush right** or aligned on the right (i.e. the last digit is at the extreme right of the cell), whereas text is automatically displayed **flush left** or aligned on the left (i.e. the first character of the label is at the extreme left of the cell). However, it is possible to change the alignment of any cell to flush right, flush left or centred.

Here we will give the command to change the week labels to flush right and change the money amounts to cash format. Our spreadsheet should now look like this:

	A	B	C	D	E	F
1	PERSONAL BUDGET	WEEK 1	WEEK 2	WEEK 3	WEEK 4	TOTAL
2						
3						
4	OPENING BALANCE	£0.00	£12.14	£9.82	£3.28	
5	WAGES	£170.00	£155.00	£150.00	£182.00	£657.00
6						
7	TOTAL MONEY	£170.00	£167.14	£159.82	£185.28	
8						
9	EXPENSES					
10						
11	CAR EXPENSES	£22.45	£22.00	£11.00	£18.33	£73.78
12	FOOD	£40.86	£43.77	£51.67	£35.45	£171.75
13	BILLS	£13.00	£23.00	£26.00	£33.00	£95.00
14	ENTERTAINMENT	£18.00	£10.00	£5.32	£29.55	£62.87
15	BANK SAVINGS	£8.00	£8.00	£8.00	£8.00	£32.00
16	MORTGAGE	£50.55	£50.55	£50.00	£50.55	£202.20
17	MISC.	£5.00	£0.00	£4.00	£10.00	£19.00
18						
19						
20	TOTAL EXPENSES	£157.86	£157.32	£156.54	£184.88	£656.60
21	CLOSING BAL.	£12.14	£9.82	£3.28	£0.40	
22						
23						
24						
25						

5. Replication

You will have noticed when entering the data in our example that there is a lot of repetitive typing of formulae. If you had to expand the model to accommodate fifty-two weeks you would be very tired after typing in all the formulae! However, all spreadsheets allow you to 'replicate' or copy formulae or text from one area of the spreadsheet to another.

There are three levels of copying or replicating to begin with: straight copying, range copying and formula copying.

◪ Straight copying

This is where one item (whether a number or label) is copied from one cell to another, and can be used when you want to avoid retyping names or headings. It is done by entering the appropriate command and the identification of the cells you want to copy from ('source cells') and copy to ('target cells').

◪ Range copying

This involves entering the 'source range' of cells to be copied and the 'target range' of cells to be copied to.

◪ Formula copying

There are three types of formula copying: **absolute**, where there is no change in the cell references when copied; **relative**, where the copied formulae change cell references according to their position; and **absolute and relative**, where some cell references in the formula do not change when copied and others do. For example, copying down a column:

ABSOLUTE	RELATIVE	ABSOLUTE-RELATIVE	RELATIVE-ABSOLUTE
A1*B1	A1*B1	A1*B1	A1*B1
A1*B1	A2*B2	A1*B2	A2*B1
A1*B1	A3*B3	A1*B3	A3*B1
A1*B1	A4*B4	A1*B4	A4*B1
A1*B1	A5*B5	A1*B5	A5*B1

(The formula to be copied is the first one in each column. Notice that only the row numbers change by one when copying relative cell references down a column.)
Copying across rows:

Absolute	A1*B1	A1*B1	A1*B1	A1*B1
Relative	A1*B1	B1*C1	C1*D1	D1*E1
Absolute-relative	A1*B1	A1*C1	A1*D1	A1*E1
Relative-absolute	A1*B1	B1*B1	C1*B1	D1*B1

(The formula to be copied is the first one in each row. Notice that only the column letter changes by one when copying relative cell references across a row.)
In the personal budget example above we could have copied most of our formulae. We

could have typed the formula +B4+B5 in B7, then copied it across to C7, D7 and E7 using relative cell references, so that each cell reference would change across the row. This would be done by identifying B7 as the cell to copy from and the range C7 to E7 as the range to copy to.

If we were to copy B7 using absolute cell references or a combination of absolute and relative cell references we would get incorrect totals. The results from the different alternatives would be:

COPY	FROM B7	TO C7	TO D8	TO E7
Absolute	+B4+B5	+B4+B5	+B4+B5	+B4+B5
Relative	+B4+B5	+C4+C5	+D4+D5	+E4+E5
Absolute-relative	+B4+B5	+B4+C5	+B4+D5	+B4+E5
Relative-absolute	+B4+B5	+C4+B5	+D4+B5	+E4+B5
Results	**B7**	**C7**	**D8**	**E7**
Absolute	170	170	170	170
Relative	170	167.14	159.82	185.28
Absolute-relative	170	155	150	182
Relative-absolute	170	182.14	179.82	173.28

Replication could also be used for the formulae in rows 20 and 21. For row 20 we would copy the formula from cell B20 to the cells in the range C20 to F20, using relative cell references. In the same way we would copy the formula in cell B21 (+B7-B20) to the cells in the range C21 to E21.

Copying with relative cell references could also be used for the formulae in column F, from cell F11 to the cells in the range F12 to F16.

◪The importance of replication
It is the replication function that gives the computer spreadsheet its real power. Once the core or original formulae have been entered it is only a matter of replicating them as far as the memory of your computer will allow. Spreadsheets can be constructed very quickly and easily using replication, which is their main advantage over manual systems. In our example we could expand the model to cover fifty-two weeks by simple replication of the formulae: no new formulae would need to be typed in.

6. Editing the spreadsheet
◪Simple editing
If we want to change any information on the spreadsheet we simply type over it or use the editing facility to insert or delete some characters. In this example we want to change the contents of cell A5 to read NET WAGES instead of WAGES. We will use the editing facility, type the word NET and then press [enter].

Inserting rows or columns

In our example we might decide to enter a blank row in row 9 to separate the expenses more clearly from other data on the sheet. To do this we use the appropriate command for inserting a row. The result will be that the present contents of row 9 will move down one row; all subsequent rows will also move down one row.

When we do this the computer automatically changes all formulae that are affected by the move. The formula for total expenses will change from @SUM(B11..B16) to @SUM(B12..B17), while the formula to calculate the closing balance will change, from +B21 to +B22. In fact most of the formulae in the spreadsheet will change because of the insertion of the row.

If we insert a new column, the information is moved across to the right, and again any formulae that are affected will change automatically.

Our spreadsheet will look like this after these two changes have been carried out:

	A	B	C	D	E	F
1	PERSONAL BUDGET	WEEK 1	WEEK 2	WEEK 3	WEEK 4	TOTAL
2						
3						
4	OPENING BALANCE	£0.00	£12.14	£9.82	£3.28	
5	NET WAGES	£170.00	£155.00	£150.00	£182.00	£657.00
6						
7	TOTAL MONEY	£170.00	£167.14	£159.82	£185.28	
8						
9						
10	EXPENSES					
11						
12	CAR EXPENSES	£22.45	£22.00	£11.00	£18.33	£73.78
13	FOOD	£40.86	£43.77	£51.67	£35.45	£171.75
14	BILLS	£13.00	£23.00	£26.00	£33.00	£95.00
15	ENTERTAINMENT	£18.00	£10.00	£5.32	£29.55	£62.87
16	BANK SAVINGS	£8.00	£8.00	£8.00	£8.00	£32.00
17	MORTGAGE	£50.55	£50.55	£50.00	£50.55	£202.20
18	MISC.	£5.00	£0.00	£4.00	£10.00	£19.00
19						
20						
21	TOTAL EXPENSES	£157.86	£157.32	£156.54	£184.88	£656.60
22	CLOSING BAL.	£12.14	£9.82	£3.28	£0.40	

Perhaps we forgot to include some expenses. In that case we would need to insert a new row and heading containing the new information. Let us say the forgotten expense was pocket money of £1 a week given to one of the children, and the information is to be inserted after the food expense. When this row is inserted the formulae and amounts will change automatically to reflect this: for example, the total expenses formula will now be @SUM(B12..B19). Note that in week 4 we have overspent by £3.60.

The spreadsheet will look like this after inserting the new pocket money row:

	A	B	C	D	E	F
1	PERSONAL BUDGET	WEEK 1	WEEK 2	WEEK 3	WEEK 4	TOTAL
2						
3						
4	OPENING BALANCE	£0.00	£11.14	£7.82	£0.28	
5	NET WAGES	£170.00	£155.00	£150.00	£182.00	£657.00
6						
7	TOTAL MONEY	£170.00	£166.14	£157.82	£182.28	
8						
9						
10	EXPENSES					
11						
12	CAR EXPENSES	£22.45	£22.00	£11.00	£18.33	£73.78
13	FOOD	£40.86	£43.77	£51.67	£35.45	£171.75
14	POCKET MONEY	£1.00	£1.00	£1.00	£1.00	£4.00
15	BILLS	£13.00	£23.00	£26.00	£33.00	£95.00
16	ENTERTAINMENT	£18.00	£10.00	£5.32	£29.55	££62.87
17	BANK SAVINGS	£8.00	£8.00	£8.00	£8.00	£32.00
18	MORTGAGE	£50.55	£50.55	£50.00	£50.55	£202.20
19	MISC.	£5.00	£0.00	£4.00	£10.00	£19.00
20						
21						
22	TOTAL EXPENSES	£158.86	£158.32	£157.54	£185.88	£660.60
23	CLOSING BAL.	£11.14	£7.82	£0.28	(£3.60)	
24						

7. Considering 'what if?' situations

When the spreadsheet is set up we can experiment with the data to consider the effect of different figure or policy changes. These are called 'what if?' calculations.

In the example above we could ask ourselves, what if we decided not to bring the car to work? This would mean we would only spend £10 a week on car expenses. All we would need to do is type over the amounts in the car expenses row with the new amount, £10. All the totals will be recalculated for us. Note the saving on the weekly balances.

Any number in the spreadsheet can be changed to see what effect it might have on our total budget. On a more complex example involving many thousands of calculations, this ability to recalculate is invaluable for decision-making.

Our spreadsheet will look like this after the car expenses are changed:

	A	B	C	D	E	F
1	PERSONAL BUDGET	WEEK 1	WEEK 2	WEEK 3	WEEK 4	TOTAL
2						
3						
4	OPENING BALANCE	£0.00	£12.14	£9.82	£3.28	
5	NET WAGES	£170.00	£155.00	£150.00	£182.00	£657.00
6						
7	TOTAL MONEY	£170.00	£167.14	£159.82	£185.28	
8						
9						
10	EXPENSES					
11						
12	CAR EXPENSES	£10.00	£10.00	£10.00	£10.00	£40.00
13	FOOD	£40.86	£43.77	£51.67	£35.45	£171.75
14	POCKET MONEY	£1.00	£1.00	£1.00	£1.00	£4.00
15	BILLS	£13.00	£23.00	£26.00	£33.00	£95.00
16	ENTERTAINMENT	£18.00	£10.00	£5.32	£29.55	£62.87
17	BANK SAVINGS	£8.00	£8.00	£8.00	£8.00	£32.00
18	MORTGAGE	£50.55	£50.55	£50.00	£50.55	£202.20
19	MISC.	£5.00	£0.00	£4.00	£10.00	£19.00
20						
21						
22	TOTAL EXPENSES	£146.41	£146.32	£156.54	£177.55	£626.82
23	CLOSING BAL.	£23.59	£32.27	£25.73	£30.18	
24						

8. The 'logical if' function

Is the profit this year greater than last year? Has the aeroplane been overloaded with luggage? The answers to these questions are either true or false. These are considered logical questions, i.e. those having true or false answers.

Most spreadsheet programs allow you to employ a formula to ask a question and generate a true or false response. The general pattern this formula takes is:

If (condition, true response, false response)

This function is very similar to the IF — THEN — ELSE command in the programming language Basic.

In the example above we could get the computer to make a decision for us. We decide to save money based on the previous week's closing balance. We have decided that if the amount left over in the previous week is greater than £10, we will save £6 in the next week; otherwise we will not save anything in the coming week.

The first week's savings will be entered by the user, and all other weeks' savings will be calculated automatically by using the 'if' function. The formula in cell C17 will be as follows:

@IF(B23>10,6,0)

This means that if the content of cell B23 (the closing balance) is greater than £10, £6 will be entered in cell C17; otherwise £0 is entered in cell C17. This formula can then be copied across the row as far as cell E17, using relative cell references.

When the formula is copied the numbers in row 17 will change to reflect this new decision, and other totals that are affected will also change. The spreadsheet will now look like this:

	A	B	C	D	E	F
1	PERSONAL BUDGET					
2		WEEK 1	WEEK 2	WEEK 3	WEEK 4	TOTAL
3						
4	OPENING BALANCE	£0.00	£23.59	£34.27	£29.73	
5	NET WAGES	£170.00	£155.00	£150.00	£182.00	£657.00
6						
7	TOTAL MONEY	£170.00	£178.59	£184.27	£211.73	
8						
9						
10	EXPENSES					
11						
12	CAR EXPENSES	£10.00	£10.00	£10.00	£10.00	£40.00
13	FOOD	£40.86	£43.77	£51.67	£35.45	£171.75
14	POCKET MONEY	£1.00	£1.00	£1.00	£1.00	£4.00
15	BILLS	£13.00	£23.00	£26.00	£33.00	£95.00
16	ENTERTAINMENT	£18.00	£10.00	£5.32	£29.55	£62.87
17	BANK SAVINGS	£8.00	£6.00	£6.00	£6.00	£26.00
18	MORTGAGE	£50.55	£50.55	£50.55	£50.55	£202.20
19	MISC.	£5.00	£0.00	£4.00	£10.00	£19.00
20						
21						
22	TOTAL EXPENSES	£146.41	£144.32	£154.54	£175.55	£620.82
23	CLOSING BAL.	£23.59	£34.27	£29.73	£36.18	
24						

◥'What if?' again

We could then ask the question, what would the situation be if we used the car again for work, but this time making use of the new saving policy? We would only have to change all car expense amounts back to the original figures: all the other calculations will be done for us, including the amount we would save each week. (Note that we will save nothing on the third week.)

	A	B	C	D	E	F
1	PERSONAL BUDGET	WEEK 1	WEEK 2	WEEK 3	WEEK 4	TOTAL
2						
3						
4	OPENING BALANCE	£0.00	£11.14	£9.82	£10.28	
5	NET WAGES	£170.00	£155.00	£150.00	£182.00	£657.00
6						
7	TOTAL MONEY	£170.00	£166.14	£159.82	£192.28	
8						
9						
10	EXPENSES					
11						
12	CAR EXPENSES	£22.45	£22.00	£11.00	£18.33	£73.78
13	FOOD	£40.86	£43.77	£51.67	£35.45	£171.75
14	POCKET MONEY	£1.00	£1.00	£1.00	£1.00	£4.00
15	BILLS	£13.00	£23.00	£26.00	£33.00	£95.00
16	ENTERTAINMENT	£18.00	£10.00	£5.32	£29.55	£62.87
17	BANK SAVINGS	£8.00	£6.00	£0.00	£6.00	£20.00
18	MORTGAGE	£50.55	£50.55	£50.55	£50.55	£202.20
19	MISC.	£5.00	£0.00	£4.00	£10.00	£19.00
20						
21						
22	TOTAL EXPENSES	£158.86	£156.32	£149.54	£183.88	£648.60
23	CLOSING BAL.	£11.14	£9.82	£10.28	£8.40	
24						

9. Other facilities

Most spreadsheet programs have several other useful features, which we can use to make this application work more effectively.

◼ Quick cursor movement

It is possible on most spreadsheets to move directly to another cell. This is done by giving a command or using a function key. The name of the desired cell is requested, and the cursor moves directly to that cell. This facility is very useful when using a very large spreadsheet.

◤Non-scrolling titles

Selected rows and columns can be fixed on the screen so that they do not scroll off when we move to another part of the spreadsheet. If we had the budget information for fifty-two weeks in our sample spreadsheet we might need to fix column A so that the labels for each expense would be on display permanently as we go from column to column.

◤Printing part or all of the spreadsheet

Large spreadsheets can be printed on several sheets and the parts joined together. Selected parts of the spreadsheet can also be printed.

Only columns A and F in the example above might be required on paper, so that the total amount for each expense could be noted separately. This would require copying column A into column G and marking columns F and G to be printed. This would be displayed as follows:

```
Totals              Personal Budget


                    Opening Balance


£657.00             Net Wages
                    Total Money
                      Expenses
£73.78              Car Expenses
£171.75             Food
£4.00               Pocket Money
£95.00              Bills
£62.87              Entertainment
£20.00              Bank Savings
£202.20             Mortgage
£19.00              Misc.


£648.60             Total Expenses
                    Closing Bal.
```

◤Turning off automatic recalculation

When a new number is typed into a spreadsheet the computer automatically recalculates all other cells affected by this change. But recalculation can take a considerable time on small computers. It is possible to turn off automatic recalculation until all changes have been made; then a command can be entered to recalculate.

◪Using the 'look-up' function

A range of cells that have codes and corresponding values in them can be searched with the 'look-up' function. This will return a value that relates to the code requested. This function is often used to produce invoices, where product codes are entered and the price per unit is 'looked up' by the computer.

◪Summary of the standard facilities of a spreadsheet program

- The cursor can be moved quickly to anywhere in the spreadsheet
- Rows and columns can be inserted in existing spreadsheets
- Rows and columns and ranges of data can be deleted
- Cell display can be changed to show different formats
- Single items or ranges of data can be copied
- Formulas can be copied or replicated
- Mathematical functions are available, e.g. sum, average, sin, cos, tan (on some spreadsheets other functions are available, such as financial and statistical functions)
- Editing facilities are available, while information is being typed in and afterwards
- Column widths can be changed
- Data can be stored for later retrieval
- Part or all of the spreadsheet can be printed
- Logical decisions can be made on data using the 'if' function
- Coded data can be looked up using the 'look-up' function
- Non-scrolling rows and columns can be fixed on the screen when more than one screen of data is used
- Data in the spreadsheet can be protected to prevent further changes
- Some spreadsheets allow integration or links with other types of program, such as graphics and word-processor programs

◪Creating a spreadsheet

Before typing in a spreadsheet you should plan what you want to do. This will involve some of the following decisions:

1. What title will I give the spreadsheet?
2. What headings will I use for the rows and columns? These should be concise but descriptive.
3. Will I need to increase or decrease the width of a column, and by how much?
4. Which of the items will be labels and which values?
5. Where will I use a formula, and can I use a built-in function?
6. Can I replicate this formula? If so, will it be relative, absolute or a combination?
7. Should the data be displayed in a special format, e.g. cash format, and where?
8. What file name will I use for the spreadsheet? This name will have to be concise but should remind you of the contents of the spreadsheet when retrieving it later.

▦ Example 2

A more complex spreadsheet

◪ Explanation

A small airline operates a twelve-seater aeroplane between Dublin and Knock. It wants to store passenger information on a spreadsheet. The following conditions apply:

1. The basic price of a ticket is £50.
2. There is VAT at 21 per cent on the basic price of all tickets (excluding discount).
3. There is a 10 per cent discount on the basic price of all tickets for children under 12.
4. A passenger is charged an extra £1 for every 1 kg over the 20 kg luggage allowance. No VAT is charged on this extra charge.

◪ Data entry

The only items to be typed in are the passenger information and the standard data such as ticket price, penalty charge, etc. All other figures are to be automatically calculated by the spreadsheet through the use of formulae.

▦ Questions

1. Set up a spreadsheet for a particular flight, including the following passenger information:

SEAT NO.	NAME	AGE	LUGGAGE (KG)
1	Brendan Bradley	45	17
2	Ciarán Collins	5	7
3	Denis Collins	11	9
4	Martin Collins	26	23
5	Aisling Doyle	42	18
6	Kevin Geraghty	7	14
7	Paul Hillery	35	21
8	Brian Laffey	17	16
9	Sean Byrne	27	10
10	Bernadette Ryan	10	20
11	Sheila Ryan	24	17
12	Deirdre WhITE	33	4

2. Use appropriate formulae and replication to show for each passenger the ticket price, discount, VAT and baggage penalty. Use suitable headings.
3. Save the spreadsheet as AIR.
4. Produce a print-out of the entire spreadsheet.

Solution

Decide on the following before typing in data:

1. The title: KNOCK AIRLINES. This will be put into cells A1 and B1.

2. The following row headings will be used for the standard data in cells A2 to A5. Column A must be 11 characters wide. The figures will be put opposite this information in cells B2 to B5.

PRICE	50
VAT	.21
DISCOUNT	.10
PENALTY	1

3. Column headings will be needed for the following: SEAT NO., NAME [15 characters wide], AGE, PRICE, DISCOUNT, PRICE LESS DISCOUNT, VAT, PENALTY and TOTAL PRICE.
   The spreadsheet should now look like this:

```
      A          B       C      D        E       F          G          H    I        J

 1 KNOCK AIRLINES

 2 PRICE     50

 3 VAT       0.21

 4 DISCOUNT 0.1

 5 PENALTY   1

 6

 7

 8 SEAT NO. NAME       AGE LUGGAGE  PRICE  DISCOUNT  PRICE-DIS. VAT PENALTY TOTAL PRICE

 9

10    1     B BRADLEY  45    17

11    2     C COLLINS   5     7

12    3     D COLLINS  11     9

13    4     M COLLINS  26    23

14    5     A DOYLE    42    18

15    6     K GERAGHTY  7    14

16    7     P HILLERY  35    21

17    8     B LAFFEY   17    16

18    9     S BYRNE    27    10

19   10     B RYAN     10    20

20   11     S RYAN     24    17

21   12     D WHITE    33     4
```

4. Align all headings flush right.

5. All money amounts should be changed to cash format.

6. Decide on formulae. These will be:

E10: +B2. This must be copied down the column, using an absolute cell reference, as everybody has the same basic ticket price before other considerations are taken into account.

F10: @IF(C10<12,e10*B4,0). All parts of this formula will be copied, using relative cell references, except B4, which should remain absolute down the column.

G10:+10-F10. This will be copied down the column, using relative cell references. The formula simply subtracts the discount (if any) from the price.

H10: +G10*B3. G10 will be relative and B3 will be absolute when copied, as the VAT rate remains 21 per cent for all tickets.

I10: @IF(D10>20,(D10-20)*B5,0). All will have relative cell references, except B5 (the penalty amount, £1), which should be absolute. (D10-20) calculates the number of kilograms over the 20 kg limit.

J10: +G10+H10+I10. This gives the total price, and should be copied using relative cell references. It includes the discounted price plus the VAT and penalty charge (if any).

The final spreadsheet should look like this after the editing and copying discussed above:

	A	B	C	D	E	F	G	H	I	J
1	KNOCK AIRLINES									
2	PRICE	50								
3	VAT	0.21								
4	DISCOUNT	0.1								
5	PENALTY	1								
6										
7										
8	SEAT NO.	NAME		AGE	LUGGAGE	PRICE	DISCOUNT	PRICE-DIS.	VAT	PENALTY	TOTAL PRICE
9										
10	1	B BRADLEY	45	17	£50.00	£0.00	£50.00	£10.50	£0.00	£60.50
11	2	C COLLINS	5	7	£50.00	£5.00	£45.00	£9.45	£0.00	£54.45
12	3	D COLLINS	11	9	£50.00	£5.00	£45.00	£9.45	£0.00	£54.45
13	4	M COLLINS	26	23	£50.00	£0.00	£50.00	£10.50	£3.00	£63.50
14	5	A DOYLE	42	18	£50.00	£0.00	£50.00	£10.50	£0.00	£60.50
15	6	K GERAGHTY	7	14	£50.00	£5.00	£45.00	£9.45	£0.00	£54.45
16	7	P HILLERY	35	21	£50.00	£0.00	£50.00	£10.50	£1.00	£61.50
17	8	B LAFFEY	17	16	£50.00	£0.00	£50.00	£10.50	£0.00	£60.50
18	9	S BYRNE	27	10	£50.00	£0.00	£50.00	£10.50	£0.00	£60.50
19	10	B RYAN	10	20	£50.00	£5.00	£45.00	£9.45	£0.00	£54.45
20	11	S RYAN	24	17	£50.00	£0.00	£50.00	£10.50	£0.00	£60.50
21	12	D WHITE	33	4	£50.00	£0.00	£50.00	£10.50	£0.00	£60.50

This spreadsheet could be used again and again by the airline. The person operating the spreadsheet would enter the standard information, including name, age and weight of luggage, and all other figures would be calculated automatically.

Also, the formulae would not need to be changed when ticket prices and other variables changed. For example, if the rate of VAT were to change, the operator would only have to change the actual rate in cell B4: no formulae would need to be altered.

Graphing the data

Most spreadsheet programs allow users to present numerical data on a spreadsheet in graph form.

⊞ Example 3

There are currently 402 students enrolled at Leeside College. The following table shows the numbers of students taking the various courses offered at the college:

COURSE	NUMBER
Accounting	62
Catering	98
Computing	75
Hairdressing	46
Marketing	37
Secretarial	84

The bar graph

Peter Connolly, the college principal, has asked us to produce a bar graph of the data shown in the table. We follow these steps:

1. Enter the data onto a spreadsheet.
2. Select the cells containing the data.
3. Choose the **Create Chart/Graph** command or icon.
4. Indicate where the graph should appear on the spreadsheet.
5. Specify the graph type (bar).
6. Add a graph title.
7. Add labels for the x and y axes.

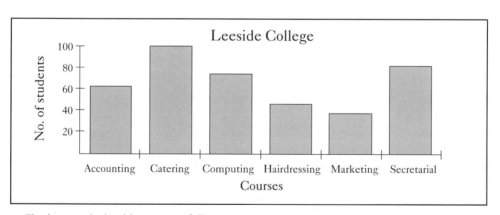

The bar graph should appear as follows:

If the data to be graphed is changed, the bar graph will automatically reflect the changes.

The pie graph

In a similar manner, we can produce a pie graph to show the percentage of students taking each course. No axes labels are required. We have, however, included a graph title and a *legend*; the latter is a key that identifies the items shown on the graph by colour, hatch pattern or symbol.

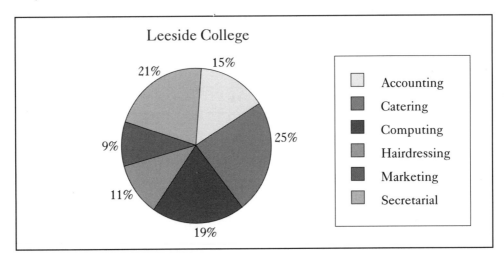

▓ Financial matters

Depreciation

Depreciation is the cost to a business of wear and tear on assets that it owns. There are a variety of methods by which depreciation amounts can be calculated on items purchased. One popular method is known as the fixed-declining balance method. The DB function, in Microsoft EXCEL, returns the real depreciation of an asset for a specific period using the fixed-declining balance method. The syntax of the function is as follows:

=DB(cost,salvage,life,period)

The four items enclosed in parenthesis are now explained:
1. *Cost* is the initial cost of the asset.
2. *Salvage* is the value of the asset at the end of the life of the asset.
3. *Life* is the number of periods over which the asset is being depreciated. This is frequently known as the useful life of the asset.
4. *Period* is the period for which you want to calculate the depreciation. It must be in the same units as life (e.g. years).

▦ Example 4

Conor Lawlor has just purchased a new car costing £18,000. The estimated life of the car is 12 years. It has been decided that the salvage value of the car in twelve years' time will only be £2000. Conor asked us to produce a spreadsheet to show the depreciation on the car at the end of each year for the first ten years. The completed spreadsheet appears as follows:

	A	B
1	Depreciation Analysis	
2		
3	Item Purchased =	Car
4	Estimated Life (yrs) =	12
5	Initial Cost =	£18,000.00
6	Salvage Value =	£2,000.00
7		
8	Year	Depreciation
9		Amount
10	1	£3,006.00
11	2	£2,504.00
12	3	£2,085.83
13	4	£1,737.50
14	5	£1,447.33
15	6	£1,205.63
16	7	£1,004.29
17	8	£836.57
18	9	£696.87
19	10	£580.49

The depreciation amounts displayed in column B were obtained as follows:
(a) The formula, =DB(B5,B6,B4,A10), was entered in cell B10.
(b) It was then copied into the range of cells B11:B19.

Loan repayments

Lending agencies frequently use spreadsheets to calculate loan repayments. The PMT function, available on most spreadsheet programs, returns the payment for an investment based on periodic, constant payments and a constant interest rate.

The syntax of this function in Microsoft EXCEL is:

$$=PMT(rate, nper, -pv) \text{ where}$$

1. *rate* is the loan interest rate
2. *nper* is the number of payment periods
3. *pv* is the loan amount.

Make sure that you are consistent about the units you use for specifying *rate* and *nper*. If *rate* is per year then *PMT* returns the number of payments per year and *nper* is the number of years.

▦ Example 5

Patricia O'Leary wishes to borrow £30,000 from the EasyLoan Building Society. Patricia asked us to produce a spreadsheet showing the monthly repayments over the twenty-five year term of the loan for four different interest rates (7%, 8%, 9% and 10%). Our completed spreadsheet is now shown:

	A	B
1	Mortgage Repayments	
2		
3	Years =	25
4	Months =	300
5	Loan =	£30,000.00
6		
7	Interest	Monthly
8	Rate	Repayment
9	7%	£212.03
10	8%	£231.54
11	9%	£251.76
12	10%	£272.61

The monthly repayment amounts displayed in column B were obtained as follows:
(a) The formula, *=PMT(A9/12,B4,-B5)*, was entered in cell B9.
(b) It was then copied into the range of cells B10:B12.

As the monthly repayments were required, the rate (i.e. the contents of cell *A9*) was divided by twelve to maintain consistency with the number of repayment periods (i.e. the contents of cell *B4*).

Investment venture

Investors must frequently decide between investing in new ventures or leaving the money on deposit in the bank or building society. A measure of the potential of an investment venture is to compare the projected income with bank interest earnings. Current spreadsheet programs offer the user an efficient means of making this comparison through the use of the Net Present Value (NPV) function.

The syntax of this function in Microsoft EXCEL is:

$$=NPV(rate, range\ of\ values)$$

The function returns the net present value of an investment based on a series of periodic cash flows, *range of values*, and a discount rate equal to *rate*. The cashflow periods must be equally spaced in time.

▦ Example 6

Gerard Clarke, the owner of Breffni Farm Machinery Ltd, is considering investing £1 million in his business. This amount of money must be invested in full at the outset. The projected sales from it are expected to last from 1997 to 2000 inclusive. The corresponding sales for each successive year are £300,000, £500,000, £900,000 and £1,200,000. The Thrifty Building Society, however, are offering 15% interest on all deposits over £750,000. Gerard has asked us to advise him on whether he should go ahead with the venture or simply deposit the money with the Building Society. We have produced the following spreadsheet to aid Gerard in his decision:

	A	B	C	D	E
	Farm Machinery Ltd				
1	Farm Machinery Ltd				
2					
3	Projected Sales				
4					
5	Investment	1997	1998	1999	2000
6	£1,000,000.00	£300,000.00	£500,000.00	£900,000.00	£1,200,000.00
7					
8	Interest Rate Given =		15%		
9					
10	Net Present Value =		£1,916,809.90		
11	Bank Savings Return =		£1,749,006.25		

The initial investment and the current interest rate are displayed in cells A6 and C8, respectively. The projected incomes from sales over the four-year period have been entered in the range of cells B6:E6.

The net present value, displayed in cell C10, was obtained by entering the formula: =NPV(C8,B6:E6). The bank savings return, displayed in cell C11, was obtained by entering the formula =A6*1.15^4 (the initial investment plus the compound interest earned). The spreadsheet shows that the return on the investment venture would be better than the deposit earnings at the building society in this particular case.

▦ Using macros

Macro basics

A macro is a sequence of specially phrased instructions which when executed will accomplish a specific task or set of tasks. Macros are frequently used to automate tedious and time-consuming work. A macro is normally assigned a name and a short-cut key; when either is invoked (called upon) the macro is executed.

Let us say that we wish to alter a numeric display in a cell on a Microsoft EXCEL spreadsheet to currency format. We would follow these steps:

1. Place the cell pointer in the appropriate cell.
2. Choose the *Number* option from the *Format* menu.
3. Select *Currency* from the category list presented.
4. Choose the exact currency format required.

A macro to automate this procedure, when produced, would appear as follows:

MACRO	COMMENT
Money (m)	Macro name and key
=FORMAT.NUMBER("£0.00")	Change to currency format
=RETURN()	End of macro

The macro is executed by pressing CRTL+m (Windows version).

Creating a macro

Most current spreadsheet programs offer the user two methods by which a macro can be created:

(a) building a macro manually
(b) recording a macro.

Building a macro manually

The processing of building a macro manually can normally be broken down into six separate stages:

1. Planning   4. Naming
2. Entering   5. Executing
3. Documenting   6. Saving

An editing stage may also be required if the macro is not executing properly.

▦ Example 7

The Adair Arms Hotel offers excellent accommodation to visitors. Each week Karen O'Brien, the hotel manageress, produces a Visitor Category Card using the spreadsheet program on her computer. A completed card is shown opposite:

Adair Arms Hotel		
Guest Category		
	Home	Foreign
Business	27	8
Holiday	31	62
Other	23	11

We will now create a macro, using Microsoft EXCEL, to produce a template based on the above table. When the macro is executed, the following details should appear on the spreadsheet:

	A	B	C
1	Adair Arms Hotel		
2			
3	Guest Category		
4		Home	Foreign
5	Business		
6	Holiday		
7	Other		

◣Planning

The following fifteen instructions will go to make up the macro:

NUMBER	INSTRUCTION REQUIRED
1	Move the cell pointer to cell A1
2	Enter "Adair Arms Hotel"
3	Move the cell pointer to cell A3
4	Enter "Guest Category"
5	Move the cell pointer to cell A5
6	Enter "Business"
7	Move the cell pointer to cell A6
8	Enter "Holiday"
9	Move the cell pointer to cell A7
10	Enter "Other"
11	Move the cell pointer to cell B4
12	Enter "Home"
13	Move the cell pointer to cell C4
14	Enter "Foreign"
15	End macro

◣Entering

Each of the instructions outlined above should have a corresponding macro instruction. The instructions must be entered, using the appropriate syntax, onto a Microsoft EXCEL macro sheet. The macro sheet is almost identical in appearance to a spreadsheet. The default column widths, however, are a little wider on a macro sheet than those on a spreadsheet.

◣Documenting

Documenting a macro involves adding comments to explain its purpose and/or its mode of execution. These comments are essential for anyone using a macro that was created by someone else.

◣Naming

The macro is then assigned a name and/or key. Microsoft EXCEL users place the name and key in the cell above the first macro instruction. The precise command is then given to associate the macro name and key with the list of instructions. We will assign 'template' and 't' as the name and key of our macro.

Our completed macro should appear as follows:

```
Macro                                    Comments

template (t)                             Macro name and key
=SELECT(!A1)
=FORMULA("Adair Arms Hotel")             This macro creates a data entry template for the
=SELECT(!A3)                             Adair Arms Hotel to show the number of
=FORMULA("Guest Category")               home and foreign guests, in each guest
=SELECT(!A5)                             category, who stayed at the hotel.
=FORMULA("Business")
=SELECT(!A6)
=FORMULA("Holiday")
=SELECT(!A7)
=FORMULA("Other")
=SELECT(!B4)
=FORMULA("Home")
=SELECT(!C4)
=FORMULA("Foreign")
=RETURN()
```

◤Executing

When the macro name or key is invoked, the macro instructions are carried out. Our macro may be executed by pressing the 'CTRL' and 't' keys simultaneously.

◤Saving

Most current spreadsheet programs allow users to save new macros to a central macro library. This means that a macro originally produced for application on a particular spreadsheet may be used while working on other spreadsheets.

Recording a macro

Macros can also be produced by using the macro recording facility of a spreadsheet program. This facility allows the user to record keystrokes and mouse selections as macro instructions. The latter can then be assigned a name and/or key and can be executed as a macro. Creating macros in this way has a number of advantages:

- It is less time consuming.
- The macros are error-free.
- Complex macros can be produced by novices.

Interactive macros

Interactive macros pause during execution and allow the user to enter input before execution resumes.

▦ Example 8

We will now create an interactive macro to convert any number of inches to centimetres. The macro will pause during execution and allow the user to enter the number of inches.

- Measurements required: 1 inch = 2.54 centimetres

  Our macro will consist of twelve instructions:

NUMBER	INSTRUCTION REQUIRED
1	Move the cell pointer to the A1 cell
2	Enter "Length Conversion"
3	Move the cell pointer to the A3 cell
4	Enter "Inches ="
5	Move the cell pointer to the B3 cell
6	Pause for input
7	Move the cell pointer to the C3 cell
8	Enter "Centimetres ="
9	Widen column C to 13 to fit the label 'Centimetres ='
10	Move the cell pointer to the D3 cell
11	Enter a formula to multiply the contents of cell B3 by 2.54
12	End the macro

A fully documented macro, in Microsoft EXCEL, to carry out the instructions above should appear as follows:

Macro	Comments
Length (l)	**Macro name and key**
=SELECT(!A1)	
=FORMULA("'Length Conversion")	This macro converts any number of inches
=SELECT(!A3)	to the equivalent number of centimetres.
=FORMULA("Inches =")	
=SELECT(!B3)	
=FORMULA(**INPUT("",1)**)	The highlighted instruction pauses execution
=SELECT(!C3)	of the macro and 'expects' input.
=FORMULA("'Centimetres =")	
=COLUMN.WIDTH(13)	
=SELECT(!D3)	
=FORMULA(!B3*2.54)	
=RETURN()	

▦ Conclusion

Spreadsheets are extremely powerful and useful analytical tools. They are used by people in many different occupations, including accountants, statisticians, engineers and scientists. They are easy to use, and complex spreadsheets can be constructed quickly by using replication and the many built-in functions and facilities we have discussed.

In the next chapter you will have an opportunity to practise using spreadsheets by working through the different assignments.

▦ Glossary of spreadsheet terms

absolute cell reference: a cell reference that does not adjust or change when a formula is copied to another cell.

alignment: the cell formatting function that controls the position of labels within a cell.

automatic recalculation mode: a feature whereby cell values are recalculated every time any cell relating to those values is changed.

block: a series of adjacent cells manipulated as an entity; also called a 'range'.

built-in functions: ready-to-use formulae that perform mathematical, statistical and logical calculations, e.g. the summation function.

cash format: a value format in which a number is displayed with two decimal places and usually with a pound sign and thousand markers.

cell: a rectangle formed by the intersection of a row and a column and in which numbers, labels and formulae can be entered and edited.

cell address: a code used to identify a cell by specifying the row and column, e.g. B34.

cell format: the way in which values and labels are displayed in a cell; the more common formats for numbers include integer format, cash format and exponent format; common formats for labels are flush right, flush left and centred.

cell pointer: a rectangular highlight that indicates the current cell, in the same way that the cursor indicates the current position in text.

cell reference: a cell address when used in a formula, e.g. A1 and A10 in the formula @SUM(A1..A10).

cell type: the classification of a cell according to whether it contains a label, a value or a formula.

centred: a label format in which the text is half way between the left and right edges of the column.

column: a vertical series of cells running the full length of the spreadsheet, and usually identified by a letter or letters.

exponent format: a value format in which a number is displayed in the form of a real number between 1 and 9 multiplied by 10 to the power of the appropriate integer.

flush left: a label format in which the text is aligned with the left-hand edge of the column.

flush right: a label format in which the text is aligned with the right-hand edge of the column.

formula: an algebraic expression that defines the relationship between two or ore values, using cell references to represent the values or formulae they contain, e.g. +A2+B7.

integer format: a value format in which a number has no decimal fraction.

label: any non-numeric data in the spreadsheet.

non-scrolling titles: a function that allows rows or columns to remain fixed on the display when the rest of the screen scrolls out of view; also called 'fixed titles'.

real format: a value format in which a number includes a decimal fraction.

relative cell reference: a cell reference that is adjusted or changed when a formula is copied to another cell.

replication: the function that allows labels, values and formulae to be copied to another part of the spreadsheet (also called 'copying').

rounding error: the difference between the exact number and the displayed number.

row: a horizontal series of cells running across the full breadth of the spreadsheet, and usually identified by a number.

spreadsheet: a screen image of a form or matrix made up of rows and columns in which automatic and interconnected calculations are made.

spreadsheet program: the computer program needed to set up a spreadsheet and to allow the use of commands, formulae and special functions.

value: any arithmetic quantity in the spreadsheet.

'what if?' analysis: the manipulation of data so that numeric variables are changed to show the effect of different policies.

window: a rectangular frame in the display that allows other parts of the spreadsheet to be viewed on the same screen.

Chapter 5
Practical Spreadsheet Assignments

These assignments are graded, and we advise that you work through them in the order in which they are given. **Note: you may enter the data given for each assignment onto a new spreadsheet or you can download the spreadsheet (labels and values only) in EXCEL format for each assignment from Gill & Macmillan's website on the World Wide Web at www.gillmacmillan.ie/eca.**

Functions and commands required
As you progress through these assignments you will need to check on the commands, functions, icons and pull-down menus specific to your spreadsheet program. You will also be practising commands and functions learned in earlier assignments. (Note: If you do not have access to a printer you can display a preview of the printout on the screen.)

The following points should be noted:

- When entering data on amounts of money, do not add the '£' sign as the data item will then be treated by the spreadsheet program as a label. Spreadsheet cells holding details on amounts of money should be formatted to currency display.
- Once constructed, some of the larger spreadsheets in the later assignments may not be entirely visible on the screen. You will need to 'freeze titles' and/or hide certain columns as required.

The new functions and commands encountered in successive assignment are as follows:

ASSIGNMENT 1
- Entering data onto a spreadsheet
- Altering the column width
- Editing the contents of a cell
- Saving a spreadsheet
- Exiting the system

ASSIGNMENT 2
- Recalling a spreadsheet
- Inserting a column of data
- Aligning headings

- Formatting a range of cells to show one decimal place
- Inserting a row of data

ASSIGNMENT 3
- Copying cell contents
- Adding a new column of data
- The summation function
- Finding the average of a row

ASSIGNMENT 4
- Consolidation assignment

ASSIGNMENT 5
- Multiplying the contents of two cells
- Formatting a range of cells to currency display

ASSIGNMENT 6
- Deleting a row of data

ASSIGNMENT 7
- Arithmetic formulae

ASSIGNMENT 8
- Absolute and relative cell references

ASSIGNMENT 9
- Consolidation assignment

ASSIGNMENT 10
- The 'IF' function — one condition
- The date function
- Sorting rows into alphabetical order
- Protecting cell contents
- Printing the entire spreadsheet

ASSIGNMENT 11
- The 'IF' function — two conditions using AND
- Sorting rows into numerical order
- Copying cell displays
- Printing selected columns

ASSIGNMENT 12
- The 'IF' function — nested conditions
- Manual recalculation

- Hiding cell contents
- Printing selected rows

ASSIGNMENT 13
- The horizontal lookup function
- Hiding entire columns

ASSIGNMENT 14
- The vertical lookup function
- Producing a pie graph

ASSIGNMENT 15
- Producing a bar graph

ASSIGNMENT 16
- Financial functions — NPV, PMT and DB

ASSIGNMENT 17
- Simple macros

ASSIGNMENT 18
- NCVA Spreadsheet Methods Paper I

ASSIGNMENT 19
- NCVA Spreadsheet Methods Paper II

ASSIGNMENT 20
- NCVA Spreadsheet Methods Paper III

Assignment 1

The following spreadsheet shows rainfall (in millimetres) for the months January to June:

	A	B	C	D	E	F	G
1	Rainfall Record (mm)						
2	All						
3	Regions	Jan	Feb	Mar	Apr	May	Jun
4							
5	North	7	9	7	16	12	6
6	West	19	16	11	11	7	3
7	South	3	0	6	3	8	9
8	East	7	8	9	10	5	2
9	N-East	17	17	15	1	9	5
10	S-East	2	2	2	12	4	5
11	N-West	12	9	6	13	13	7
12	S-West	7	13	15	9	14	15

You are required to enter data as shown onto a spreadsheet.

Carry out the following tasks:

Change:

1. the contents of cell A9 to North-East, cell A10 to South-East, cell A11 to North-West and cell A12 to South-West.

Alter:

2. the width of column A to best accommodate the longer labels.

Edit:

3. the rainfall value for February in the East region to show 13 and for June in the South-East region to show 15.

Delete:

4. the contents of cell A2.

Save:

5. the spreadsheet as RAIN.

Exit:

6. the spreadsheet program.

Assignment 2

◼Carry out the following tasks:

Recall:

1. the spreadsheet RAIN.

Add:

2. a new column between the *Regions* column and the *Jan* information column (i.e. a new column B).

Enter:

3. the area of each region in this new column as given in the following table:

REGIONS	AREA
North	4768
West	5674
South	3213
East	4356
N-East	675
S-East	567
N-West	453
S-West	689

Align:

4. all month labels and the Area label flush right (if you have not already done so).

Insert:

5. a new row of rainfall data for West Islands, to be the new row 9; the present row 9 will move down to become row 10, and all other rows below this will also move down automatically.

The data for this region is:

REGIONS	AREA	JAN	FEB	MAR	APR	MAY	JUN
West Islands	345	17	13	19	20	15	12

Format:

6. the rainfall data on the spreadsheet to show one decimal place.

Save:

7. the edited spreadsheet as NEWRAIN.

Exit:

8. the spreadsheet program.

Assignment 3

◼Carry out the following tasks:

Recall:

1. the spreadsheet NEWRAIN.

Add:

2. a new *Total* column after the June data to show the total rainfall for each of the nine regions. (Hint: Use the summation function.)
3. a new *Average* column after the *Total* column to show the average rainfall in each region for the six-month period. (Hint: For each region, use a formula that divides the total rainfall for that region by 6.)

Enter:

4. the heading *Total Area* in cell A14.

Show:

5. the total area of all the regions in cell B14.

Enter:

6. your name and today's date in cells A16 and A17, respectively.

Save:

7. the spreadsheet as ENDRAIN.

Exit:

8. the spreadsheet program.

Assignment 4

The following table shows student results in four tests. The maximum mark possible for each test is 10; the minimum possible is 0.

TEST RESULTS				
Student	Test 1	Test 2	Test 3	Test 4
J Kelly	9	9	7	8
S Nicholl	0	8	5	4
O Browne	2	7	7	7
M Carey	9	10	8	7
C Smyth	9	7	8	9
E Quinn	3	6	0	0
U Daly	3	6	5	3
F Murphy	9	10	8	5

You are required to enter the details in the table onto a spreadsheet.

◪Carry out the following tasks:

Add a new:

1. *Overall Marks* column to show the total marks obtained by each student in all four tests.
2. *Average Marks* column to show the average mark for each student in the four tests. (Hint: Use the average function.)

Amend:

3. the marks for J. Kelly, O. Browne and F. Murphy in test 3; each mark should be increased by 2.
4. the mark for S. Nicholl in test 4; it should be 7.

Add:

5. a new *Test Average* row to show the average mark for each test.

Save:

6. the spreadsheet as RESULTS.

Assignment 5

The following table shows the cone sales for seven different flavours of ice cream at Mel's Ice Cream Parlour over a five-day period:

MEL'S ICE CREAM PARLOUR					
Flavour	Mon	Tue	Wed	Thu	Fri
Caramel	18	24	11	19	14
Choc Chip	27	33	25	20	29
Mint	5	4	9	13	8
Orange	12	9	7	5	4
Pistachio	8	11	12	10	13
Strawberry	22	31	17	22	34
Vanilla	35	20	28	25	37

You are required to enter this data onto a spreadsheet.

◪Carry out the following tasks:

Save:

1. the spreadsheet as ICE1.

Add:

2. a column after Friday's data to show the *total sales* of each ice cream flavour over the five day period.

Insert:

3. a column between *Friday's data* and *total sales*.

Enter:

4. in the new column the following ice cream sales for Saturday: Caramel — 20,
   Choc Chip — 26, Mint — 17, Orange — 6, Pistachio — 17, Strawberry — 28, Vanilla — 31.
   Amend the totals formulae to take account of this insertion.

Add:

5. a column after the *total sales* column to show the *cone cost* for each ice cream flavour:
   Caramel — £0.80, Choc Chip — £1.05, Mint — £1.15, Orange — £0.75,
   Pistachio — £1.10, Strawberry — £0.90, Vanilla — £0.65.

6. a column, after the *cone cost* column, to show the *total income* from the sales of each ice
   cream flavour during the six-day period.

Enter:

7. a formula, in the appropriate cell, to show the total income for the week at Mel's Ice Cream
   Parlour.

Format:

8. the *cone cost* and *total income* columns to currency format.

Save:

9. the spreadsheet as ICE2.

Assignment 6

The table below shows the sales commission of seven salespersons who sell different products
for Annex Ltd. The salespersons are paid their commission at the end of a three-month period.

ANNEX LTD					
COMMISSION PAYMENTS					
Name	EE No	Qtr 1	Qtr 2	Qtr 3	Qtr 4
A Behan	901	157	295	10	290
B Collins	264	71	221	130	355
C Daly	745	247	242	256	176
A Nolan	256	39	227	64	297
A Sheils	633	142	24	120	241
T Timmons	908	178	56	67	359
J Wynne	353	335	367	190	186

Enter the details shown in the table onto a spreadsheet.

◤Carry out the following tasks:

Change:

1. the name C. Daly to C. Davis.
2. the amount for J. Wynne for the second quarter to 153.62.

Format:

3. all money amounts to currency format.

Insert:

4. a new *Division* column between the employee number (EE No) and the first-quarter details to give the following division names:

   A. Behan: Paper

   B. Collins: Equipment

   C. Davis: Paper

   A. Nolan: Stationery

   A. Shiels: Equipment

   T. Timmons: Stationery

   J. Wynne: Paper

Alter:

5. the width of the *Division* column to accommodate the longest entry.

Add:

6. a new *Total Commission* column to show the total commission for each salesperson for the four quarters.
7. a *Bonus* column to show the end-of-year bonus payable to all salespersons; those in the Paper Division are to get £30 extra; all other divisions get a bonus of £20.
8. a *Commission Earnings* column to show the total commission plus bonus for each salesperson
9. a new *Commission Payable* row to display the total commission issued in each quarter.

Insert:

10. (preserving the alphabetical order of employee names) a new row containing the following details for G Ennis who joined the Equipment Division of the company in the third quarter:

Name	EE No	Qtr 1	Qtr 2	Qtr 3	Qtr 4
G Ennis	449	0	0	200	345

Add:

11. a new row that shows the average commission issued in each quarter.

Delete:

12. the row containing A. Nolan's details.

Save:

13. the spreadsheet as EARNINGS.

Assignment 7

Quality Copiers Ltd, a company that rents photocopiers to many different businesses, has given you the following details:

COMPANY NAME	LAST READING	CURRENT READING
BC Services Ltd	31977	33668
Brogan & Co	43222	46472
Connolly & Sons	83661	84700
Energywise Ltd	15003	16191
Fastline Ltd	19981	21130
Kitt Packaging	64812	66917
Lee Electrical	36391	38110
Marsden & Co	28901	30121
Safeclean Ltd	18368	21555
Windowland Ltd	51252	54213

Rental bills, issued monthly, are calculated on:

1. a £0.05 per copy charge **and**
2. a £30.00 monthly service charge.

All bills are subject to VAT at 21%.

You must enter the details in the table above onto a spreadsheet.

◪Carry out the following tasks:

Save:

1. the spreadsheet as COPY1.

Add:

2. a *Copies Made* column after the *Current Reading* column showing the number of photocopies made since last month's reading of the photocopier counter.
3. a *Unit Cost* column after the *Copies Made* column showing the cost of one copy.
4. a *Copies Cost* column after the *Unit Cost* column showing the actual cost of copying for each business.
5. a *Service Charge* column displaying the amount.
6. a *Bill Total* column showing the cost of copying plus the service charge for each business.
7. a *VAT* column showing the VAT payable on each bill.
8. an *Amount Payable* column showing the actual amount payable by each business.

Format:

9. all columns containing money details to currency format.

Save:

10. the spreadsheet as COPY2.

Assignment 8

Carrigallen Mart hold livestock sales every week. The table below shows the monthly sales of cattle, pigs and sheep for the past year:

MONTH	CATTLE	PIGS	SHEEP
January	1466	2621	1121
February	1839	3819	1619
March	2844	1726	2144
April	4525	1341	3282
May	2193	1716	2792
June	1153	1205	1844
July	1008	1017	1102
August	1796	1914	1219
September	4377	2838	1372
October	5542	3561	2611
November	3829	4219	2433
December	2081	4532	1518

You are required to enter these details onto a suitably titled spreadsheet.

◪Carry out the following tasks:

Save:

1. the spreadsheet as MART1.

Insert:

2. a row, labelled *Total Sold*, beneath the December details.

Enter:

3. formulae into this row to obtain the total number of each animal type sold during the year.

Insert:

4. a new column after each of the three livestock columns.

Label:

5. these three new columns — *Cattle (%), Pigs (%)* and *Sheep (%)*, respectively.

Obtain:

6. the percentage of each animal type sold each month as a fraction of the total sales for that particular animal type for the year. (Hint: each formula will have absolute and relative cell references.)

Format:

7. these three percentage columns to percentage format (one decimal place).

Add:

8. a new column, labelled *Total Livestock*, after the last column on the spreadsheet showing the total number of livestock sold each month and obtain the total for the year.

9. a new column, labelled *Total Livestock (%)*, after the *Total Livestock* column showing the percentage of livestock sold each month as a fraction of the yearly total. This column should also be formatted to display percentages (one decimal place).

Save:

10. the spreadsheet as MART2.

Assignment 9

Riversdale Farms Ltd supply fresh vegetables to a number of greengrocers in the Dublin area. The table below shows the number of kilograms of carrots, onions, parsnips and tomatoes delivered to ten different greengrocers' shops on a particular day:

SHOP	CARROTS	ONIONS	PARSNIPS	TOMATOES
J Bean & Sons	80	40	65	50
Cabbage Patch	65	45	40	85
Get Fresh	120	75	70	100
Just In	75	80	30	75
Lentils & Co	90	45	25	70
Picked Today	50	70	40	45
Salad Days	85	35	15	30
SpringFresh Ltd	110	90	100	85
The Runner Bean	70	20	45	55
Vegworld	60	50	10	40

You must enter these details onto a suitably titled spreadsheet.

◪Carry out the following tasks:

Save:

1. the spreadsheet as VEG1.

Insert:

2. a new column after each of the four weight columns.

Label:

3. these new columns — *Carrots (£), Onions (£), Parsnips (£)* and *Tomatoes (£)*, respectively.

Insert:

4. two new rows between the spreadsheet heading and the column headings.

Enter:

5. the following price details into the two new rows:

SHOP	CARROTS	ONIONS	PARSNIPS	TOMATOES
Price/kg	£0.35	£0.55	£0.40	£0.50

Enter:

6. appropriate formulae into the four new price columns to calculate the total cost of each vegetable type bought by each individual shop. (Hint: each formula will have absolute and relative cell references.)

Insert:

7. a column, labelled *Total Price* after the *Tomatoes* (£) column, showing the total cost of all four vegetable types for each shop.

8. a new row, labelled *Overall Income* below the bottom row on the spreadsheet, showing the total income generated from sales of all four vegetable types to all ten shops.

Format:

9. all columns containing money details to currency format.

Save:

10. this spreadsheet as VEG2.

Assignment 10

Mac's Tool Hire Company, set up by Susan MacMahon in 1996, provides a wide range of electrical and mechanical tools suitable for use by the professional builder or the DIY enthusiast. A 25% discount is offered on all equipment hired for more than two weeks. Susan needs your expertise in using a spreadsheet program to help in the preparation of customer invoices. You must transfer the following invoice details to a spreadsheet:

MAC'S TOOL HIRE COMPANY		
CUSTOMER INVOICE: SEAN MURPHY		
Tool Hired	Weekly Cost	Weeks Hired
Skill Saw	£5.00	2
Drill	£4.00	4
Cement Mixer	£75.00	5
Electric Plane	£11.00	1
Generator	£25.00	1
Rotovator	£22.00	3
Roofing Torch	£8.00	4
Compressor	£18.00	1
Pressure Washer	£27.00	2
Floor Edger	£13.00	3

⬛Carry out the following tasks:

Save:
1. the spreadsheet as TOOLS1.

Add:
2. a *Total Cost* column showing the total cost of hiring each item listed.
3. a *Discount Given* column showing the discount, if any, available on each item. (Hint: Use the IF function.)
4. an *Actual Cost* column showing the amount payable on each item.
5. three rows below the last row of data showing:
   (a) the total of actual costs for all items listed (*Total Bill*);
   (b) the VAT payable at 21% on the bill (*VAT Payable*);
   (c) the total amount payable by the customer (*Amount Payable*).

Insert:
6. a row beneath the row containing the customer's name.

Enter:
7. today's date in this new row. (Use the appropriate date function.)

Sort:
8. the rows containing the equipment details into alphabetical order of equipment name.

Protect:
9. all cells containing formulae.

Save:
10. the spreadsheet as TOOLS2.

Print:
11. the entire spreadsheet.

Assignment 11

Bethany Travel Ltd specialise in organising pilgrimages for Irish parishes to a number of shrines in Europe and the Holy Land. The following table shows booking details for last week:

PARISH NAME	PILGRIMAGE DESTINATION	GROUP SIZE	TICKET COST
Ballinteer	Medjugorie	72	£249.00
Clifden	Fatima	29	£283.00
Drumshambo	Fatima	16	£283.00
Ennis	Rome	25	£380.00
Gorey	Lourdes	38	£315.00
Gort	Medjugorie	50	£249.00
Killeshandra	Lourdes	33	£315.00
Kimmage	Lourdes	85	£315.00
Mostrim	Fatima	20	£283.00
Navan	Fatima	12	£283.00
Omagh	The Holy Land	19	£380.00
Thurles	Lourdes	27	£315.00

A 20% reduction was given to parish groups where the pilgrimage destination was not Lourdes **and** the group consisted of more than thirty people, otherwise a 10% reduction was given.

A 5% government tax was levied on all bookings.

You must enter the details in the table onto a suitably titled spreadsheet.

◪Carry out the following tasks:

Save:

1. the spreadsheet as PILGRIM1.

Add:

2. a *Group Cost* column showing the total ticket costs for each parish group.
3. a *Group Reduction* column showing the total reductions for each parish group. (Hint: Use a compound IF statement.)
4. a *Govt Tax* column showing the total government tax levied on each parish group. (Hint: This is calculated on the group cost.)
5. a *Group Total* column showing the actual amount paid by each parish group after the appropriate reduction was made and the government tax levied.
6. an *Individual Cost* column showing the actual amount paid by each member of the parish group.

Sort:

7. the rows on the spreadsheet into descending order of parish group size.

Copy:

8. the details displayed in the *Parish Name* column and the corresponding details in the *Individual Cost* column to Columns L and M, respectively, on the spreadsheet.

Protect:

9. all cells containing formulae.

Save:

10. this spreadsheet as PILGRIM2.

Print:

11. the contents of columns L and M.

Assignment 12

Ashton Electrical Ltd, based in Cork, are one of Ireland's leading importers of electrical goods. The company supplies electrical shops throughout the country with a wide variety of modern domestic appliances. A new shipment of goods is due at the company's warehouses next week and it has been decided to hold a sale in order to clear the existing stock.

The following percentage reductions are available during the sale of existing stock:

```
Individual items costing:
£200 or less — 20%
between £200 and £400 — 25%
£400 or more — 30%
```

The company's fleet of lorries delivers the goods to the individual shops. If the delivery distance is more than 20 miles then the charge is £3.00 per mile, otherwise the charge is £2.50 per mile.

JD Abbot, the head of Sales at Ashton Electrical, has employed you for the sale period to produce customer invoices on a spreadsheet. The following incomplete invoice has just been given to you:

ASHTON ELECTRICAL LTD				
Customer:	Harry Murphy & Co		Address:	4 Main St, Athlone
Date:	Today's Date		Delivery Distance:	32

Electrical Item	Usual Price	Units Bought
Cooker	£450.00	5
Deep fat fryer	£40.00	18
Dish washer	£150.00	3
Fridge freezer	£240.00	6
Microwave	£80.00	9
Stereo	£220.00	7
Television	£300.00	4
Tumble dryer	£110.00	2
Vacuum cleaner	£100.00	12
Video	£270.00	10
Washer dryer	£410.00	7
Washing machine	£320.00	3

Enter the invoice details given onto a spreadsheet. Use the appropriate function to include *today's date*.

◼Carry out the following tasks:

Save:

1. the spreadsheet as SALE1.

Add:

2. a *Total Price* column showing the total price of all the units bought of each item **before** any sales reduction.

3. a *Reduction Available* column showing the total reduction on all the units bought of each item. (Hint: Use a nested IF statement.)

4. a *Total Sale Price* column showing the total price of all the units bought of each item **after** the sales reductions are made.

Add:

5. a *Total Charge* row beneath the bottom row of the spreadsheet showing a total for the *Total Sales Price* column.

6. a *VAT Payable* row showing the VAT due on this invoice (VAT is charged at 21%).

7. a *Delivery Charge* row showing the total cost of delivering the items listed to Harry Murphy & Co. (Hint: Use a simple IF statement.)

8. a Total Amount Payable row showing the actual amount payable on this current delivery to Harry Murphy & Co.

Save:

9. the file as SALE2.

Switch:

10. to manual recalculation mode.

Make:

11. alterations to the contents of the appropriate cells to take account of the following:
    - 4 dishwashers and 9 vacuum cleaners were bought;
    - the usual price of a washer dryer is £430.

Switch:

12. to automatic recalculation mode.

Sort:

13. the rows containing the item details into descending order of *Total Sales Price.*

Protect and hide:

14. the contents of all cells containing formulae.

Save:

15. the spreadsheet as SALE3.

Print:

16. the cell displays for the T*otal Charge, VAT Payable, Delivery Charge* and *Total Amount Payable* rows only.

Assignment 13

CareFree Car Rentals, established in 1995, have given you the following table showing rental details for ten tourists who have hired cars from the company:

CAREFREE CAR RENTALS				
Daily Car Hire Rates				
Category	A	B	C	D	E
Rate	£35.00	£30.00	£25.00	£20.00	£15.00
Customer Name	Car Type	Car Category	Days Hired	
Pierre Almont	Mazda 323F	C	8	
Maria Bonetti	Nissan Micra	D	5	
Daniel Davies	VW Passat	B	4	
Keith Frazier	Toyota Starlet	D	9	
Petra Lamvelt	Toyota Carina	B	4	
Ida Luff	Ford Mondeo	B	6	
Shari McKenzie	Puegot 106	E	7	
Carlo Ponti	Mazda 626	B	8	
Sven Stonson	Mitsubishi Pajero	A	4	
Hillary Wallace	VW Golf	C	6	

You are required to enter the details shown in the table onto a spreadsheet.

◣Carry out the following tasks:

Save:

1. the spreadsheet as CARHIRE1.

Add:

2. a *Basic Cost* column showing the basic cost of car rental for each of the customers listed. (Hint: Use the horizontal lookup function.)

3. an *Extra Days Reduction* column showing the reduction amount, if any, that each customer receives. This reduction amount of £5.00 per day is given for each extra day that a car is rented over the standard five-day rental period. (Hint: Use a simple IF statement.)

4. an *Amount Payable* column showing the actual rental payable by each customer after the correct reduction, if any, has been made on the *Basic Cost*.

Save:

5. the spreadsheet as CARHIRE2.

Switch:

6. to manual recalculation mode.

Make the following alterations to the appropriate cells:

7. the daily car rental costs have increased by £2.50 for all categories.

8. the VW Passat and Toyota Carina were hired for 3 and 7 days, respectively.

9. The reduction amount has been increased to £7.50 per day for each extra day that a car is rented over the standard five-day rental period.

Switch:

10. to automatic recalculation mode.

Hide:

11. all columns except the *Customer Name* and *Amount Payable* columns.

Save:

12. the spreadsheet as CARHIRE3.

Print:

13. the customer names and corresponding amounts payable from the two columns that are visible on the spreadsheet. This printout should show column and row identifiers.

Assignment 14

The Corn Mill Theatre caters for a wide range of theatrical tastes. The current play running at the theatre is John B. Keane's *'Sive'*. The table below shows the audience attendances in the four different categories for the three areas of the theatre for last evening:

CORN MILL THEATRE — AUDIENCE RECEIPTS			
Audience Category	Base Level	Lower Circle	Upper Circle
Adult	51	35	42
Child	14	22	27
Student	28	19	23
Unwaged	20	12	17

You are required to enter the details shown in the table onto a spreadsheet.

◤Carry out the following tasks:

Save:

1. the spreadsheet as THEATRE1.

Insert a column labelled:

2. *Base Level (£)* after the *Base Level* column.
3. *Lower Circle (£)* after the *Lower Circle* column.
4. *Upper Circle (£)* after the *Upper Circle* column.

Insert:

5. eight rows between the spreadsheet heading and the column headings.

Enter:

6. the following details concerning ticket prices into the new rows. (Use the correct date function to enter *Today's Date*):

TODAY'S DATE			
Ticket Prices			
	Base Level	Lower Circle	Upper Circle
Adult	£12.00	£15.00	£18.00
Child	£5.00	£6.50	£8.00
Student	£7.50	£10.00	£13.00
Unwaged	£9.00	£12.00	£15.50

The details from this table can be used as a lookup table.

Enter:

7. formulae in the three new columns to calculate the receipts taken in the various audience categories for each section of the theatre. (Hint: Using the ticket price details in the lookup table and the attendance figures, construct the formulae using the vertical lookup function).

Add:

8. a column, labelled *Total Receipts*, showing the total receipts taken in each of the four audience categories for the whole theatre.

Insert:

9. a formula in the appropriate cell to show the total receipts taken for last evening.

Add:

10. a column, labelled *% Receipts*, showing the percentage of total receipts taken in each of the four audience categories.

Format:

11. the display, in this latter column, to percentage format (one decimal place).

Copy:

12. the cell displays in the *Audience Category* and *% Receipts* columns to the L and M columns, respectively.

Protect and hide:

13. the contents of all cells containing formulae.

Save:

14. the spreadsheet as THEATRE2.

Produce:

15. a pie graph, titled *Corn Mill Theatre — Audience Receipts*, showing the percentage breakdown of audience receipts.

Save:

16. the graph as CORNMILL.

Print:

17. the graph.

Assignment 15

Wheel World Ltd, a shop specialising in the sale of new bicycles and cycling accessories, has been in existence for over twenty years. Susan Kelly, the owner of the shop, provides a hire purchase method of payment to any customer who has just bought a new bicycle at the shop. Different rates of interest are charged depending on the number of agreed monthly payments. The interest payable is calculated as a percentage of the cost of the bicycle. The interest rate categories are as follows:

Monthly Payments	2	6	10	12	18	24
Interest Rate	0%	3%	6%	7%	10%	15%

If the customer uses Susan's hire purchase method of payment, an initial deposit must be paid. The deposit is calculated as 20% of the cost on all bicycles over £250, otherwise the deposit payable is only 15% of the cost of the bicycle.

Susan has given you the following details on ten new customers who have opted for her hire purchase system:

CUSTOMER NAME	BICYCLE MAKE	BICYCLE COST	NUMBER OF PAYMENTS
Sandra Allen	Falcon 65	£160.00	10
Seamus Cullen	Townsend G5	£145.00	6
John Dunne	Alexa MB4	£275.00	2
Marie Higgins	President CX	£320.00	24
Linda Logan	Alexa MB1	£235.00	12
Martin Murphy	Saracen 96	£185.00	18
Noel O'Brien	Falcon 105	£335.00	10
Carol O'Gorman	Marlboro DT	£250.00	2
Brian Ryan	Diamond 109	£170.00	6
Margaret Tracy	Saracen 98	£215.00	12

Enter the details in this table onto a suitably titled spreadsheet.

◪ Carry out the following tasks:

Save:

1. the spreadsheet as CYCLE1.

Insert:

2. two new rows between the spreadsheet title and the column titles.

Enter:

3. the details on monthly payments and interest rates outlined earlier into the two new rows.

Add:

4. an *Interest Payable* column showing the actual amount of interest due on each purchase. (Hint: Use the most suitable lookup function in the construction of the formula.)
5. a *Total Payable* column showing the actual amount of money that each customer must pay.
6. a *Deposit Due* column showing the deposit that must be paid by each customer.
7. a *Monthly Amount* column showing the actual amount of money that must be paid monthly by each customer **after** the initial deposit has been paid.

Save:

8. the spreadsheet as CYCLE2.

Change:

9. the interest rates, in the lookup table, for 2, 6, 10, 12, 18 and 24 monthly payments to 5%, 10%, 15%, 20%, 25% and 30%, respectively.

Copy:

10. the details in the *Customer Name* column and the corresponding details in the *Interest Payable* column to the K and L columns, respectively.

Protect and hide:

11. the contents of all cells containing formulae.

Save:

12. the spreadsheet as CYCLE3.

Produce:

13. a bar graph of the details in columns K and L. The graph should have a suitable title and should show the customer names along the x-axis and the interest payable amounts along the y-axis.

Save:

14. the graph as INTEREST.

Print:

15. the graph.

Assignment 16

Section A — Investment venture

Mervyn Richardson, the owner of Jetwash Ltd, is considering an investment venture costing £250,000 which must be paid in advance. The projected sales from the venture, expected to last for 1997, 1998 and 1999 are £120,000, £140,000 and £160,000 respectively. Mervyn wishes to know if it is better to invest in the venture or to leave the money in the bank at the current interest rate of 12% over the same period.

You must enter the details given below onto a spreadsheet:

JETWASH LTD			
Projected Sales			
Investment	1997	1998	1999
£250,000.00	£120,000.00	£140,000.00	£160,000.00
Interest Rate Given =	12%		
Net Present Value =			
Bank Savings Return =			
Worthwhile Investment =			

■**Carry out the following tasks:**

Enter a formula in the cell to the right of:

1. the *'Net Present Value ='* label to show the net present value of the investment at a rate of 12%. (Hint: Use the NPV function in constructing the formula.)

2. the *'Bank Savings Return ='* label to show the compound interest that the money would earn over the same period.
3. the *'Worthwhile Investment ='* label to show whether the investment is worthwhile or not (Yes/No). (Hint: the investment is worthwhile if the *Net Present Value* is greater than the Bank Savings Return.)

Save:

4. the spreadsheet as JETWASH.

Section B — Mortgage repayments

Patrick Doyle, the manager of the EasyLoan Building Society, wishes to produce a mortgage repayments table to show the monthly repayments on a £30,000, a £50,000 and a £70,000 mortgage. The table must show repayments for varying interest rates (from 7 to 9% in increments of 0.5%). All mortgages are for 20 years.

You are required to enter the details in the following incomplete table onto a spreadsheet:

EASYLOAN BUILDING SOCIETY			
Monthly Repayments Table			
Loan Term			
Years	20		
Months	240		
Interest Rate	£30,000.00	£50,000.00	£70,000.00
7.0%			
7.5%			
8.0%			
8.5%			
9.0%			

◼Carry out the following tasks:

Enter:

1. suitable formulae in the appropriate cells to show the monthly repayment for each mortage amount and interest rate. (Hint: Use the PMT function in constructing the formulae.)

Save:

2. the spreadsheet as MORTGAGE.

Print:

3. the spreadsheet showing the actual formulae used.

Section C — Depreciation

Office Machines Ltd supply businesses nationwide with a range of modern office equipment. Sean O'Gorman, the managing director, is intensely interested in the amounts of depreciation on equipment over a number of years.

Sean has given you the following incomplete table showing details of an autoprinter that has just been sold by the company:

OFFICE MACHINES LTD			
Equipment Sold =	Autoprinter	Cost =	£40,000.00
Estimated Life (yrs) =	8	Salvage Value =	£5,000.00
Year Number	Depreciation Amount	Cumulative Depreciation	Net Book Value

You are required to enter these details onto a spreadsheet.

◣Carry out the following tasks:

Enter:

1. the values 1 to 8 in the eight cells beneath the *Year Number* column heading.
2. a formula in the *Depreciation Amount* column to calculate the depreciation at the end of the first year. (Hint: Use the DB function, i.e. the fixed-declining balance function.)

Copy:

3. this formula down the column to show the depreciation amounts for years 2 to 8.

Enter suitable formulae in the:

4. *Cumulative Depreciation* column to show the total depreciation on the autoprinter at the end of each year.
5. *Net Book Value* column to show the actual value of the printer at the end of each year.

Save:

6. the spreadsheet as PRINTER.

Print:

7. the spreadsheet showing the actual formulae used.

Assignment 17

Section A

Produce:

1. a macro that widens a column to 'best fit' the longest entry.

Save:

2. the macro as COLWIDEN.

Section B

Produce:

1. a macro that, upon execution, produces the following template:

	A	B	C	D
1	Claire's Cake Shop			
2				
3	Cake	Day 1	Day 2	Day 3
4				
5	Carrot			
6	Cheese			
7	Coffee			

Save:

2. the macro as CAKESHOP.

Section C

Produce:

1. an interactive macro that accepts any number of Irish pounds and returns the equivalent amounts of US dollars and German Marks. Use the following exchange rates:
   IR£1.00 = $1.57 = 2.32DM

Save:

2. the macro as MONEY.

When the macro is executed and IR£25 is entered; you should obtain the following:

	A	B	C
1	Exchange Rate		
2			
3	Irish Punt	US Dollar	German Mark
4	25.00	39.25	58.00

Assignment 18
NCVA Spreadsheet Methods Sample Paper I

◤ Task 1 (30 marks)

1. Set up the spreadsheet and input the data as shown in Figure 1.
   a. The *Selling Price* is calculated as 1.3 times the *Cost Price* and should be displayed in currency format.
   b. The *Total* is calculated as the *Selling Price X Qty* and should be displayed in currency format.
   c. The *Sub Total, VAT @ 21%* and the *Total Incl. VAT* should be calculated values and displayed in currency format.
2. Insert your name and the date in the positions indicated.
3. Save the spreadsheet under the filename SREPORT1, for printing now or later.

COMPUTER WIZARDS				
September Sales Report				
Item Description	Cost Price	Selling Price	Qty	Total
Printer DM9	£180.00		13	
Printer DM 24	£230.00		6	
Printer IJ Model 1	£220.00		15	
Printer IJ Model 2	£250.00		8	
Printer L Model 1	£340.00		6	
Printer L Model 2	£430.00		9	
Plotter A4	£660.00		4	
Plotter A3	£760.00		3	
Disk DD (Box 10)	£4.00		22	
Disk HD (Box 10)	£5.50		18	
		Sub Total		
		VAT @ 21%		
		Total Incl. VAT		
Name:				
Date:				

Figure 1

◪Task 2 (25 marks)

1. Input the additional information shown in Figure 2.

   a. Change the subheading to *October Sales Report*.

   b. Insert extra columns as required.

   c. The Disc.% should be calculated on the following basis:

      i.   if the *Qty* is less than 5 then the *Disc.%* is 0%.

      ii. if the *Qty* is between 5 and 9 inclusive then the *Disc.%* is 2%.

      iii. if the *Qty* is 10 or greater then the *Disc.%* is 5%.

   d. The *Disc.%* should be displayed in percentage format.

   e. The *Disc. Price* is calculated as *Selling Price* — the discount allowed.

   f. Reposition the *Sub Total, VAT @ 21%* and *Total incl. VAT* headings.

2. Recalculate the *Total* to use the *Disc. Price* for the calculation.

3. Save the spreadsheet under the filename SREPORT2 for printing now or later.

	COMPUTER WIZARDS					

September Sales Report

Item Description	Cost Price	Selling Price	Qty	Disc%	Disc Price	Total
Printer DM9	£180.00		13			
Printer DM 24	£230.00		6			
Printer IJ Model 1	£220.00		15			
Printer IJ Model 2	£250.00		8			
Printer L Model 1	£340.00		6			
Printer L Model 2	£430.00		9			
Plotter A4	£660.00		4			
Plotter A3	£760.00		3			
Disk DD (Box 10)	£4.00		22			
Disk HD (Box 10)	£5.50		18			

Sub Total
VAT @ 21%
Total Incl. VAT

Name:
Date:

Figure 2

◼Task 3 (35 marks)

1. Input the additional information as shown in Figure 3.

   a. Change the subheading to *November Sales Report*.

   b. Insert the table of *Computer Type, Model* and *Prices* under the subheading

      i. The *Selling Price* should be calculated as 1.3 times the *Cost Price* and displayed in currency format.

   c. Delete the **Disks** from the spreadsheet.

   d. Insert the five *Computer Types*.

      i. Use the LOOKUP function to insert the *Cost Price* form the table into the *Cost Price* column.

      ii. Use the LOOKUP function to insert the *Selling Price* from the table into the *Selling Price* column.

   e. Change the quantities sold as indicated in Figure 3.

   f. The *Average Quantity Sold* should be the average of the *Qty* column and should be an integer.

   g. The *Average Disc. on Computers* should take account of the quantity of each type of computer sold. The value should be rounded to one decimal place and should be in percentage format.

2. Sort the spreadsheet into alphabetical order on the *Item Description*.

3. Save the spreadsheet under the filename SREPORT3 for printing now or later. This printout will require formulae to be printed.

COMPUTER WIZARDS

November Sales Report

Computer Type	1	2	3	4	5
Model	386sx 20	386dx 20	386 sx 25	486 sx 33	486 dx 33
Cost Price	£580.00	£620.00	£650.00	£720.00	£760.00
Selling Price					

Item Description	Cost Price	Selling Price	Qty	Disc%	Disc Price	Total
Computer Type 1			12			
Computer Type 2			11			
Computer Type 3			8			
Computer Type 4			5			
Computer Type 5			3			
Plotter A3	£760.00		6			
Plotter A4	£660.00		5			
Printer DM 24	£230.00		2			
Printer DM9	£180.00		8			
Printer IJ Model 1	£220.00		9			
Printer IJ Model 2	£250.00		11			
Printer L Model 1	£340.00		3			
Printer L Model 2	£430.00		12			

Sub Total
VAT @ 21%
Total Incl. VAT

Average Quantity Sold
Average Disc on Computers

Name:
Date:

Figure 3

◤Task 4 (10 marks)

1. Produce a *Bar Chart* to show the quantity of computers sold:
   a. The quantity should be taken from the *Qty* column.
   b. The Bar Chart should have the heading *Sales Figures — Computers by Quantity*.
   c. The x-axis should show *Type 1* under the first bar, *Type 2* under the second etc. and should have the label *Computer* underneath.
   d. The y-axis should show the *Quantity* in figures and have the label *Quantity*.

2. Save the *Bar Chart* under the filename SGRAPH for printing now or later.

◼Printing:

Printouts of the following files are required:

- SREPORT1
- SREPORT2
- SREPORT3
- SGRAPH.

Assignment 19
NCVA Spreadsheet Methods Paper II

◼Task 1 (30 marks)

1. Set up the spreadsheet and input the data as shown in Figure 1.

    a. Align main heading (Hi-Tech Production) and subheading (Production Report - January 1994) centrally over the data.

    b. Set column widths to appropriate values.

    c. Column 1 heading and values should be centrally aligned.

    d. Column 2 heading and values should be left aligned.

    e. Column 3, 4, 5 and 6 headings and values should be right aligned.

    f. The profit figures should be the profit for the quantity produced in each factory and should be calculated values.

    g. The values in columns 4, 5 and 6 should be displayed in currency format.

    h. The *Total:* and *Total Profit:* should be calculated values. They should be aligned and displayed in the same format as the column in which they appear.

2. Insert the labels *Name:, Examination No:* and *Date:* in the positions indicated and insert the appropriate information after each.

3. Save the spreadsheet under the filename 94TASK1, for printing now or later. (The printout should show borders — Row/Column labels.)

```
                        Hi-Tech Productions


              Production Report      —      January 1994


                         Factory          Unit          Unit
                         Production    Production     Selling
         No.   Factory   Quantity         Price         Price      Profit


         1     Clondalkin      2500        £0.28         £0.48
         2     Santry          3400        £0.25         £0.46
         3     Cork            2800        £0.30         £0.49
         4     Galway          2300        £0.26         £0.52
         5     Limerick        4400        £0.32         £0.53
         6     Athlone          800        £0.28         £0.46
         7     Sligo           1800        £0.29         £0.51
         8     Waterford       3500        £0.30         £0.50
         9     Dundalk         2700        £0.33         £0.52


                     Total:                   Total Profit:


    Name:
    Examination No:
    Date:
```

Figure 1

◤Task 2 (25 marks)

1. Input the additional information shown in Figure 2.
   a. Change the month in the subheading to *February*.
   b. Insert an extra column where required.
   c. Insert the heading *Royalty Fee* in the new column and align to the right.
   d. Re-align the main and subheadings centrally over the data.
   e. The *Royalty Fee* should be calculated on the following basis and displayed in the
      column as a percentage (i.e. 6%, 4%, 2%): if the production quantity is greater than
      2000 then the royalty fee is 6%, if the quantity is between 1000 and 2000 inclusive
      then the royalty fee is 4% and if the quantity is less than 1000 then the fee is 2%.
   f. The *Royalty Fee* should be displayed in percentage format and right aligned.
2. Reposition the *Total Profit:* heading.
3. Recalculate the profit on the following basis: the royalty fee is a percentage of the *Unit
   Selling Price* and reduces the profit by that amount.
4. Save the spreadsheet under the filename 94TASK2, for printing now or later. (The printout
   should show borders — Row/Column labels.)

```
                        Hi-Tech Productions

              Production Report    —    January 1994

                        Factory      Unit      Unit
                        Production   Production Selling  Royalty
        No.  Factory    Quantity     Price      Price    Fee    Profit


         1   Clondalkin    2500       £0.28     £0.48
         2   Santry        3400       £0.25     £0.46
         3   Cork          2800       £0.30     £0.49
         4   Galway        2300       £0.26     £0.52
         5   Limerick      4400       £0.32     £0.53
         6   Athlone        800       £0.28     £0.46
         7   Sligo         1800       £0.29     £0.51
         8   Waterford     3500       £0.30     £0.50
         9   Dundalk       2700       £0.33     £0.52


              Total:                        Total Profit:

Name:
Examination No:
Date:
```

Figure 2

◢Task 3 (35 marks)

1. Input the additional information shown in Figure 3.

   a. Change the month to *March*.

   b. Delete the *Athlone, Sligo, Waterford* and *Dundalk* factories from the spreadsheet.

   c. Insert the *Blackrock* factory into the spreadsheet.

   d. Change the production quantities as shown.

   e. Insert the headings *Spare Capacity*: and *Value of Spare Capacity:* in the positions shown.

   f. Insert an extra column for the *Factory Production Capacity* and place this heading in the position shown.

   g. Right align the new column and heading.

   h. Re-align the main and subheadings centrally over the data.

   i. Insert the table: *No., Manager* and *Capacity* in the position shown and fill in the information in the table, aligned as in Figure 3.

2. Use the LOOKUP function to insert the *Factory Production Capacity* for each factory in the *Factory Production Capacity column*, from the table in (1) above.
3. Calculate the total production capacity and place it in the position indicated at the bottom of that column.
4. The *Spare Capacity* should be the difference between the sum of the factory production capacities and the sum of the factory production quantities.
5. The *Value of Spare Capacity* should be calculated using the selling price only.
6. Sort the spreadsheet into alphabetical order on the *Factory* names.
7. Save the spreadsheet under the filename 94TASK3, for printing now or later. (Make two printouts of 94TASK3 to show (1) values and (2) formulae and cell references.)

```
                        Hi-Tech Productions


              Production Report     —     March 1994


                 Factory      Factory      Unit     Unit
                 Production Production Production Selling Royalty Profit
   No. Factory   Capacity   Quantity     Price    Price    Fee


   6   Blackrock              5000       £0.23   £0.51
   1   Clondalkin              900       £0.28   £0.48
   2   Santry                 1800       £0.25   £0.46
   3   Cork                   3200       £0.30   £0.49
   4   Galway                 2300       £0.26   £0.52
   5   Limerick               3500       £0.32   £0.53


      Total:                                    Total Profit:


   Spare Capacity:
                                               Value of Spare
                                                   Capacity:



      No.            1          2          3        4       5        6
      Manager:   M. Murphy  P. Doyle   J. Daly  B. Walsh H. Byrne N. Cleary
      Capacity:    4000       4500       4000     3000    4500     6000


   Name:
   Examination No:
   Date:
```

Figure 3

1. Produce a Bar Chart from spreadsheet 94TASK3 to show the quantities produced in each factory:
   a. The quantities should be taken from the *Factory Production Quantity* column.
   b. The bar chart should have the heading *Production Quantities*.
   c. The x-axis should the factory name under each bar and have the word *Factory* as the x-axis label.
   d. The y-axis should show the quantities in figures and have the word *Quantity* as the y-axis label.
2. Save the Bar Chart under the filename 94GRAPH (either separately or as part of the spreadsheet 94TASK3), for printing now or later.

Assignment 20
NCVA Spreadsheet Method Paper III

◼Task 1 (30 marks)

```
                        William's Grain Merchants

                          Daily Grain Intake


  (Date)


  Cust.                   Weight        Price      Bonus      Total
  Code      Product       (Tonne)    per Tonne   per Tonne    Price


   225      Wheat          12.6       £102.00
   106      Barley         15.3        £95.00
   357      Wheat          21.7       £102.00
   246      Wheat          11.6       £102.00
   341      Oats            9.5        £90.00
   128      Barley         18.3        £95.00
   207      Oats            7.9        £90.00


            Totals:


     Name:
  Exam No:
```

Figure 1

1.1 Set up the spreadsheet and input the data as shown in **Figure 1**.

   (a) Align the main heading **(William's Grain Merchants)** and the subheading **(Daily Grain intake)** centrally over the data.

   (b) Insert today's date, in the cell marked **(Date)**, from the computer clock.

   (c) Set column widths to appropriate values.

   (d) Column headings and contents should be as shown.

   (e) Column headings and contents should be aligned as shown.

   (f) All monetary values should be displayed in currency format, with two places of decimals.

1.2 The **Bonus per Tonne** should be displayed as £1.00 if the weight is less than 15 tonnes and £2.00 if the weight is 15 tonnes or over.

1.3 Calculate **Total Price** as **Price per Tonne** plus **Bonus per Tonne** multiplied by the **Weight** and display in the column under the heading Total Price.

1.4 Calculate the **Totals** for Weight and Total Price, using the SUM function and display in the **Totals:** row, in the appropriate column.

1.5 Insert your Name and Examination Number in the second column, beside the appropriate label.

1.6 Save the spreadsheet under the filename **REPORT1**, for printing now or later. The printout should show borders (row/column identifiers).

◤Task 2 (5 marks)

```
                        William's Grain Merchants

                          Daily Grain Intake
  (Date)


Cust.    Customer                Moisture   Weight  Price per   Bonus     Total
Code       Name      Product     Content    (Tonne)   Tonne    per Tonne  Price


 225                 Wheat         24%        12.6
 106                 Barley        18%        15.3
 357                 Wheat         21%        21.7
 246                 Wheat         20%        11.6
 341                 Oats          15%         9.5
 128                 Barley        19%        18.3
 207                 Oats          13%         7.9


                          Totals:


   Code:     106     128          207        225      246       341      357
   Name:   P. Daly  A. Doyle   H. Jones   P. Coyle  J. Murphy  R. Dunne  W. Wise


   Name:
Exam No:
```

Figure 2

2.1 Input the additional information as shown in **Figure 2**.

(a) Insert two extra columns, one between Cust. Code and Product columns and the second between the Product and Weight columns.

(b) Insert the heading **Customer Name** in the position shown and align as shown.

(c) Insert the values in the **Moisture Content** column and display as shown.

(d) Delete the values in the **Price per Tonne** column.

(e) Move the **Totals:** side heading one column to the right.

(f) Insert three extra rows between the Totals: row and your name.

(g) Insert the table **Code:** and **Name:** in the position shown and fill in the information in the table, aligning as shown.

2.2 (a) Use the LOOKUP function to insert the **Customer Name** from the table in 2.1(g), into the column under the **Customer Name** column heading.

   (b) Align the **Customer Names** to the left of the column.

2.3 (a) Use the IF function to display the correct value in the **Price per Tonne** column, based on the following information:

   Wheat £103.00 per tonne

   Barley £97.00 per tonne

   Oats £92.00 per tonne

   (b) Display the Price per Tonne in currency format, whole pounds only (i.e. no decimal places).

2.4 Save the spreadsheet under the filename **REPORT2**, for printing now or later. The printout should show borders (row/column identifiers).

◼Task 3 (35 marks)

```
                        William's Grain Merchants
                           Daily Grain Intake


(Date)
Cust.   Customer          Moisture  Weight   Price per  Bonus    Total  Collection
Code      Name    Product Content   (Tonne)    Tonne   per Tonne Price    Charge


 225             Wheat      24%      12.6
 106             Barley     18%      15.3
 357             Wheat      21%      21.7
 246             Wheat      20%      11.6
 341             Oats       15%       9.5
 128             Barley     19%      18.3
 207             Oats       13%       7.9


                           Totals:

                                  Average Price per Tonne:
                                  Average Collection Charge per Tonne:


   Code:   106      128      207      225       246      341      357
   Name:  P. Daly  A. Doyle H. Jones P. Coyle  J. Murphy R. Dunne W. Wise
Col. Charge: 2.0%   1.5%     3.0%     2.5%      1.5%     0.5%     3.5%


   Name:
Exam No:
```

Figure 3

3.1 Input the additional information as shown in Figure 3.

(a) Insert the column heading **Collection Charge** to the right of the **Total Price** column and align as shown.

(b) Insert two extra rows between the **Totals:** row and the **Table**.

(c) Insert the heading **Average Price per Tonne:** in the position shown and right align.

(d) Insert the heading **Average Collection Charge per Tonne:** in the position shown and right align.

(e) Insert an extra row between the Table and your name at the bottom of the spreadsheet.

(f) Insert the side heading **Col. Charge:** and associated data in the table as shown.

(g) Ensure that the main heading and subheading are centrally aligned across all column headings.

3.2 (a) Delete the data from the **Bonus per Tonne** column.

(b) Use the IF function to display the correct value in the **Bonus per Tonne** column, based on the following information:

(i) If the Moisture Content is greater than or equal to 23%, then the Bonus per Tonne is *minus* £3.00 (i.e. -£3.00 or £[3.00]).

(ii) If the Moisture Content is greater than or equal to 20%, but less than 23%, then the Bonus per Tonne is *minus* £2.00 (i.e. -£2.00 or £[2.00]).

(iii) If the Moisture Content is greater than or equal to 17%, then the Bonus per Tonne is £3.00.

3.3 Calculate the collection charge using the LOOKUP function to take the rate from the **Col. Charge** in the Table multiplied by the **Total Price**, and display as £ with two decimal places.

3.4 Calculate the average price per tonne and insert it in the **Total Price** column beside the heading **Average Price per Tonne:**.

3.5 Calculate the weighted average collection charge per tonne and insert it in the **Collection Charge** column beside the heading **Average Collection Charge per Tonne:**.*

3.6 **Sort** the spreadsheet in alphabetical order on the **Cust. Code**.

3.7 Save the spreadsheet under the filename **REPORT3** for printing now or later. Produce two printouts of REPORT3 to show **(i) values** and **(ii) formulas and cell references**, both with borders (row/column identifiers).

*This should be calculated as the average of the individual collection charges **per tonne** for each customer.

◥Task 4 (10 marks)

4.1 Produce a Macro which will perform the following tasks on REPORT3. (NB Do & run/execute the macro on REPORT3)

(a) Delete the values from the Cust. Code column.

(b) Delete the values from the Product, Moisture Content and Weight (Tonne) columns.

(c) Insert the date from the computer clock in cell marked (Date).

4.2 Save the macro under the name NEWDAY (either separately or as part of the spreadsheet — REPORT3), for printing now or later.

◣Printing

Printing may be carried out after the time allocation for the examination, but no alterations may be made to the saved files.

The following printouts are required:

1. Printout of REPORT1, complete with border (row/column identifiers).
2. Printout of REPORT2, complete with border (row/column identifiers).
3. Printout of REPORT3, to show all *values* complete with border (row/column identifiers).
4. Printout of REPORT3, to show all *formulae* and cell references.
5. Printout of the MACRO.

Chapter 6
Computer Applications Projects

▦ Introduction

The production of a good project demands the use of expressive and creative abilities as well as an understanding of how to use a particular computer program. Many students erroneously believe that they must be 'tapping away' on their computer keyboards for the entire duration of a project. A builder will only commence work on a house after he has received detailed house plans from an architect. Similarly, a project idea must be planned accurately and written up as an in-depth design. This project design must then be marked by your teacher **before** you embark on implementing the design using a computer program. In short, your tools during the design phase of your project are pen and paper and **not** a computer equipped with a particular applications program. It is recommended that you spend twice as much time on project design as you do on implementing the design on your computer.

▦ A project idea

The starting point is a period of quiet reflection to decide on a suitable topic for the project. Sources of project ideas are many and varied; some popular sources are:
- your work experience **(do not use real data)**
- hobbies.

A good guide to the suitability of an idea for a database project is to ask yourself the following questions:
- *Will the completed project be useful to others?*
- *How many fields will go to make up a record?*
- *Are all the fields relevant?*
- *Can suitable queries and reports be generated?*

Some popular topics for database projects include:

Club membership	Concert bookings
Employee details	Car rental
Dentistry patients	Student profiles
Product orders	Restaurant reservations
Shop stocks	Veterinary surgery — pet details

Similarly, a good guide to the suitability of an idea for a spreadsheet project is to ask yourself the following questions:

- *Will the completed project be useful to others?*
- *Will the final spreadsheet be easy to use?*
- *How many rows and columns will go to make up the spreadsheet?*
- *Will cumbersome formulae be required? (If so, it may not be a suitable project idea.)*

Some popular topics for spreadsheet projects include:

Employee salaries	Customer invoices
Cashflow projections	Insurance quotes
Pension schemes	Sales analysis
Stock re-ordering	Equipment hire
Budget forecasting	Loan repayments

A golden rule is to keep the project specifications before you while you work on the project.

▓ Producing a database project

This can be broken down into three distinct phases: the design phase, the implementation phase and the conclusion phase.

Design phase

A database project design should include:

1. An outline of the problem to be solved including document analysis, e.g. data capture forms
2. Identification of:
   - record structure
   - relevant key fields for sorting and/or indexing the file
   - likely queries, reports and labels to be generated.
3. Design of the data entry screen layout (ideally this should be based on the data capture form to aid data entry).

Implementation phase

During this phase, a computer equipped with a suitable database program is required. Hard copy will obviously be produced using a printer. Ability to carry out the following should be demonstrated:

1. Create the record structure and data entry screen
2. Input data accurately
3. Modify the structure and amend data
4. Handle a variety of data types

5. Query the database on a variety of data types
6. Organise the data on different field types
7. Create relevant reports and labels.

Conclusion phase

The conclusion should include an evaluation of the project in terms of:

1. its usefulness
2. all necessary modifications
3. any likely improvements.

Common questions

How big should my database file be?
The completed database file should contain at least five fields and a minimum of twenty-five records.

What field types should I use?
Field types should consist of at least character, numeric and one other (e.g. date or logical).

Should I generate query files?
Two relevant queries should be produced as a minimum. Each resulting query file should contain at least four records. One of the queries should contain a logical operator (e.g. AND, OR, NOT).

Must the file be sorted?
The file must be sorted on a minimum of two separate fields and two printouts should be produced using the appropriate report format.

What should the finished project look like?
It should be of a professional standard, typed and bound, within the constraints of the equipment available.

▦ Producing a spreadsheet project

This can also be broken down into the same three distinct phases.

Design phase

A spreadsheet project design should include:

1. A concise description of the problem and a proposed solution, identifying a source of data.
2. Identification of:
   • input data

- the processing required (in words)
- output data generated.

An example of each should be given.

3. Design of the screen layout, which should be based on a data capture form.
4. Specification of:
   - data format (e.g. alignment, currency, decimal places)
   - column widths
   - data to be hidden, frozen and or protected.

Implementation phase

During this phase, a computer equipped with a suitable spreadsheet program is required. Again, hard copy will obviously be produced using a printer. Ability to carry out the following should be demonstrated:

1. Create the spreadsheet
2. Print the spreadsheet
3. Print the spreadsheet showing formulae
4. Change a variable and print the altered spreadsheet.

Conclusion phase

The conclusion should include an evaluation of the project in terms of:

1. its usefulness
2. all necessary modifications
3. any likely improvements.

Common questions

How big should my spreadsheet be?
It is generally accepted that the completed spreadsheet should contain enough data to fill a monitor screen.

How complex should my formulae be?
This depends greatly on the problem which you are solving. The NCVA spreadsheet project guidelines suggest that a simple IF function should be included in at least one column of formulae as the basic minimum.

What should the finished project look like?
It should be of a professional standard, typed and bound, within the constraints of the equipment available.

Chapter 7
Introduction to
Word Processing

A word processor is a program that makes it possible to use a microcomputer for entering, storing and manipulating text.

In typing a document we usually make some mistakes: spelling errors, missing or duplicated words, and paragraphs in the wrong order, or even omitted. A word processor allows us to correct these errors and to make any other changes before the document is printed. It also allows us to store a copy of the document onto disk and to recall it later and edit it as required.

Facilities of a word processor

In this chapter we will examine the following facilities of a word processor:
1. Elementary editing: deleting and inserting
2. More advanced editing: moving text
3. Enhancing the appearance of a document
4. The 'find and replace' facility
5. Setting tabs
6. Stored paragraphs
7. Merge printing
8. Other facilities

1. Elementary editing: deleting and inserting

Patrick Matthews is secretary to the managing director of a company that manufactures building insulation: Cavityfoam Enterprises Ltd. He produces all documents on his microcomputer, which is equipped with a word processor program.

This is the first draft of a document describing the company and its products:

Cavityfoam Enterprises Ltd was founded in 1981 by JohnHall and Fionnuala O'Connor. The aim of the company was to produce good-quality home insulation products at a competitive price.

The company initially employed only twelve people. As markets were quickly established, the number of people employed by the firm grew rapidly. In 1985 the company employed forty-three people, and by 1995 the work force numbered seventy-eight.

In response to a need in the market, the company directors decided to branch into factory farm building insulation products. John Hall spent nine months in Toronto observing the mannufacture and testing of Canadian insulation products.

Today Cavityfoam enterprises Ltd is one of Ireland's leading companies in the manufacture of insulation building products. The Company employs 265 people, and last year's profits were £1.7 million.

Fionnuala now edits this first draft. There are standard ways of indicating what changes are to be made: the most important of these are shown here.

Cavityfoam Enterprises Ltd was founded in 1981 by John Hall and Fionnuala O'Connor. The aim of the company was to produce good-quality home insulation products at a competitive price.

The company initially employed ~~only~~ twelve people. As markets were quickly
established, the number of people employed by the ~~firm~~ (company) grew rapidly. In 1985 the company employed forty-three people, and by 1995 the work force numbered seventy-eight.

In response to a need in the market, the company directors decided to branch into
factory (and) farm building insulation products. John Hall spent nine months in Toronto observing the mannufacture and testing of Canadian insulation products.

Today Cavityfoam enterprises Ltd is one of Ireland's leading companies in the manufacture of insulation building products. The Company employs 265 people, and last year's profits were £1.7 million.

⊢—⊣	Delete a word	=	Change from lower case (ordinary letters) to capitals
company ⊢—⊣	Substitute a word	⌐⌐	Transpose (swap) words
Y	Insert a space between words	≢ or ○	Change from capitals to lower case
ʌ	Insert a character or word	◡	Close up (remove a space)
/	Delete a character		

New text can be inserted into a document by moving the cursor to the correct position and simply typing the text. Unwanted text can be deleted by positioning the cursor at the appropriate place and giving one of the delete commands. Word processors have commands to delete a character, word, line or block of text.

The word processor will rearrange the text after you have edited a line so that the remainder of the text will move forwards or back to fill the space.

The corrected text will now appear as follows:

Cavityfoam Enterprises Ltd was founded in 1981 by John Hall and Fionnuala O'Connor. The aim of the company was to produce good-quality home insulation products at a competitive price.

The company initially employed twelve people. As markets were quickly established, the number of people employed by the company grew rapidly. In 1985 the company employed forty-three people, and by 1995 the workforce numbered seventy-eight.

In response to a need in the market, the company directors decided to branch into factory and farm building insulation products. John Hall spent nine months in Toronto observing the manufacture and testing of Canadian insulation products.

Today Cavityfoam Enterprises Ltd is one of Ireland's leading companies in the manufacture of building insulation products. The company employs 265 people, and last year's profits were £1.7 million.

2. More advanced editing: moving text

The managing director has asked Patrick to draw up a letter to the wholesalers who stock Cavityfoam products. The letter should tell them of future price increases on some products and of the development of a new insulation material suitable for bungalows. Here is his draft:

Dear Wholesaler,

We regret to inform you that, because of spiralling raw material costs, we have increased the price of some products. Our very popular Astrofoam has been increased from £11.75 to £12.50 per cubic metre. Our insulation foam for farm buildings, Agrifoam, has been increased from £8.50 to £9.20 per cubic metre. The company has decided to extend its guarantee from ten to fifteen years on all of its insulation products. This fact should be made clear to the retailers, as our largest competitors only guarantee their products for seven years.

We are introducing a new insulation product called Bungafoam onto the market. This is suitable for bungalows, and is competitively priced at £11.50 per cubic metre.

Our sales representative will be calling on you on 28 March. He will furnish you with all the details of our other insulation products and will accept your order this month.

I wish to remind you of our 5 per cent discount on all products that are paid for in full on the delivery date.

I am confident that you will continue to stock the Cavityfoam range of insulation products.

Yours faithfully,

Fionnuala O'Connor
Managing Director

Fionnuala feels that some changes need to be made to this letter.

- Paragraph 2 should be moved so that it becomes the first paragraph of the letter. This is achieved by marking the paragraph to be moved and positioning the cursor at the new position in the document. The command to move a marked block of text must then be given.
- One paragraph should be divided into two. The paragraph that starts 'We regret to inform you . . .' should be split at the point that begins 'The company has decided to extend . . .' This is achieved by inserting two carriage returns (pressing the 'enter' key twice) at the appropriate position in the text.
- Two separate paragraphs should be joined together. The paragraph that starts 'Our sales representative will be calling . . .' and the one that starts 'I wish to remind you . . .' should be run together. This is achieved by deleting the carriage returns between the paragraphs.

Fionnuala marks the draft with the following symbols:

Dear Wholesaler,

Ⓐ We regret to inform you that, because of spiralling raw material costs, we have increased the price of some products. Our very popular Astrofoam has been increased from £11.75 to £12.50 per cubic metre. Our insulation foam for farm buildings, Agrifoam, has been increased from £8.50 to £9.20 per cubic metre. Ⓑ The company has decided to extend its guarantee from ten to fifteen years on all of its insulation products. This fact should be made clear to the retailers, as our largest competitors only guarantee their products for seven years.

We are introducing a new insulation product called Bungafoam onto the market. This is suitable for bungalows, and is competitively priced at £11.50 per cubic metre.

Our sales representative will be calling on you on 28 March. He will furnish you with all the details of our other insulation products and will accept your order this month.

Ⓒ I wish to remind you of our 5 per cent discount on all products that are paid for in full on the delivery date.

I am confident that you will continue to stock the Cavityfoam range of insulation products.

Yours faithfully,

Fionnuala O'Connor
Managing Director

A Move text to new position

B Start new paragraph

C Run on (not a new paragraph)

The letter will appear as follows after all these changes have been made:

Dear Wholesaler,

We are introducing a new insulation product called Bungafoam onto the market. This is suitable for bungalows, and is competitively priced at £11.50 per cubic metre.

We regret to inform you that, because of spiralling raw material costs, we have increased the price of some products. Our very popular Astrofoam has been increased from £11.75 to £12.50 per cubic metre. Our insulation foam for farm buildings, Agrifoam, has been increased from £8.50 to £9.20 per cubic metre.

The company has decided to extend its guarantee from ten to fifteen years on all of its insulation products. This fact should be made clear to the retailers, as our largest competitors only guarantee their products for seven years.

Our sales representative will be calling on you on 28 March. He will furnish you with all the details of our other insulation products and will accept your order this month. I wish to remind you of our 5 per cent discount on all products that are paid for in full on the delivery date.

I am confident that you will continue to stock the Cavityfoam range of insulation products.

Yours faithfully,

Fionnuala O'Connor
Managing Director

It is obvious that these changes could not have been carried out on an ordinary typewriter without retyping the whole document.

3. Enhancing the appearance of a document

Most word processors offer the user a number of features to enhance the appearance of the text — although these should be used sparingly in business documents, especially by a beginner. They include:

- changing the font and font size
- centring and underlining key words and phrases
- altering the line spacing
- setting new margins and rearranging text accordingly.

◪Changing the font and font size

Word processors allow the use of different fonts. A font is a set of characters with a consistent and identifiable typeface. Each font has a name which you can use to select the font and apply it to text. Times Roman and Dom Casual are examples of fonts. Further examples of common fonts are given in the table. The size of the font, known as the point size, can also be changed, as shown in the table.

TABLE OF COMMON FONTS		
10 point size	12 point size	16 point size
Times	Times	Times
Caslon 540	Caslon 540	Caslon 540
Stone Serif	Stone Serif	Stone Serif
Futura Book	Futura Book	Futura Book
Brush Script	Brush Script	Brush Script
Bodoni	Bodoni	Bodoni
Helvetica	Helvetica	Helvetica
Baskerville	Baskerville	Baskerville
Freestyle Script	Freestyle Script	Freestyle Script
Optima	Optima	Optima

◪Centring and underlining

Centring a line means moving it so that it is halfway between the left and right margins, making it stand out more clearly. This is very commonly used for headings.

Underlining a section of text means that a continuous line will be printed under this area.

Word processors also allow selected words to be printed in **bold type**. On dot-matrix printers this is usually achieved by printing over the same letters two or more times.

To enhance a piece of text using one of these features, the text is usually first marked, and then the command to centre, underline or change to bold must be given.

Word processors also have a feature called **justification**, where the shorter lines of a document are spread out towards the right margin to make all the lines the same length (as in this paragraph). In business documents this is rarely an improvement over ordinary ('flush left') alignment,   and   it   is   never   appropriate   for   letters.

The default setting on most word processors for justification is off (i.e. flush left alignment), and for line spacing is 1. These settings can be altered by using the correct commands before text is entered. It is also possible to alter justification and line spacing settings after the text has been entered: the text can then be realigned to the new settings.

Patrick has prepared a statement describing the company's plans for overseas expansion. He has centred the heading at the top of the document and changed its font (Caslon 540) and size (11.5pt) , and he has also used bold type, italics and underlining for key phrases:

New Project

Cavityfoam Enterprises Ltd has decided to open a <u>new plant at Reims in France for the production of building insulation materials</u>. The outlay is projected to be £7.8 million, and at first the plant will employ thirty-five people. The town council has given **approval** for the construction of the factory, and it is hoped that production at the new plant will start in eighteen months. This venture will allow *Cavityfoam Enterprises* to gain a foothold in the European market for insulation products.

◩Altering the line spacing

The amount of spacing between the lines can also be altered on your word processor. Letters and statements for publication in newspapers often have 'double line spacing' — with approximately the depth of another line of type between each line — as printers prefer to receive text in this form.

◩Setting new margins

The managing director may wish to have the statement submitted to the local newspaper for publication in the next edition. Newspapers sometimes like text for publication to be formatted in newspaper style. Patrick can reset the margins on his word processor to allow a maximum line width of 5 cm, as well as changing to double line spacing and justifying the text (straight right and left margins). Centring, underlining and other enhancements are not used.

The document would now appear as follows:

New project

Cavityfoam Enterprises Ltd has decided to open a new plant at Reims in France for the production of building insulation materials. The outlay is projected to be £7.8 million, and at first the plant will employ thirty-five people. The town council has given approval for the construction of the factory, and it is hoped that production at the new plant will start in eighteen months. This venture will allow Cavityfoam Enterprises to gain a foothold in the European market for insulation products.

The 'find and replace' facility also allows you to replace entire phrases with alternative phrases. The length of phrase permitted may be limited, however.

4. The 'find and replace' facility

Sometimes you may have used a word in the course of typing a document and then decide to replace it with another. A word processor offers you a facility with which you can replace one word with another, at one place in the document or at every occurrence of that word in the document.

In the document above, Patrick has used the word 'plant' three times. He can easily replace it with the word 'factory' by using the 'find and replace' facility on his word processor. The document would now appear as follows:

New project

Cavityfoam Enterprises Ltd has decided to open a new factory at Reims in France for the production of building insulation materials. The outlay is projected to be £7.8 million, and at first the factory will employ thirty-five people. The town council has given approval for the construction of the factory, and it is hoped that production at the new factory will start in eighteen months. This venture will allow Cavityfoam Enterprises to gain a foothold in the European market for insulation products.

5. Setting tabs

All keyboards have a 'tab' key (short for 'tabulation'). When this key is pressed the cursor will jump a number of spaces horizontally. This saves the inconvenience of continually using the space bar to get to a certain position in the text.

There are a number of positions or 'tabs' already set at equal distances across the line. We can abandon these, however, and set our own tabs. This is an essential facility when we want to enter text in columns.

Tabs can be set quite easily on a word processor. You can change the number of tabs and their positions, thus varying the widths of columns and the space between them.

Patrick has been asked to list the prices of Cavityfoam products for the last three years in columns. The document appears as follows:

PRODUCT	1993	1994	1995
Agrifoam	7.80	8.50	9.20
Astrofoam	10.50	11.75	12.50
Bungafoam	—	—	11.50
Chip carpet	4.99	5.50	5.50
Floor seal	3.60	4.20	4.20
Mason tiles	1.80	2.20	2.20
Shedfoam	7.20	7.20	7.20

Patrick realises that the columns are too close together. He resets the tabs to adjust the distances between the columns. The document would now appear as follows:

PRODUCT	1993	1994	1995
Agrifoam	7.80	8.50	9.20
Astrofoam	10.50	11.75	12.50
Bungafoam	—	—	11.50
Chip carpet	4.99	5.50	5.50
Floor seal	3.60	4.20	4.20
Mason tiles	1.80	2.20	2.20
Shedfoam	7.20	7.20	7.20

An alternative is to set up a table. The gridlines on the table can be set to on or off. The main advantage of the table is that it can be easily changed.

An example of a table is given below (gridlines are set on):

PRODUCT		1993		1994		1995
Agrifoam		7.80		8.50		9.20
Astrofoam		10.50		11.75		12.50
Bungafoam		—		—		11.50
Chip carpet		4.99		5.50		5.50
Floor seal		3.60		4.20		4.20
Mason tiles		1.80		2.20		2.20
Shedfoam		7.20		7.20		7.20

6. Stored paragraphs

One of the most useful features of a word processor is the ability to store frequently used paragraphs in separate files on disk. When we are entering text into a file on our word processor we can copy one of the stored paragraphs into the file as required.

Many letters and documents produced on word processors are the result of 'pasting together' a number of stored paragraphs (sometimes called 'boilerplate paragraphs'). Cavityfoam Enterprises Ltd interviewed five suitably qualified people for two positions in the quality control department. The interview board has made its selection and has asked Patrick to send letters to the applicants, telling them of the board's decision. Patrick will store the following paragraphs in separate files on disk:

[Paragraph 1]
We should like to thank you for attending for interview on Thursday last. We were very impressed by your qualifications and experience.

[Paragraph 2]
We wish to offer you the position of quality control assistant. Please confirm your acceptance of the position as soon as possible so that we can organise a suitable date for a medical examination. We look forward to hearing from you.

[Paragraph 3]
We are, however, unable to offer you a position with our company at the present time. We wish you every success in your future career.

[Paragraph 4]
Yours faithfully,

Fionnuala O'Connor
Managing Director

Patrick can open individual documents on his word processor and use these paragraphs to compose appropriate letters.

Two of the applicants for jobs were Anne Breen and John Cuddy. Anne's efforts have been successful; John, however, has been unsuccessful. Both applicants will receive appropriate letters. The texts of these letters are as follows:

◗Letter 1: comprising stored paragraphs 1, 2 and 4

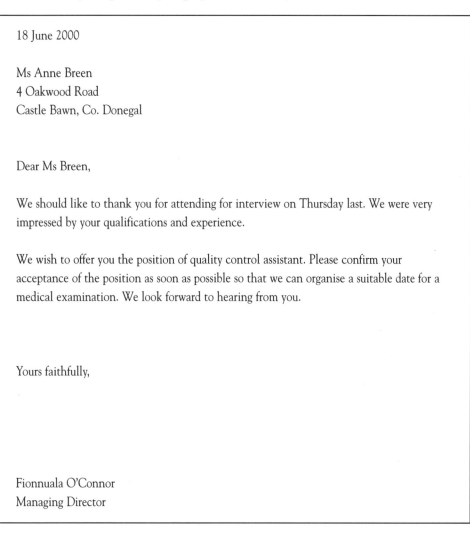

18 June 2000

Ms Anne Breen
4 Oakwood Road
Castle Bawn, Co. Donegal

Dear Ms Breen,

We should like to thank you for attending for interview on Thursday last. We were very impressed by your qualifications and experience.

We wish to offer you the position of quality control assistant. Please confirm your acceptance of the position as soon as possible so that we can organise a suitable date for a medical examination. We look forward to hearing from you.

Yours faithfully,

Fionnuala O'Connor
Managing Director

◣Letter 2: comprising stored paragraphs 1, 3 and 4

> 18 June 2000
>
> Mr John Cuddy
> 31 Eskermore Terrace
> Castlebawn, Co. Donegal
>
>
> Dear Mr Cuddy,
>
> We should like to thank you for attending for interview on Thursday last. We were very impressed by your qualifications and experience.
>
> We are, however, unable to offer you a position with our company at the present time. We wish you every success in your future career.
>
>
>
> Yours faithfully,
>
>
>
>
> Fionnuala O'Connor
> Managing Director

The other three applicants would receive replies identical to one or other of the above letters.

This method of composing letters and documents from a set of stored paragraphs is widely used by people who use word processors as a central part of their work. A lawyer's secretary may store on disk a range of paragraphs relating to contracts and other legal documents. Different sets of paragraphs can then be combined in a document, depending on the nature of the contract being drawn up.

7. Merge printing

One of the most powerful features of a word processor is the merge printing facility. This allows you to draw up a **source file**, which usually consists of a single document or letter containing **variables**. The precise information to be included instead of the variables is entered in a **data file**. When you invoke merge printing, the various sets of data from the data file are merged into copies of the source file.

The managing director of Cavityfoam Enterprises Ltd has asked Patrick to send letters to wholesalers in three regions — south-west, south-east, and central — informing them of a demonstration of the new insulation product, Bungafoam. The details of the demonstration in each region are as follows:

REGION	TIME	DATE	VENUE
South-west	2 p.m.	3 April	Whiterock Hotel
South-east	3 p.m.	5 April	Silver Swan Hotel
Central	2 p.m.	10 April	Kilmore Hotel

Patrick would enter a source file in his word processor like the one shown below:

---

19 March 2000

Dear Wholesaler,

You are invited to a demonstration of our new insulation product for bungalows, called Bungafoam, at &time& on &date& in the &hotel&. This demonstration is for the benefit of all wholesalers in the &area& region.

There will be time after the demonstration for a discussion on the product. Any opinions or criticisms of the product will be welcome.
We look forward to seeing you at the demonstration.

Yours sincerely,

Fionnuala O'Connor
Managing Director

Patrick would then set up a data file and include the times, dates, hotels and regions in a manner similar to that outlined below.

---

2 p.m., 3 April, Whiterock Hotel, south-west
3 p.m., 5 April, Silver Swan Hotel, south-east
2 p.m., 10 April, Kilmore Hotel, central

You should check the exact format on your particular word processor for variables in the source file and for data in the data file.

When Patrick invokes the merge printing facility, the details from the data file will be merged with the source file, and three separate documents will be produced for the three regions. The three letters should appear as follows:

◣Letter 1: South-west region

19 March 2000

Dear Wholesaler,

You are invited to a demonstration of our new insulation product for bungalows, called Bungafoam, at 2 p.m. on 3 April in the Whiterock Hotel. This demonstration is for the benefit of all wholesalers in the south-west region.

There will be time after the demonstration for a discussion on the product. Any opinions or criticisms of the product will be welcome.
We look forward to seeing you at the demonstration.

Yours sincerely,

Fionnuala O'Connor
Managing Director

19 March 2000

Dear Wholesaler,

You are invited to a demonstration of our new insulation product for bungalows, called Bungafoam, at 3 p.m. on 5 April in the Silver Swan Hotel. This demonstration is for the benefit of all wholesalers in the south-east region.

There will be time after the demonstration for a discussion on the product. Any opinions or criticisms of the product will be welcome.
We look forward to seeing you at the demonstration.

Yours sincerely,

Fionnuala O'Connor
Managing Director

19 March 2000

Dear Wholesaler,

You are invited to a demonstration of our new insulation product for bungalows, called Bungafoam, at 2 p.m. on 10 April in the Kilmore Hotel. This demonstration is for the benefit of all wholesalers in the central region.

There will be time after the demonstration for a discussion on the product. Any opinions or criticisms of the product will be welcome.
We look forward to seeing you at the demonstration.

Yours sincerely,

Fionnuala O'Connor
Managing Director

8. Other Facilities

Other commonly used facilities include the use of columns, frames, clip art and bullet points as shown in the following sample.

Information Technology in Schools

Computers and related technologies have greatly changed our society and our world. We have now truly reached the information age. Computers are now poised to promote revolutionary change in our educational systems. This change may be compared to changes wrought by books. IT has similar characteristics. Books empower people who know how to read. In the same way schools of the future will place major emphasis on helping all students to read IT.

Recently, there has been a worldwide metamorphosis, having computers in schools is now seen as a service to the whole school and not just as a specialist subject. This specialist focus of the past had the undesirable effect of constraining wider curricular development in IT in other subjects, and denied the majority of pupils any substantial access to IT as a tool for learning.

More and more people are coming to realise that the current educational system is not adequate to the challenge of the information age. Emphasis is now shifting from a focus on the computer itself, to a focus on learning environments that are facilitated by computers. This change of focus has put major demands on schools to change, in order to facilitate this challenge of integration. Massive amounts of money have been spent on the purchase of hardware and software. However, this has not solved the problem of true integration of computers into the curriculum. Major barriers to integration have been identified such as school structure, teachers attitudes, teacher support, teacher training, lack of policy, lack of time and co-ordination.

The introduction and integration of computers into education is similar to other innovations and requires a human solution as well as a resource solution. The rapid growth of computers in schools has brought about the equally rapid growth in the need for people to co-ordinate computer education programs.

Most schools go through stages in their progression on to full integration. These stages are:

- **Innovation:** just one or two members of staff exploring the educational use of IT.
- **Fire Lighting:** attempts are being made to get more staff involved, and someone, perhaps an IT co-ordinator, has been identified.
- **Promotion:** serious attempts to engage large numbers of staff, where it is seen as an important element in the school development plan.
- **Growth:** as result of promotion the school faces serious demands for resources, staff development.
- **Co-ordination:** associated with collaboration across the school about IT experiences.
- **Integration:** methods of work have been established, most subjects using IT extensively for teaching.

⸬ Applications of word processing

Almost any application requiring the manipulation of text can be handled efficiently with a word processor. Only a few of the most common applications are described here.

◤ Standard letters

These are letters containing the same information that are sent to many customers. With the merge printing facility the letters can be 'personalised', i.e. the name and address of the customer can be added to the letter. Matching envelope labels can also be printed.

◤ Contracts and agreements

Most legal contracts contain standard information. When a solicitor's secretary prepares a contract, some of these paragraphs can be read into the document by using the stored paragraphs facility. The paragraphs need only be typed in once and can then be used any number of times.

◤ Reports

Reports usually require a variety of styles of presentation. Some of the various text enhancement facilities can be used here, as well as the ability of most word processors to read text into the report from other sources, e.g. from a spreadsheet or database.

◤ Mail shots

These are regular advertising leaflets posted to a compiled list of customers. The information may need to be changed from time to time, and word processor editing facilities will help here. More importantly, the word processor will produce printed labels showing the name and address of each customer.

◤ Regularly updated lists

Lists of all kinds that require regular updating can be produced, such as price lists, directories, customer lists, inventories and catalogues.

⸬ Advantages of word processor use

We have already examined many of the advantages of word processors in the creation and editing of documents of all kinds. Some of the most important advantages are summarised here.

◤ Storage of text

The ability to store and retrieve text means that it can be used again, either exactly as first used or with changes. Magnetic storage media are also less bulky and easier to retrieve than paper copies.

◣Time savings
The ability to edit easily, both while entering text and subsequently, means a very significant saving in time, which is of great importance to a business.

◣Quality
The layout and general appearance of documents can be enhanced by changing typefaces, margins, alignment, and line spacing, as well as by other enhancement features, particularly if a high-quality printer such as a laser printer is available.

◣Security
Confidential documents are easily protected on word processor files, which can be secured against accidental viewing or changing by use of the 'protect' tab on diskettes or programmed to require a password to permit viewing or changing them. Magnetic media can be easily stored in fireproof safes.

◣Ease of use
Most word processor programs are easy to operate and learn. Good programs have a key that provides on-screen help when you are entering text.

▦ Disadvantages of word processor use
Despite their many advantages, word processors have a number of drawbacks that should also be taken into account.

◣Cost
Business-quality computers and peripherals can be expensive, and the rapid pace of technological change can make systems obsolete very quickly and frequent updates are required.

◣Staff training
Staff must be trained to use the computers and the word processor programs. Equipment and programs will need to be upgraded occasionally and the staff retrained in their use. This can be a considerable cost for a business.

◣Poor checking
Because so many editing facilities are available during the typing of text, there may be a temptation to be less thorough in correcting the final print-out.

◣Health
There is some evidence that prolonged use of monitors can have adverse physical effects (e.g. eye strain, migraine).

Conclusion

In this section we have examined the main features of a word processor, and we hope that you will work through all the assignments in the next chapter on your own equipment and using your own programs. The word processor is by far the most widely used computer application, and the ability to operate one is essential in many occupations as the trend away from the use of typewriters continues.

Questions

Multi-choice questions

1. word processing is:
   (a) the sending of text from a microcomputer to a large mainframe computer for processing
   (b) the use of microelectronic equipment to increase the amount of work carried out by office staff in a given time
   (c) the use of microelectronic equipment to enter, edit and store text
   (d) the use of microelectronic equipment to eliminate errors in writing
2. Which of the following could be carried out just as efficiently using a typewriter as using a word processor?
   (a) producing customised letters
   (b) producing short occasional letters
   (c) producing long legal documents with many identical clauses
   (d) producing complex medical documents containing many pharmaceutical terms
3. Centred text in a document may help to highlight:
   (a) text that has to be moved
   (b) the start of a new section
   (c) text that contains errors
   (d) where we must justify the text
4. A triple-underline symbol on a corrected document means that we must:
   (a) start a new paragraph
   (b) use a capital letter
   (c) use a lower-case letter
   (d) correct the spelling of a word
5. The 'find and replace' facility —
   (a) finds all occurrences of words longer than eight characters and offers a list of alternatives from the thesaurus
   (b) finds a block of text you may have marked for moving and allows you to replace the markers with 'move' symbols

(c) searches for all words at the beginning of sentences and checks that they start with a capital letter

(d) finds one or all occurrences of the given text and changes it to the given replacement

6. The term 'text' means:

(a) letters, numbers and symbols (excluding pictures and diagrams) that make up a document

(b) documents that consist of letters only

(c) all documents (excluding business letters)

(d) a document that does not contain any typing errors?

7 A font is the same as

(a) the pitch

(b) the typeface

(c) the size of the characters

(d) none of the above

Short-answer questions

1. Briefly describe the main text editing facilities of a word processor.
2. Suggest three advantages and two disadvantages of a word processor compared with a typewriter.
3. Briefly describe the main features you would look for in buying a word processor program.
4. Describe the following styles of text alignment, and give examples of where each one might be used: justified, flush left, flush right and centred.
5. Illustrate, by means of an example, the 'stored paragraphs' facility of a word processor.
6. What is merge printing? Give an example of an application where it might be used.
7. Distinguish between the spelling check and thesaurus facilities of a word processor.

▦ Glossary of word-processing terms

alignment: the way in which the text of a document is adjusted relative to the left and right margins, whether flush left, flush right, justified, or centred.

bold type: a typeface design matching the one in normal use but made up of thicker lines to give emphasis; on dot-matrix printers, bold type is simulated by overstriking the same characters two or more times.

carriage return: the keystroke or command that ends the current line of text and sends the cursor to the first character position on the next line, invoked in word processing by pressing the 'enter' key.

centred: the style of alignment in which the text is placed halfway between the left and right margins of the document.

data file: a computer file on disk that contains text or other data that the user has created and stored, as distinct from program files, which contain the computer code that runs the program.

editing: making corrections and other changes to a text, including substitutions, deletions, and insertions.

'find and replace': a facility that automatically replaces a selected word or phrase with an alternative word or phrase, at selected occurrences or at every occurrence in the document.

flush left: the style of alignment in which lines are of different length and the text has a straight left margin and uneven right margin, exactly as it was typed into the word processor.

flush right: the style of alignment in which lines are of different length and the text has a straight right margin and uneven left margin.

font: a special type of program file that contains instructions for creating a particular typeface on the printer, usually with a separate font for each size.

justification: the style of alignment is which all the lines are forced out to equal length by increasing the space between words, with straight left and right margins.

line spacing: the adjustable vertical distance between lines of text.

menu: a list of the options available at any stage in the execution of a program.

merge printing: a facility that allows the user to customise standard documents by automatically reading in variable data.

page break: a code in a word processor file that causes the printer to start printing on a new page: it may be a 'forced page break' entered by the user or one that occurs automatically when the amount of text entered would fill the defined page size.

spelling check: a facility of most word processors that checks the spelling of words in a document by comparing them against a list of words in one of the program files.

stored paragraph: a paragraph stored in a separate file on disk that can be combined with other paragraphs to make up a composite document.

tab key: a key that causes the cursor to jump a number of spaces horizontally to user-defined positions on the typing line in order to set the width of columns and the space between them.

thesaurus: a facility that allows the user to choose alternative words from lists of words with a related meaning.

typeface: a distinctive style of type with its own name.

underlining: the printing of a continuous line under a selected group of words to emphasise them.

word processor: a computer program used in the creating, editing and printing of text.

word wraparound: a feature of a word processor that causes the cursor to move automatically to the beginning of the next line in the display when the end of a line is reached.

work area: the area of the display excluding the status line, menu and ruler line, where text is typed and edited.

Chapter 8
Practical Word-processing Assignments

These assignments are graded, and we advise that you work through them in the order in which they are given. Unless otherwise stated, set up the document for A4 page size with one inch left and right borders for all assignments. Justification should be off unless otherwise stated. **Note: the text for assignments 3, 4, 6, 7, 8, 9, 10 and 16 are available in ASCII format and Word format from the Gill & Macmillan website at www.gillmacmillan.ie/eca.**

◣Functions and commands required

As you progress through these assignments you will need to check on the functions and commands specific to your word processor program. You will also be practising commands and functions learned in earlier assignments. (Note: If you do not have access to a printer, you can display the results of that task instead.)

The functions and commands required for each assignment are as follows:

ASSIGNMENT 1
• Text entry in a document file
• Cursor movement
• Saving a document to disk

ASSIGNMENT 2
• Deleting and inserting text
• Retrieving a file

ASSIGNMENT 3
• Consolidation assignment

ASSIGNMENT 4
• Moving a block of text

ASSIGNMENT 5
• Dividing and joining paragraphs
• Letter format

ASSIGNMENT 6
• Consolidation assignment
• Find and replace

ASSIGNMENT 7
- Centring
- Fonts

ASSIGNMENT 8
- Underlining and bold
- Bullets
- Case changes
- Hanging indent

ASSIGNMENT 9
- Setting margins
- Block format

ASSIGNMENT 10
- Consolidation assignment
- Indent paragraphs
- Line spacing

ASSIGNMENT 11
- Tables

ASSIGNMENT 12
- Setting tabs/tables

ASSIGNMENT 13
- Tabs and tables, layout

ASSIGNMENT 14
- Decimal tabs, tables

ASSIGNMENT 15
- Clip art
- Font sizes

ASSIGNMENT 16
- Clip art
- Columns
- Frames

ASSIGNMENT 17
- Stored paragraphs

ASSIGNMENT 18
- Merge printing

ASSIGNMENT 19
- Merge printing

ASSIGNMENT 20
- Consolidation assignment— NCVA Examination 1997

Assignment 1

- Key in the following text
- Proofread carefully
- Use the backspace key or delete key to delete any errors, and retype
- Save on disk using the filename LOCHHUNT

Nessie lies low

A prize of £1,500 in the Loch Ness monster hunt was won yesterday by Oceanscan, an American survey company. The prize, however, feel far short of the £250,000 on offer for conclusive proof of Nessie's existence.

Oceanscan made sonar contact on Saturday with a large unidentified object measuring up to 8 m long. The sonar contact was made near the loch's northern shore, where most sightings of Nessie have been reported.

Andy James (42), the team leader, said yesterday: 'We are thrilled to win the prize for the best search method. The object, which showed up on Saturday, registered as two blips on the sonar screen, but it moved out of range quickly.'

The organising committee of the hunt have decided to hold the event again next year. It will be held over a ten-day period in July, and the prize money for conclusive proof of Nessie's existence will be increased to £300,000. Many teams, including those from Canada and the United States, have agreed to participate again.

Assignment 2

- Key in the following text
- Proofread carefully
- Save on disk using the filename OILFIND1

New oil reserves

Saudi Arabia has discovered extensive new crude oil reserves in previously unexplored areas, according to a report from Reuters news agency today.

One Saudi government source said that the new find was bigger than the total known reserves of some other OPEC member-states. The Saudi state company has reportedly been drilling in areas well away from its existing oil pipeline network.

The agency quotes unnamed Saudi officials as saying that the find could boost the country's oil reserves by as much as 20 per cent. The discovery could have a significant impact on oil markets, in lowering the price of crude oil from its recent record price of around $40 per barrel.

This is good news for the consumer, who has recently been experiencing steadily increasing prices on all oil products. Increased oil prices automatically lead to increased inflation and invariably to increases in unemployment.

- Retrieve the file OILFIELD1
- Edit the file by making the alterations shown below and proofread carefully

---

New oil reserves

Saudi Arabia has discovered extensive new crude oil reserves in previously unexplored areas, according to a report from Reuters news agency ~~today.~~ *yesterday*

One Saudi government source said that the new find was bigger than the total known reserves of some other OPEC member-states. The Saudi state ^oil company has reportedly been drilling in areas well away from its existing oil pipeline network.

discovery

The agency quotes unnamed Saudi officials as saying that the ~~find~~ could boost the country's oil reserves by as much as 20 per cent. The discovery could have a significant impact on ^world/ oil markets, in lowering the price of crude oil from its recent record price of around $40 per barrel.

This is good news for the consumer, who has recently been experiencing steadily increasing prices on all oil products. Increased oil prices ~~automatically~~ lead to increased inflation and invariably to increases in unemployment.

- Save this edited version of the file onto your diak, using OILFIELD2 as the file name.

220

Assignment 3

■ **Carry out the following tasks:**

• Retrieve the file DUNBEG1 from the Gill & Macmillan website (www.gillmacmillan.ie/eca).

• Edit the document by making the alterations shown below and proofread carefully.

Dunbeg development proposals

There is an immediate [urgent] need for a children's playground in the area. The association considers Knockmore Meadow [as] to be a suitable site for a playground, as it is close to Dunbeg swimming pool and gymnasium. The association is prepared to organise and supervise sports events and barbecues at the playground during the summer holidays.

There is an immediate need for a pedestrian crossing on Castledean Road near the shopping arcade [centre]. Residents of Beechwood Road and Fitzgerald Avenue have great difficulty crossing Castledean Road during working hours.

The association urges the county council to honour its 1989 commitment to install street lighting on Bishopstown Road and Gasfinn Road. These roads are close to the railway station, and the lack of adequate street lighting, especially during winter months, is a problem for those who commute by rail to Castledean every day

---

• Save the edited version of the file to disk, using DUNBEG2 as the file name.

Assignment 4

◼Carry out the following tasks:

• Retrieve the file NEWS from the Gill & Macmillan website (www.gillmacmillan.ie/eca).

• Edit the document by making the alterations shown below and proofread carefully.

Mason & Co.

COMPANY NEWSLETTER   *position here*

INTERCOMPANY FOOTBALL. The annual intercompany football tournament took place at Murrenstown [football] *sports* grounds. Many local firms entered a team. The tournament was eventually won by Slaney Meats PLC. Our team reached the semi-final but was beaten by Marymount Electrical Ltd. *in a penalty shootout*

FISHING TRIP. Twenty-five people have enlisted for the fishing trip to the [Slane] *Boyne* valley on Saturday next. A coach will leave from the town hall at 10 a.m. A limited number of places is still available; if you are interested, please forward your name to John Martin or Susan Conway. *and address and telephone number*

NEW ARRIVAL. Best wishes to Andrew and Niamh Boylan on the birth of their first child, a baby girl. She is to be called Ciara.

DRAMA SECTION. Mary McEvoy would like to hear from anyone who would be willing to participate in this year's drama production of John B. Keane's 'Many Young Men of Twenty'. Performances would be in [late March] *early April* of next year.

SECURE PARKING. In the light of last month's vandalism of two cars in the company car park, a new gate has been installed at the entrance to the car park. This gate will be locked from 10 a.m. to 1 p.m. and from 2.15 to 4.45 p.m. each day. *position where shown by asterix *

---

3. Save the edited version of the file to your disk, using NEWS 1 as the file name.

4. Produce a print-out of NEWS1.

Assignment 5

- Create the following letter
- Proofread
- Save the letter using CARSALE1 as the filename

Cox Motors Ltd
Gort Road
Ballymore
Co. Tipperary

Mr Ruairi O'Connell
25 Golden Vale Road
Ballymore
Co. Tipperary

11 May 1999

Dear Mr O'Connell,

Thank you for your enquiry about the Astra car range. As requested, we are sending you a brochure giving full details of all six cars in the range.

You will notice that the fuel consumption is excellent and all new Astra cars have a three-year warranty on all parts. A leaflet is also enclosed outlining the retail prices of our new cars, together with a comprehensive list of quality used Astra cars in stock.

Please feel free to drop into the garage at any time for a test drive.

Yours sincerely,

Robert Cox
Sales Department

- Make the following edits to the letter, you may practise using the editing symbols for this exercise:
- (a)   replace the date given with today's date;
- (b)   in paragraph 2, replace 'cars' with 'models' throughout the paragraph;
- (c)   delete the word 'also' in paragraph 2;
- (d)   insert the word 'now' before 'in stock' at the end of paragraph 2;
- (e)   replace 'drop' with 'call' in paragraph 3;
- (f)   join the first two paragraphs together;
- (g)   make the sentence that begins 'A leaflet is...' the start of a new paragraph.

Save this version of the letter to your disk, using CARSALE2 as the file name.

Assignment 6

- Retrieve the file AGM1 from the Gill & Macmillan website and make the following edit.
- Save the changed file as AGM2.

Minutes of the annual general meeting of members of Corrugated ~~Steel Products~~ [Iron Process] Ltd, held at 34 Riverside Road, Navan, on Tuesday 30 October 199~~8~~9.

Mr Aidan Dooley, Chair ~~of the Board~~, presided.

The Secretary read the notice convening the meeting, and the auditors' report.

The Chair addressed the meeting, and proposed: That the directors' report and the accounts for the year ending 30 September 199~~8~~9 produced at the meeting [in Navan] be hereby received and adopted, and that a dividend of ~~15~~ [18] per cent less income tax be declared, to be payable to members on ~~20~~ [27] November 199~~8~~9.

The Chair proposed that Mr Patrick Matthews, the director retiring by rotation, be re-elected as a director of the company, Mr Declan Murphy seconded the motion, which was put to the meeting and carried by nine votes to three.

Ms Niamh Sheridan, a shareholder, proposed that Jackson, Brady and Company, having agreed to continue in office as auditors for a further year, receive a fixed fee of £17,000. This was seconded by Mr Seán Moran, another shareholder, put to the meeting, and carried unanimously.

There was no other business.

Operator: change all occurrences of chair to chairperson throughout

Chair

7 November 199~~8~~9

Assignment 7

◩ Carry out the following tasks:

- Retrieve the file MENU from the Gill & Macmillan website.
- The menu is to be displayed outside the hotel, but the manager is not pleased with the format. He has asked you to centre all the text, including the hotel name and address and to use fonts to enhance the appearance of the menu.
- Save the centred menu to disk, using MENUC as the file name.

Assignment 8

- Retrieve the file REPORT from the Gill & Macmillan website and make the following edits.
- Save the edited files as REPORTA.

REPORT OF THE SUBCOMMITTEE ← (Point size 18, bold, Centre and underscore)

This is the report of the subcommittee appointed according to the terms of the Board resolution of 5 July 1995 'that a subcommittee be appointed to investigate and report on the decline of paper sales in the southern region for the period ending 30 November 1995, and to make recommendations.'

Subcommittee members   **Bold Headings**

Indent 2.5 cm

⌜ Frank Brady (chairman)
  Valerie Byrne
  Ian Caprani   (Operator: Change all company names)
  Ciarán Dunne   (in the report to bold print   )
  Madeleine Dunne
  Dermot Moyne
⌞ Mary Purcell

Summary
The full report is in the hands of the marketing manager. Some of the more important findings are:

(a) Competition has increased considerably, especially with the entry into the market of Reprotext Ltd.
                    clients
(b) Two of our reliable ~~customers~~ have ceased trading in the last twelve months: Southprint Ltd and Speedprint Ltd.
((c) There is a cheaper imported paper on the market, which is affecting sales from
  department C.)

(d) Because of the high rate of absenteeism in the dispatch department some orders were cancelled.

and more expensive

(e) The haulier for the southern region is less reliable /than those of any of the other regions.

Recommendations
1. Find a new haulier for the southern region.
2. Obtain more information on possible cheaper sources of paper.
3. Assign two more sales representatives to the region.
4. Establish the reason for the absenteeism in the dispatch department.
5. Make a closer examination of the activities of Reprotext Ltd.

change numbering to bullet format

Data
Details of data relevant to this report are attached.

Signed: ....
1 December 1995

Assignment 9

- Retrieve the file OUTDOOR from the Gill & Macmillan website and make the following edits.

---

91 St Peter's Drive
Dublin 24

5 July 1995

Dear Sir,/Madam,

I am writing to describe a recent experience that ~~might~~ *will* be of interest to your readers.

I decided to do something different for my holidays this year. I booked an adventure holiday at the Slievemore Mountain Lodge adventure centre in Co. Wicklow, *Ireland*. From the very minute I arrived at the centre I began to unwind. The scenery was beautiful, with peaceful lakes, rolling heather-covered hills, and sparkling streams. *run on*

The centre has a choice of daily activities, including hill walking, canoeing, sailing, orienteering, and rock climbing, to mention only a few. I tried ~~nearly~~ all of these activities during the week. *N.P.* The walks covered an area where we saw no signs of human habitation, which made a pleasant contrast with the 'concrete jungle' I am used to most of the year! The accommodation was very comfortable: it was a real pleasure to return from a day's activity to a roaring log fire and a hot meal.

We hear so much about disappointed holidaymakers nowadays. This was *one of* the best holiday of my life, and I would wholeheartedly recommend such a holiday ~~to anyone who wants a real break from it all~~.

Yours sincerely,

Pádraig Whelan ——— *leave 4 lines for the signature*

⬛Carry out the following tasks:

- To make it more acceptable to the editor of the paper, the letter should be put into two narrow columns of equal width.
- Change the alignment to block format.
- Save the edited file as OUTDOOR1.

Assignment 10

- Retrieve the file SURVEY from the Gill & Macmillan website and make the following edits.

HEART DISEASE SURVEY ← (Bold, centre, point size 20)

More than half of a group of patients screened for heart disease risk factors were found to
be overweight, and nearly a ~~quarter~~ third had high blood pressure, it emerged today. ⌐ run on

examined
The researchers ~~looked at~~ examined forty patients in the Dún Laoghaire area. GPs screened the
patients for such things as excess weight, high blood pressure, and high cholesterol levels.

already
Now researchers are planning a second screening project, to study a larger number of
patients, following the disturbing results of the pilot study carried out by the Department of
Preventive Medicine in University College, Dublin.

italics
Nearly 60 per cent of the people examined were overweight, according to the 'Irish
Medical Times'. A quarter had high cholesterol levels, while 20 to 30 per cent had high
blood pressure.

Now, GPs in the wider area of south ~~east~~ Co. Dublin are to become involved in a second
trial to screen a larger number of patients.

◼ Carry out the following tasks:
- Alter the left margin to 4cms.
- Produce a 1.5cm hanging indent on each paragraph.
- Change the entire documnet to double line spacing.
- Save the edited file to disk.
- Name the file SURVEY2.

Assignment 11

Create a new document for each of the following tables.

◣Task 1

COUNTY	COUNTY TOWN	PROVINCE
Meath	Navan	Leinster
Mayo	Castlebar	Connacht
Tyrone	Omagh	Ulster
Clare	Ennis	Munster

Save this table as COUNTY and close the file.

◣Task 2

COURSE	CO-ORDINATOR	SUBJECTS	EXAM	STUDENTS
Accounting	J. Smyth	6	CIMA	22
Beauty Care	M. Clarke	9	CIDESCO	18
Computers	D. Cooney	8	NCVA	30
Catering	M. Maguire	7	CERT	35
Sports Therapy	F. Ward	9	NCVA	24

Save this table as COURSES and close the file.

◣Task 3

TRIM AGRICULTURAL SHOW					
Category	**Entrants**	**First Prize**	**Second Prize**	**Third Prize**	**Closing Date**
Cattle	35	£1000	£500	£250	14 June
Horses	20	£2000	£1000	£750	22 June
Sheep	25	£800	£500	£200	25 June
Dogs	15	£500	£250	£100	01 July

1. Sort the table in alphabetical order of category.
2. Save this table as SHOW and close the file.

◣Task 4

MODERN DESIGNS LTD — CUSTOMER ORDER FORM					
Item	Quantity	Unit Price	Total Price	VAT	Total Due
Door	3	£85.00	£255.00	£54.00	£309.00
Window	10	£40.00	£400.00	£84.00	£484.00
Radiator	8	£55.00	£440.00	£92.00	£532.00
				Total	**£1325.00**

Save this table as MODERN and close the file.

Assignment 12

- Create the following document using tabs or a table.
- Save on disk using the file name TABS.

COURSE: INTRODUCTION TO COMPUTING			
Time	Details	Tutor	Room
9:30	Introduction to computer hardware	Ms M. Purcell	Com1
10:30	Coffee break		
10:50	Introduction to computer software	Dr D. Cox	Com1
11:30	Keyboarding	Mr G. Coakley	Com2
12:30	Lunch		
1:30	Hands-on word processing	Prof. J. O'Brien	Com2
2:30	Hands-on spreadsheets	Dr A. Clifford	Com2
3:30	Coffee		
3:50	Hands-on database	Dr D. Cooney	Com2
4:30	Networking; electronic mail; computer safety	Mr M. Keenan	Com2
5:30	Review		

Assignment 13

- Create the following document using a combination of tabs and tables.
- Save on disk using the file name QUEST.

QUESTIONNAIRE

A. Personal Profile

Q1. Sex | Male | | Female |

Q2. Number of years teaching [ ]   Number of years teaching with computers [ ]

Q3. Number of years as computer/IT coordinator [ ]

Q4. Qualifications [ ]

Q5. Age | 20-30 | | 31-40 | | 41-50 | | 50+ |

Q6. Computer owner | No | | Yes |

B. School Profile

Q7.

1	Location of school (e.g. Dublin 12)	
2	School type (e.g. vocational)	
3	Is your school coeducational? (Y/N)	
4	Number of students in the school	

C. Hardware Facilities

Q8 Please indicate the number of each of the following computers in your school.

	No.	Networked (Y/N)
IBMs or compatibles		
Apples		
Nimbus		
BBCs		
Commodores		

Thank you for your cooperation!

Assignment 14

- Create the following document using tabs or using a table.
- Show the gridlines on the table.
- Save on disk using the file name TAX.

Tax Deduction Card for: Mary Woods			
Week No.	Gross Pay	Cumulative Gross Pay	PAYE tax
	£	£	£
1	200.34	200.34	28.75
2	200.34	400.68	28.75
3	184.77	585.45	23.77
4	73.91	659.36	0.00
5	0.00	659.36	0.00
6	0.00	659.36	0.00
7	73.91	733.27	0.00
8	248.96	982.23	31.43
9	195.47	1,177.70	27.19
10	0.00	1,177.70	0.00
11	200.34	1,378.04	28.75
12	200.34	1,578.38	28.75
13	200.34	1,778.72	28.75
14	200.34	1,979.06	28.75
15	200.34	2,179.40	28.75

Assignment 15

- Create the poster below using clip art, font sizes and borders.
- Save the file as POSTER.

Congratulations!

to
all the students of City Community College

on your Graduation

You are invited to the graduation ceremony at The College Hall

On 25th November 1999 At 8.00pm sharp

Assignment 16

- Retrieve the file IDEAL from the Gill & Macmillan website.
- Change the documnet to appear as given below using columns, bullet points, frames and clip art.

The Ideal of Integration The Way Forward

Computers were introduced into the education systems of some countries in the late 1960s and early 1970s. However, the development of the microcomputer in the 1980s has produced the most significant developments in computer use in education systems worldwide.

The global effect of the use of computers on the curriculum as outlined by Wellington has been threefold.

- Firstly, the emergence of a new subject called *Computer Science*. This has been incorporated in to the vocational and upper secondary level curriculums worldwide.
- Secondly, the development of computers and information technology as an integral part of culture and society, which all students should experience. The subjects **Computer Awareness** and *Computer Literacy* seem to fulfil this role.
- Thirdly, the development of computers and information technology as teaching and learning resources where computers are integrated across the curriculum.

Some countries opted initially to concentrate on the first option only. Such countries include Greece, Japan, Denmark, Ireland, Austria and Belgium. Other countries such as France, UK and Canada developed comprehensive policies where all three options have been followed. However, more recently the general trend in all countries is towards a comprehensive approach where all three options are being introduced as outlined in a recent report by the OED in 1989.

With respect to the detailed curriculum many claims have been put forward about the possible impact of using computers in the school curriculum. Educational goals may change by having more emphasis on productive rather than reproductive tasks (as there is often quicker learning of practice and drill activities) such as problem solving, information handling and inquiry skills.

It is claimed that greater opportunities will be more available to work on more real life problems. The benefit to special needs students is particularly evident where multimedia (combination of video and text images) computer systems are used. This will mean that the curriculum can be expanded for special needs students. It is possible for students to do things never possible before, such as severely handicapped students learning and communicating via the computer. The assessment of students' achievement may change to more responsive and quicker methods. The role of the teacher may change to that of a facilitator and hence the operational curriculum may also change.

Assignment 17

You have just been appointed to the complaints department of Hewson Electrical Ltd. Your duties include responding to letters of complaint from dissatisfied customers.

- Create the following paragraphs in separate files on your disk. The files should be named PT1, PT2, PT3, PT4 and PT5, respectively.

[File 1]
We have received your letter concerning the item that you bought at our store. We are sorry to hear that it is causing problems.

[File 2]
As the goods are still under guarantee, please call our maintenance department to arrange a suitable time for our repair technician to call to you.

[File 3]
As the goods are no longer under guarantee, repair work cannot be carried out free of charge. Our repair technician, however, can call to you to give a quotation for the cost of repairs.

[File 4]
As this is an old model, parts are extremely difficult to obtain. We have an excellent range of new models in our showrooms, and we would be happy to offer you a reasonable trade-in discount off the cost of a new model.

[File 5]
Your faithfully,

Desmond Joyce
Repair Control Department

- Use the correct combination of stored paragraphs and today's date to compose letters of reply to the following customers. Your are also given suitable names for your letter files.

LETTER	PERSON	STORED PARAGRAPHS
LTR1	Ms Joyce Noonan 55 Kilmore Road Castlebawn, Co. Donegal	Files: PT1, PT2, PT5
LTR2	Mr Seán Ryan 73 Ormond Road Invermore, Co. Limerick	Files: PT1, PT3, PT5
LTR3	Ms Róisín Nestor 6 Mount Nugent Road Dunfinn, Co. Cavan	Files: PT1, PT4, PT5

Assignment 18

As personnel manager of Green Valley Foods Ltd you must recruit a new secretary for the managing director of the company. You have advertised the position in the local press and have received a large number of applications.

- Create the standard letter below and save it as STAND

<merged name>
<merged address>

17 May 1995

Dear <merged name>,

We are pleased to invite you to an interview for the post of secretary to the managing director of our company, on <merged date> at <merged time>.

You should call at the reception desk in the front hall. The receptionist will direct you to <merged location>.

Please confirm that you will be able to attend at that time.

Yours faithfully,

Mary Thompson
Personnel Manager

(Here the symbol '<>' is used to enclose the variables: different indicators may be required on your word processor.)
- Use the merge printing facility of your word processor to compose letters to these three people requesting them to attend for interview.
- Create a data file called PEOPLE using the data given below

person:	Ms Aisling Downey	Mr Paul Ryan	Ms Patricia Burke
address1:	3 Willowbrook Rd	45 Collins Pk	12 Rosslee Rd
address2:	Kilpatrick,	Kilpatrick,	Kilpatrick,
	Co. Cork	Co. Cork	Co. Cork
name:	Ms Downey	Mr Ryan	Ms Burke
date:	26 May 1995	26 May 1995	26 May 1995
time:	10:30 a.m.	2:15 p.m.	3:30 p.m.
location:	room 19	room 22	room 22

Assignment 19

As personnel manager of Green Valley Foods Ltd you must organise and confirm the holiday arrangements for three members of staff. You will use the merge printing facility of your word processor to compose the letters. Set up two files, the standard letter and the data file and merge print them using appropriate file names.

The standard letter is as follows:

01/05/99

\<merged name>
\<merged address>

Dear \<merged name>,

Re: Summer Holidays 1999

I have received your request for holiday leave and I am pleased to be able to confirm the following dates from \<merged dates> inclusive.

Yours sincerely,

Joe Manning
Personnel Manager

The holiday rota is as follows:

Brenda Clancy	Paul Cusack	Sean Whelan
13 Willows Lodge	11 Rathdown Rd	23 Marley Close
Killiney	Bray	Rathfarnham
Co. Dublin	Co. Wicklow	Dublin 14
11/06/99 to 27/06/99	17/07/99 to 31/07/99	28/07/99 to 11/08/99

Assignment 20

NCVA Word Processing Level 2 1997
Practical Assignment 1 (30%)

1. Recall the document stored on your system or disk called **TASK1**.

2. Proofread and correct where necessary, and make the amendments as indicated.

3. Ragged or justified line endings are accepted (unless otherwise instructed within the document).

4. Take great care with pagination.

5. Save your document as **HEALTH** for printing as instructed by your Specialist Teacher.

- All abbreviations should be typed in full where appropriate.
- Block or centre style is acceptable once used consistently throughout an assignment.
- Dictionaries are not allowed.

Assignment 1.

HEALTH & SAFETY AT WORK ← *Bold, Centre + U.S*

OPERATOR: Change Font size to 12 litil throughout document

In order to ensure health and safety at work the employer must first prepare a safety statement. The safety statement identifies the risks or hazards to which the workers are exposed. When these risks or hazards have been established action must be taken. Good Codes of Practice as well as staff training and information form an *del* essential part of the strategies involved in promoting a healthier and safer working environment.

1. REPETITIVE STRAIN INJURY (RSI) *Bold Headings*

Repetitive Strain Injury (RSI) is the result of awkward or constrained working postures, repetitive movements or tasks. The strain usually affects the neck and upper limbs. The cost of hours lost to the workforce is enormous, not to mention costs involved due to early retirement and medical attention required; or reduced quality and quantity of work produced.

The factors that lead to RSI are still not quite known, but some of the risk factors can be outlined as follows:

INDENT 1"
- awkward posture
- repetitive work
- poor social relations
- heavy manual handling
- lack of influence in the organisation

} double line spacing

Justify R.H. Margin throughout document

* INSERT TEXT HERE

2. FIRE AND ELECTRICITY

use side Heading Fire. Most substances burn quickly and the fumes produced can be deadly. It is smoke and fumes that kill people, not flames.

It is imperative that the Fire Escapes are adequate and clearly marked.

Electricity. Common sense prevails in this instance. Every year many people are killed or badly injured at work due to electric shock.

Cable joints that are frayed or damaged should be replaced. Make sure all plugs are connected properly. Light bulbs or items which could be easily broken should have a protective guard. Appliances should be unplugged before making adjustments or cleaning. *N.P.*

It is the responsibility of the Employees to ensure that they know and understand the Company Safety Statement.

del With due care and consideration given to the factors outlined above better productivity will ensue and there will be reduced insurance costs as well as less disruptions to (work) which are caused by accidents or ill health. *TRS.*

3. SURVEY ← *(Block Caps + Bold Heading)*

L.C. Finally, a Recent survey indicates :

- over 16,000 accidents occurred at work
- approx. 80 people died
- some 4,000 suffered occupational diseases
- 750,000 working days lost through absences

} double line spacing

238

Assignment 1.

Insert at "*"

The on-set of RSI is usually slow + involves a series of steps. At first the person feels tired or fatigued with slight discomfort. This later develops into more severe pain + usually constrains daily activities. If allowed to continue it can lead to chronic disability for the individual. Rehabilitation at this chronic stage is more difficult than if

STET. measures ~~had been~~ <u>were</u> in place to prevent RSI. <u>Prevention</u> is better than <u>cure</u>. (Bold + Italics)

~~Psychological~~ factors such as stress, monotonous work, (which requires an amount of attention or precision + fixed posture) along with lack of work satisfaction contribute to RSI.

(PSYCHOSOCIAL)

OPERATOR: Replace the phrase "at work" with "in the workplace" throughout the document.

Note:
Print out the document with Page numbers included.

239

NCVA Word Processing Level 2 1997
Practical Assignment 2 (25%)

1. Key in and display the information attractively.

2. Information should be on a single page.

3. Save your document as **AGENDA** for printing as instructed by your Specialist Teacher.

- All abbreviations should be typed in full where appropriate.
- Block or centre style is acceptable once used consistently throughout an assignment.
- Dictionaries are not allowed.

Assignment 2.

"H + S" - Health and Safety in full

H + S Seminar   caps, centre & bold

17 - 19 June 1997   centre

Day 1.   General Office Safety + Stress Management   Block Caps + Bold

9.00 - 9.30 Registration

9.30 - 11.00 Ergonomics in the Office

11.00 - 11.30 Coffee Break

11.30 - 12.30 Stress Management

12.30 - 1.30 Q. + A. Session

"Q + A" - Question and Answer in full

Day 2. Safety Assessment + Controls in the Lab. → in full

9.00 - 9.30 Registration

9.30 - 11.00 Fundamentals of Industrial Measurement + Process Controls

11.00 - 11.30 Coffee Break

11.30 - 12.30 Respiratory Exposure to Volatile Solvent Vapours

12.30 - 1.30 Q + A Session

Day 3. Safety Skills with Mechanical Equipment

9.00 - 9.30 Registration

9.30 - 11.00 Rotating Equipment Preventative Maintenance

11.00 - 11.30 Coffee Break

11.30 - 12.30 Dust Suppression in Suction - type Machinery

12.30 - 1.30 Q + A. Session

- -

Reservation Form here

241

Assignment 2.

(H + S) Seminar Reservation Form (Bold Text)
in full

NAME (Block Caps)..
DEPT. .... Position ....

Seminar Title ....

Date of Seminar................... Time of seminar ....

(Words) 1st Choice ....
         2nd Choice ....

double
line
spacing

Lunch Required   Yes [ ]   no [ ]

Signature .... Date ....

Note: Please return to your Dept manager.
Reservations cannot (only) be confirmed when
this form is received.

Bold text

Operator : Please ensure that both the Agenda
for the seminar and the Reservation
Form are on the one page.
All Abbreviations in full

242

NCVA Word Processing Level 2 1997
Practical Assignment 3 (25%)

1. Key in the following Draft Letter being careful to insert the symbols for the variables exactly as shown.

2. Save your document as **DRAFT** for printing later as instructed by your Specialist Teacher.

3. Create **three** separate letters with the variables given: save each one for printing later.

Please save first letter as **MOONEY**
Please save second letter as **SEARCHER**
Please save third letter as **FIXET**

Assignment 3.

[1]

[2]

Dear [3]   *"H+S" - Health and Safety in full throughout document*

H + S Seminar - June 1997   *Caps, Bold + U.S. Heading*

This company has a very positive approach to H + S
del. in all its ~~aspects~~ activities. To ensure implementation
of its policies, it is proposed to hold seminars
on different aspects of H + S at work.
I shall be grateful if you will deliver a one-
day seminar to our employees in relation to [4].
NP [The date for this seminar is [5].
I enclose a programme indicating details of each
day's proceedings. The location of your seminar
is [6].
Please confirm with me at your earliest convenience
if you can give the seminar on that date.
Looking forward to a favourable response.

Yours sincerely   WINNING   WIDGET   COMPANY

Block Caps. + Bold

_____

A M O'Neill
General Manager

Enc

244

Assignment 3
Variables

Letter 1

[1] Today's Date
[2] Mr C. D. Mooney
   Director
   Human Resources
   A.D. Communications Company
   63 Central Mall
   DONEGAL
[3] Mr Mooney
[4] General Office Safety and Stress Management
[5] Tuesday 17 June 1997, from 9.00 a.m. - 2.00 p.m.
[6] First Floor, Boardroom, Head Office, Dublin

Letter 2

[1] Today's Date
[2] Dr E. F. Searcher
   Chief Analyst
   Laboratory Division
   R.O. Chemicals Ltd
   37 Alder Industrial Estate
   CORK
[3] Dr Searcher
[4] Safety Assessment and Controls in the Laboratory
[5] Wednesday, 18 June 1997, from 9.00 a.m. - 2.00 p.m.
[6] Block B of Annex at Manufacturing Site, Dundalk.

Letter 3

[1] Today's Date
[2] Mr G.H. Fixet
   Mechanical Services Section
   Melting Engineering Company
   4 New Quays
   DUBLIN
[3] Mr Fixet
[4] Safety Skills with Mechanical Equipment
[5] Thursday, 19 June 1997, from 9.00 a.m. - 2.00 p.m.
[6] Room 22, Assembly Building at Manufacturing Site, Dundalk.

Chapter 9
The Internet and the
World Wide Web

▦History and Structure of the Internet

◪What is the Internet?

The Internet is a global computer network. The computers, on this network, can be divided into two types — *clients* and *servers*. The clients are the computers that are similar to yours and mine: they can request information from the network. The servers, sometimes called *hosts*, are the computers that store and provide the information.

◪How Does the Internet Work?

The essential elements of the Internet are the *server* computers that are linked by a *permanent communications link*. This link is like a special-purpose telephone line that is always open and talking to the server computers, which are always on. The computers communicate over the network using the same 'language' called *TCP/IP (Transmission Control Protocol/Internet Protocol)*. Each server computer has a unique address that tells the other computers on the Internet how to find it. A client computer can connect to the Internet by linking to a server computer that is permanently connected to the Internet.

When you send or receive information through the Internet, it is broken down into smaller pieces called *packets*. Each packet is 'passed' from server computer to server computer on the Internet until it reaches its destination. On arrival, the packets are re-assembled into the original information. The packets travel independently through the Internet and may take different routes to their destination. Special computers, called *routers*, regulate the traffic on the Internet. A router, like a good travel agent, picks the most efficient route based on the volume of traffic and number of stopovers.

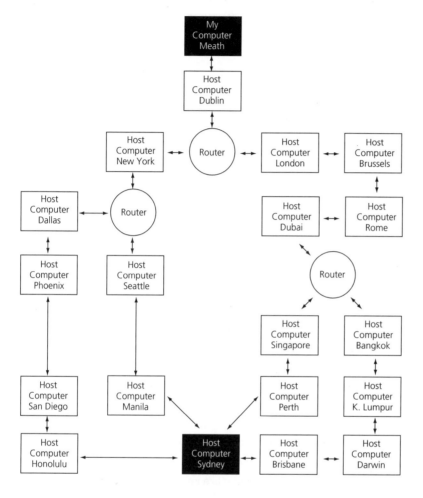

Referring to the diagram above, I may request information on the Sydney's Opera House. Let us assume that this information is held on a server computer in Sydney, Australia. The packets that go to make up the requested information may travel between the server computer in Sydney and my computer in Meath via a number of different routes:

- Sydney → Manila → Seattle → New York → Dublin → Meath

- Sydney → Honolulu → San Diego → Phoenix → Dallas → New York → Dublin → Meath

- Sydney → Brisbane → Darwin → Kuala Lumpar → Bangkok → Dubai → Rome → Brussels → London → Dublin → Meath

- Sydney → Perth → Singapore → Dubai → Rome → Brussels → London → Dublin → Meath

What is the World Wide Web?

The World Wide Web (WWW), sometimes called the 'Web', consists of millions of pages of information stored on thousands of server computers all over the world. A collection of related web pages is called a website.

The terms Internet and Web are often confused with one another. The Internet is the physical structure of the network, including server computers, routers and the communications lines that connect everything. The Web refers to the collection of websites and the information that can be accessed when one is using the Internet.

How did the Internet Develop?

During the Cold War, the American Department of Defence embarked on a project to link military and research computer systems in a fail-safe network. The principal problem to be solved was how to design a network of computer systems, situated in different geographical locations, that would not be entirely disabled in the event of a nuclear attack.

In 1964, Paul Baran wrote a proposal for such a computer network. Every computer (node) of the network could equally send or receive information. Most importantly, if one node was 'down', the rest of the nodes could still communicate. Though not the most efficient way to transmit information, the network would be reliable and not dependent on any particular computer. In 1969, the Pentagon's Advanced Research Projects Agency (ARPA) used these principles to install the first such network in the United States. It was called the ARPANET and it connected Stanford Research Institute, University College Los Angeles (UCLA), University College Santa Barbara and the University of Utah.

The ARPANET offered two main services:

- *Electronic Mail (e-mail):* This meant that people could compose documents on their computers and post them 'electronically' to each other.
- *Electronic Publishing:* This meant that people could make information from their computers available to everyone else using the service

By 1971, the ARPANET was connecting 23 agencies, including universities and government research centres, in the United States. In 1973, the ARPANET became international with initial connections to the University College of London and the Royal Radar Establishment in Norway. By the end of the decade, the ARPANET had moved from its military/research roots and was being used for commercial purposes and as a discussion platform for various groups. Computers attached directly to the network became known as servers.

In the early 1980s, a team led by Bob Kahn and Vint Cerf developed a set of rules, or protocols, for transferring data between different types of computer networks. These protocols tell computers how to locate and exchange data with one another. This standard set of protocols, as we have already seen, became known as *Transmission Control Protocol/Internet Protocol (TCP/IP).*

In 1984, the American National Science Foundation (NSF) built a network to connect its six supercomputer centres. The new network soon connected many of NSFs regional centres and became known as NSFNET. The ARPANENT and NSFNET were then connected and the growth of this 'network of networks' or Internet became exponential.

In other countries, educational and research computer networks were being constructed. For example, the Higher Education Authority Network (HEANET) and the Joint Academic Research Network (JANET) were developed in Ireland and Britain respectively. By the late 1980s, it became clear that all of these national networks would be more useful if they were connected together. Since the Internet in the United States was the largest and best tested system, the other national networks adopted its technologies and connected to it. By 1987, the number of Internet servers exceeded 10,000; two years later the number had exceeded 100,000.

The concept for the World Wide Web was developed in 1990, when Tim Berners-Lee and Robert Cailliau wrote a proposal for using a simple interface and 'HyperText' to access and 'browse' data and information. The software was developed for CERN (The European Institute for Particle Physics) in Switzerland, the original 'Web' was meant to be only for the Physics community. In 1991, Berners-Lee and Cailliau put their 'Web' software on the Internet for free. Soon afterward, Marc Andreessen incorporated graphical capabilities into a new browser, and the Mosaic browser was released from The American National Centre for Supercomputing Applications (NCSA) to the public in January 1993. The 1990s saw an exponential growth in the Internet. Some estimates now say that it is growing at a rate of 20 per cent each month!

◤Who owns and pays for the Internet?

No single person, group, company or government owns or controls the Internet. The owners of an individual server computer are responsible for maintaining it and its connection to the Internet.

The server computers on the Internet are permanently connected by thousands of miles of telephone lines and fibre optic cables that require routers to co-ordinate the flow of information. The cost of maintaining these links must be met. Some users, particularly those on government or university networks, do not pay for access to the Internet because their employers or superiors pay for the costs. The vast majority of users, however, pay a subscription fee and/or a telephone charge for access to the Internet.

◤Internet Connection

In order to connect to the Internet, you require:

- a computer
- standard telephone line and modem or an ISDN line and terminal adapter
- appropriate Internet software
- an account with an Internet Service Provider (ISP).

◪Hardware Required

The World Wide Web is expanding at a phenomenal rate. Better websites, with a high multimedia content, are appearing all the time. These websites may contain sound, graphics and video clips as well as text. Modern computers running up-to-date software are now required to view these sites successfully. As of going to print, we would recommend the following Personal Computer hardware specification for connection to the Internet using a standard telephone line:

HARDWARE	RECOMMENDED SPECIFICATION
CPU	Pentium III, 700mhz or equivalent
RAM	256MB
Hard Disk	20GB
Floppy Disk	1.44MB
Graphics	32MB AGP Graphics Card
Modem	56Kbps/V90
DVD	X8 Speed
Sound Support	Yes
Operating System	Microsoft Windows 2000

Improvements in PC technology mean that faster and better components are being included in new Personal Computers. For the latest hardware specifications, you should visit the websites of leading PC manufacturers like *Dell* or *Gateway*.

◪Integrated Services Digital Network (ISDN)

Integrated Services Digital Network or *ISDN* is a high-speed, fully digital telephone service. ISDN can operate at speeds of up to 128KB/second. Connecting to the Internet using an ISDN instead of a standard telephone link greatly enhances access speeds. The faster your Internet access is, the quicker it is to download e-mail or information from the World Wide Web. This means that you spend less time connected to the Internet, thereby reducing your Internet call charges.

◪Software Required

The software required in order to access and use the Internet can be categorised into three types:

- *Communications Software* — this should typically come with your modem. It enables your computer to make contact with your ISP's server computer.
- *Protocol Software* — this enables your computer to communicate with computers used by other Internet users.
- *Applications Software* — these enable you to actually do things on the Internet, such as send e-mail, read news and transfer files. Two examples of applications software are your web browser and e-mail programs.

The Protocol and Applications software is usually available on one CD, from an Internet Service Provider, as a 'Start-up kit' and can be installed quite easily on your computer.

◣Internet Service Provider

An Internet Service Provider (ISP) is a company that provides access to the Internet. The ISP owns a number of server computers that are linked permanently to each other and to the Internet. Each server has a number of modems connected to it. The ISP's servers are continually 'listening' for incoming calls on their modems.

When you want to 'go on the Internet', your computer places a telephone call via its modem to the ISP. When the call gets answered, your client computer and the ISP's server computer go through a process known as 'handshaking'. This process ensures that the two computers are 'talking the same language' and that you are authorised to connect to the ISP. When the connection is established, you are said to be *on-line*. Conversely, when your computer is not connected to your ISP, you are said to be *off-line*.

In connecting to an Internet Service Provider, you must consider the following costs:
- the fee if any to the ISP and/or
- the cost of the telephone charges.

◣Evaluating an Internet Service Provider

The quality and cost of service can vary significantly from one ISP to another. In evaluating an Internet Service Provider you should consider the following questions:

1. Is there a monthly/annual charge for an account?
2. Is the price quoted a flat rate or a metered fee? A flat rate fee does not take into account the length of time you spend 'live' or 'on-line' on the Internet but with a metered fee, you pay more as you spend longer on-line.
3. Can you connect to the ISP for the price of a local telephone call? Indeed, some ISPs offer access from anywhere in the country at rates significantly lower than local call access.
4. Is there an initial registration charge for setting up your account?
5. What is the user-to-line ratio? This tells you how many people there are for every telephone line. A good ratio is 15 to 1. If the ratio exceeds this, you may get a busy signal when you try to connect.
6. What Internet software does the ISP provide and support?
7. What type of technical support does the ISP provide? Is there a telephone help line?
8. Is there a charge for technical support?
9. How much free space does the ISP provide on one of its servers for posting your own website?
10. How many e-mail addresses are provided?
11. How fast is your ISP's connection to the Internet?
12. How fast are your ISP's modems?

Some ISPs do not charge a monthly or annual fee for an account. They appear to be offering Internet access for free. In some situations, however, a number of problems have arisen.

- High telephone charges — calls, in some cases, are not charged at local access rates.
- Exorbitant rates are, sometimes, charged for technical support.
- There have been reports of slow download times. This means that information passes from the Internet to a client computer very slowly.
- E-mail addresses and web space are, in some cases, not provided free.

Speed of Access to the Internet

The two main factors that effect speed of access to the Internet are:

- Modem speed
- Bandwidth

Modem speeds are indicated by a 'bits (of information) per second rating'. Currently the fastest modem that the average user can buy has an access speed of 56000bps. This number is a maximum not a minimum meaning that your modem may not connect at that speed.

Bandwidth is how much data, expressed in bits per second, you can send from one computer to another in a given amount of time. The faster your transmissions (or the greater the bandwidth of your connection), the less time you will spend waiting for text, images, sounds and video clips to upload or download from computer to computer.

Bandwidth is closely allied to the speed at which the ISP's server connects to the Internet combined with the number of users. Imagine your modem is a car and the ISP's server speed of connection to the Internet is represented by the width of the road. With a fast car you can get where you want quickly even on a narrow road. If you put a few more cars on the road, suddenly things are not moving quite so quickly. When you switch to a wider road, you are back up to speed again even if there are more cars.

Web pages, containing pictures, sound or video elements, take longer to download than those pages that contain only text. If another user is downloading a large graphics file, it is similar to a large juggernaut on the road getting in the way and slowing the traffic.

IP addresses and Domain Names

Server computers on the Internet are able to communicate with one another because each one has a unique code number called an *IP (Internet Protocol) address*. Each IP address is made up of a series of numbers separated by periods. A typical example would be: 128.92.32.187

Human beings have difficulty remembering long strings of numbers. This is where domain names come in. A *domain name* is a unique word that acts like a nickname for the IP address. A typical example would be: www.rte.ie

The domain names are significantly easier for us to remember but computers prefer to communicate with each other using the numerical IP address. In order that we can use addresses that we can remember and understand, the IP address and its corresponding domain name must be linked or cross-referenced.

The *Domain Name System (DNS)* takes care of this cross-referencing for us. DNS is a large database that holds all the IP addresses and corresponding domain names of all servers connected to the Internet. When you specify the address of a server, using its domain name, a process called *domain name resolution* takes place to find the server computer.

Domain name resolution takes place on the Internet on special computers known as Domain Name Servers. The other servers on the Internet access the *domain name servers* many times per second. If one domain name server does not know how to translate a domain name into its IP address, the task will be sent to the next closed domain name server all within milliseconds.

Intranet

An Intranet can be defined as an 'internal Internet' designed for use within the confines of a company or organisation. Technologies and software, originally developed for the Internet, are used to establish the internal network. What distinguishes an Intranet from the Internet is that the former is private. Outside users can be prohibited access, ensuring high security. It is ideal for companies who want to avail of all the benefits of the Internet, but in an internal environment. Intranets can be used to:

- Distribute information throughout a company or to specified recipients, especially in multimedia format.
- Facilitate effective and highly secure communication between employees.

The World Wide Web and Other Internet Facilities

The Basics

We have already established that the World Wide Web (WWW or Web) comprises millions of pages of information stored on thousands of server computers all over the world. We know that in order to view pages on the Web that we need special software known as a web browser, two examples are *Microsoft Internet Explorer* and *Netscape Navigator*.

Uniform Resource Locator (URL)

Each web page has its own unique address known as a *Uniform Resource Locator (URL)*. An imaginary URL is shown below:

http://www.gaa.ie/leitrim/results.htm

This URL consists of four distinct parts:

- *http://* — this is the protocol that the browser uses to read the web page.
- *www.gaa.ie* — the domain name of the server where the web page is located.
- *leitrim* — the folder, on that server, where the web page is stored.
- *results.htm* — the file or web page name.

This imaginary page might contain club results for Leitrim GAA matches.

◪HyperLinks

It is easy to move within the same page or between pages on the Web using *hyperlinks*. A hyperlink can be text, graphics or pictures. When you click with your mouse on a hyperlink, the browser takes you to another place within the same page or to another web page containing related information. A text hyperlink is frequently known as *hypertext*, it is frequently underlined and normally appears in a colour different from the normal text colour on the web page.

◪The Browser

When you load your browser software and connect to the Internet, you will most likely be brought to the home page of your Internet Service Provider (ISP). You will observe that your browser window is divided into two main areas:

• A top panel — containing an address line, a menu and a tool bar.
• A bottom area — where the web page is displayed.

If you know the URL of a web page, you can type it directly into the *address line* in the browser window. The page will be then be downloaded from the server into the browser window. The following screen shot shows the Irish Government's home page displayed in *Microsoft Internet Explorer:*

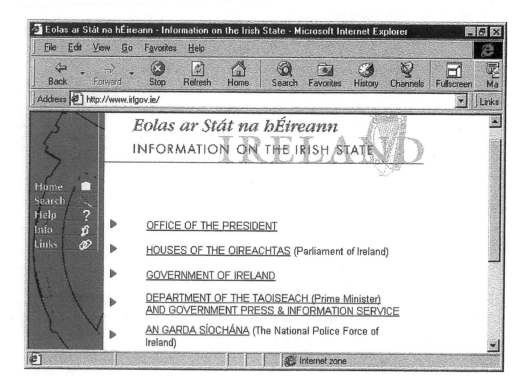

The *menu* presents you with a range of options and sub-options. The *Print* and *Save* options are particularly useful as they allow you to print a web page or save it to disk. Other menu options, that are frequently used, include *Select* and *Copy*. These latter options facilitate you in copying text from a web page into a word processor document.

The *tool bar* contains a number of useful buttons to aid your browsing:

- *Back* — allows you to revisit the page immediately before the one you are currently looking at.
- *Forward* — will move you forward again to the next page.
- *Home* — takes you back to your browser's default page. In many cases, this will be the home page of your ISP.
- *Stop* — halts the downloading of a page.
- *Refresh/Reload* — requests the server to send the same page again.
- *History* — displays a list of all the pages you have viewed since the last time you started your web browser.
- *Favorites/Bookmarks* — is a list of your favourite web pages. You can return to any of the pages listed by simply clicking on its name in the *favorites* or *Bookmarks* list. (Notice the American spelling of 'favorites')

Web browsers offer the facility to switch off graphics. This means that only the text on a web page will be downloaded and allows the Internet user to 'surf' the Web more quickly.

Plug-ins

A *plug-in* is a program that works with your web browser to give it an extra capability. For example, some popular plug-ins include:

- *RealAudio* — plays sound effects and music clips on web pages. You can also use it to hear live radio broadcasts on the Internet.
- *Crescendo* — plays midi sound files.
- *QuickTime* — allows you to view video clips on web pages.
- *Shockwave* — enables you to see animation on a web page and is useful for playing on-line games.

On the Internet, sound and video can be sent from a server to a client computer in either of two ways:

- *Complete Download* — all of the data must be downloaded from the server before you can hear sound or see video images.
- *Streaming* — this is similar to listening to the radio or watching television. You hear the sound and/or see the images as your computer receives the data from the server. You do *not* have to wait for complete files to be downloaded before you hear sound or see video images.

Conducting a Search

In searching for specific information on the Web, you should be:

- Familiar with search tools and their different searching methods.
- Comfortable in using the range of search techniques necessary to refine a query.

◤ Search Tools

A *search tool* is a computer program that helps us to find information on the Web. There are many search tools available and each one has access to its own large database of information on web pages. These databases are continually being updated with new website or web page references. Search tools may be categorised into two main types:

- Directories
- Search Engines

◤ Directories

A *directory* search tool looks for information by subject matter. An example of a directory search tool is *Yahoo*. Using a directory search tool, you can conduct a search in a hierarchical manner starting with a general subject heading and following with a succession of increasingly more specific subheadings. The search method is known as a *subject search*.

An example of a subject search, in *Yahoo*, for information on *Star Wars* films was conducted as follows:

Entertainment ➜ Movies & Film ➜ Genres ➜ Science Fiction & Fantasy ➜ Series ➜ Star Wars

The database of websites for directory search tools are usually compiled and categorised by human beings. A website owner would normally register a new website with the directory for inclusion in its database. Directory search tools are useful when you want to find entire websites on a particular topic. Other examples of Directory Search tools are *Magellan* and *Onekey*.

YAHOO!
UK & IRELAND

What's New   Check Email   Personalise   Help

Yahoo! Classifieds
Jobs, Cars, Homes

are you free tonight?

Yahoo! Mail - It's Free!
Sign Up Now

[Search field] `Search` advanced search

You are searching: ⦿ All of Yahoo! ○ Yahoo! UK ○ Yahoo! Ireland

Yahoo! Auctions - Music - Film - Toys & Games - Bid Now! -What is Auctions?

News - **Finance** - **Sport** - Weather - People Search - Free Net Access - **Business Finder** - Shopping - Auctions
Property - Jobs - Cars - Free Email: UK & IE - **My Yahoo!** - Calendar - Address Book - **Messenger** - more...

Arts & Humanities
Literature, Photography...

Business & Economy
Companies, Investments, Taxes...

Computers & Internet
Internet, WWW, Software, Games...

Education
UK, Ireland, Universities...

Entertainment
Humour, Movies, Music, Cool Links...

Government
UK, Ireland, Europe, Politics...

Health
Medicine, Drugs, Diseases, Fitness...

News & Media
Full Coverage, Newspapers, TV...

Recreation & Sport
Sport, Outdoors, Travel, Motoring...

Reference
Libraries, Dictionaries, Phone Numbers...

Regional
UK, Ireland, Countries, Regions...

Science
CS, Biology, Astronomy, Engineering...

Social Science
Anthropology, Sociology, Economics...

Society & Culture
People, Environment, Royalty, Religion...

In The News
- Ryder Cup, Davis Cup, Football, F1, more...
- UN tightens grip on devastated E.Timor
- Vicky murder hunt: body found in ditch

[headlines...]

Marketplace
- Jewellery Auctions
- Buy a car with Yahoo!

Inside Yahoo!
- Get Organised! - Free stuff from Yahoo!
- Web Access For Free - with Yahoo! Online
- Need Help? - Get started with Yahoo!

[more features...]

World Yahoo!s

Europe: Denmark - France - Germany - Italy - Norway - Spain - Sweden
Asia Pacific: Asia - Australia & NZ - China - Chinese - Hong Kong - Japan - Korea - Singapore - Taiwan
Americas: Yahoo! - Brazil - Canada - Spanish

Other Guides
Yahooligans! - My Yahoo! - Yahoo! Internet Life - Picks of the Week
Irish Picks - Scottish Picks - UK Net Events - News Ticker

Yahoo! prefers **VISA**

Information Centre - Advertiser Info - Privacy Policy - Get Some Yahoo! - Add Your Web Site - Jobs @ Yahoo!

◣ Search Engines

A *search engine* searches database(s) by using keywords. It responds to a query with a list of references or *hits*. This search method, known as a *keyword search*, differs from the *subject* method of searching used by the directory search tools.

Search engines rely on special software called *spiders* to maintain and update their databases of web information. Examples of popular search engines are *AltaVista* and *Infoseek*.

AltaVista The most powerful and useful guide to the Net

September 26, 1999 PDT

My AltaVista Shopping.com Zip2.com

Ask AltaVista® a question. Or enter a few words in [any language ▼]

Help
Advanced Text Search

Search For: ⦿ Web Pages ○ Images ○ Video ○ Audio

[   ] [Search]

Search tip:
do a video search

Example: **How can I find someone who moved or changed their phone number?**

ALTAVISTA CHANNELS - My AltaVista - Finance - Travel - Shopping - Careers - Health - News - Entertainment

FREEACCESS - Download Software^New - Support **USEFUL TOOLS** -Family Filter - Translation - Yellow Pages - People Finder - Maps - Usenet - Free Email

DIRECTORY

Automotive

Business & Finance

Computers & Internet

Health & Fitness

Hobbies & Interests

Home & Family

Media & Amusements

People & Chat

Reference & Education

Shopping & Services

Society & Politics

Sports & Recreation

Travel & Vacations

OTHER TOOLS

▶AltaVista Discovery 1.1
▶Free Photo Albums
▶Make us your Home Page
▶Get Internet Explorer 5
▶AV Tools & Gadgets
▶Industrial Communities
▶Search Products

ALTAVISTA HIGHLIGHTS

POWER SEARCH
▶Win **FREE** artwork for your home and desktop from Corbis.**A winner every day!**

NEW MEDIA NOW
▶Build an online community with **My AltaVista**
▶**FREE** Fantasy Football! Play Smart, Win **BIG!**

ALTAVISTA NETWORK
▶Help old friends find you! Click here!
▶Surf the Web all day, every day, **FREE!**

ULTRA SHOPPING FROM 🛒 **Shopping**.com

Blue Streak / CD
Shopping.com Price: $11.99 You **Save:** $5.98

Harry Potter / Book
Shopping.com Price: $9.97 You **Save:** $9.98

WWF Attitude - Nintendo
Shopping.com Price: $62.99 You **Save:** $7.00

Video Blaster Webcam III
Shopping.com Price: $64.95 You **Save:**

Click for more Ultra Shopping

NEWS BY ABCNEWS.com
▶Floyd's Flooding Unearths Coffins
▶Aftershock Rocks Taiwan
▶JFK Jr. Left Estate to Family, Friends, Charities
▶Refugees Sack Warehouse in East Timor

amazon.com

TRY THESE SEARCHES...

sailing - free games online - golf tips - Eurorail - MP3 archive

OUR SPONSORS

⋄30%-50% off Retail - FurnitureFind.com!

⋄Shop for your pet at PETsMART.com

⋄living.com, quality goods for your home

⋄webpersonals.com Find your mate!

ALTAVISTA INFORMATION

▶International
▶About AltaVista
▶Job Openings
▶Press Room

About AltaVista | Help | Feedback | Advertising Info | Add a Page
Disclaimer | Privacy | Copyright | International | Set your Preferences

◪Multi-Engine Search Tools

A *multi-engine search tool*, also called a *meta-search tool*, uses a number of search engines simultaneously. The search is conducted using keywords; it then lists the hits either by search engine or by integrating the results into a single listing. Examples of popular multi-engine search tools are *All-In-One* and *Dogpile*.

DOGPILE

FREE $5 amazon.com Gift Certificate!

Dogpile Destinations
Dogpile Remote
Open Directory
Custom Search
Search at Home
Metafind
Help

Marketplace

Xerox
Countrywide Loans
Gateway
CompareNet
$ Beenz
Amazon
MicroWarehouse

Save 90% off
Bargain Books!
MyShopnow.com

Go2Net Network
Go2Net Personal
Silicon Investor
HyperMart
Haggle Auctions
WebMarket
PlaySite
100hot Sites

Feedback
Advertising Info

Dogpile Search

[   ] [Fetch]

⦿ Web Metasearch ◌ Web Catalog ◌ Usenet ◌ Ftp ◌ Newscrawler ◌
◌ Stock Quotes ◌ Regional Web ◌ Weather ◌ Yellow Pages ◌ White Pages ◌
Click on Regional to choose a default city for the above se

FREE "Titanic" video from bigstar.com   NextCard Visa: 9.9% Fixed APR! A

Dogpile Web Catalog

Arts
[Design] [Humanities] [Museums]
[Performing Arts] [Visual Arts]

Biz
[Auto] [Electronics] [Financial]
[Internet Services] [Real Estate]

Computers & Internet
[Networking] [Net Culture] [Software]
[Games] [World Wide Web]

Entertainment
[Food] [Humor & Fun]
[Movies & Films] [Music]

Government
[Law] [Military]
[Politics] [U.S. Govt]

Health
[Alternative Medicine] [Diseases]
[Medicine] [Mental Health] [Public Health]

News & Media
[Magazines] [Newspapers]
[Radio] [Television]

Recreation
[Automotive] [Games] [Hobbies & Crafts]
[Outdoors] [Sports] [Travel]

Science
[Agriculture] [Alternative] [Astronomy]
[Biology] [Earth Sciences] [Engineering]

Society & Culture
[Cultures] [Disabilities] [Environment]
[Issues & Causes] [Organizations] [Religio

Books Furniture Travel Insurance Auctions Vitamins Site-See Mortgages Computers Library Medical Autos

Information
Contact Us Privacy Policy Press Center Advertising Job Opportunities About Us Investor Relations

Traded on NASDAQ: GNET Copyright © Go2Net, Inc. 1996-1999 Terms of use

These are the addresses of some of the most popular directories and search engines:

All-In-One — www.allonesearch.com

AltaVista — www.altavista.com

Ask Jeeves — www.ask.com

Excite — www.excite.com

HotBot — www.hotbot.com

Infoseek — www.infoseek.com

Dogpile — www.dogpile.com

Magellan — http://magellan.excite.com

Onekey — www.onekey.com

Yahoo — www.yahoo.ie

◼Portal Sites

Portal or *Gateway* sites are large websites that cover a wide range of topics and issues. A search engine may be incorporated into the website. The information, on the website is vetted by human beings to ensure that it is relevant and up-to-date. Most ISPs have a portal site. For example, Eircom's *Dorás* is a portal site dedicated to all things Irish.

◼Advice on How to Search the World Wide Web

The best advice to give regarding how to search the Web is *to read the directions*. Every search tool has its own website giving detailed information on how best to use its services. There are, however, a number of search tips that can be applied when using most search tools:

1. Be Specific

Let us assume that you are using a search engine to find information on fish. If you enter 'fish' as a keyword, a long list of references to web pages that contain the word 'fish' will result from the search. It may take hours to go through each one to find the exact information that you require. The search criterion entered was not specific enough. You must decide what information you require about fish e.g. a search for 'fresh water trout' would yield a shorter list of references, as it is more focused.

2. Use Quotation marks for Associated Words

Let us say that you require information on Irish music. If you enter Irish music, you will certainly get details on *Irish music*. You will, however, also get information on:

- All things Irish
- Music of all types

The search engine has looked for references to web pages that contain the word *Irish* and the word *music*. In this particular search, we have not emphasised that the two words must be taken together. In order to search for information on Irish music only, it is better to enter "Irish music". The quotation marks specify phrases or words that must be taken together instead of individual words.

3. Plus and Minus

Let us assume that you wish to search for a restaurant in Galway. You should enter the keywords as follows:

Galway + restaurant

The plus ensures that the search engine will look for references that contain both keywords: *Galway* and *restaurant*.

Let us say that you require a restaurant in Galway that does *not* specialise in seafood. You should enter the keywords as follows:

Galway + restaurant - seafood

The minus sign here will ensure that references containing the word *seafood* will not be shown. The plus and minus signs are invaluable tools when you wish to refine a search.

4. Stemming

This refers to the ability of a search tool to include the stem or the main part of a word. For example, sing is the stem for sings, singer, singing and singalong. Stemming may require use of a *wild card*, symbolised by an asterisk (*). In our example, the search would be conducted using 'sing*' as the reserved word.

5. Connection Operators

You can choose from a number of operators to help construct search criteria:

- AND (similar to '+') requires that both words are present somewhere within the document being sought e.g. *football* AND *Gaelic*.
- NEAR is used when you expect to find certain words occurring near each other, *or* do not know the order in which words will occur in relation to each other e.g. searching for *Shakespeare'* NEAR *comedies'* will find *"The wonderful comedies of Shakespeare are ..."* as well as *"Shakespeare's greatest comedies number only three."*
- OR requires that at least one word is present e.g. *classical* OR *opera*.
- NOT (similar to '-') excludes a word from a query e.g. *football* NOT *soccer*.
  When using these operators, remember to capitalise them as shown above.

6. Case Sensitive

If you capitalise letters in your search, then you narrow the search to only occurrences of that word with the exact same capitalisation. If your entry is in all lower case, then the search engine will search for all occurrences of the word, regardless of capitalisation.

- Adjacent capitalised words are treated as a single proper name e.g. Michael Collins
- Commas separate proper names from each other e.g. Sonia O'Sullivan, Stephen Roche

7. American English

As many websites are American, the text on these sites will be in 'American' English. Words such as *colour* and *metre* will be spelled as *color* and *meter*. Americans use words like *automobile* and *gas* for *car* and *petrol* respectively. A search for "American automobiles" may be more fruitful than one for "American cars"

⦙⦙⦙⦙ Other Internet Facilities

◪ File Transfer Protocol

File Transfer Protocol (FTP) is the name for a set of rules for transferring files from one computer to another via the Internet. The files are stored on server computers all over the world called *FTP sites*. The URLs of FTP sites have the prefix *ftp://*. FTP is a separate Internet facility from the World Wide Web. A web page, however, can have a hyperlink to a file stored on an FTP site.

Each FTP site limits the number of people who can use it simultaneously. If the site is busy, you will get an error message when you try to connect. Many FTP sites have alternative sites that provide identical information. The latter, known as *mirror sites*, help reduce the traffic on popular FTP sites.

◪ Downloading Software

You may wish to download software from an FTP site to your computer e.g. a new version of your browser software. Programs, stored at FTP sites, usually consist of a large group of files. To avoid downloading each program file individually, these are normally grouped or *archived* into one file. This file may then be *compressed* or *zipped* to reduce its size. Compressed files save storage space on the FTP site and transfer more quickly on the Internet. After downloading the software file to your own computer, you will then have to decompress it before you proceed with the its installation. Popular compression/decompression programs include:

- *WinZip* — for personal computers
- *Stuffit* — for Apple Macintosh computers.

FTP directory /pub/ at ftp.indigo.ie

```
This is the ftp-server of Indigo.

All transactions with this server are logged.
If you do not like this, you should disconnect now.

Please report problems to: tech@indigo.ie
```

Up to higher level directory

```
06/15/99 09:22        Directory  FreeBSD
05/06/98 12:00        Directory  mac
05/09/97 12:00        Directory  microsoft
03/15/99 06:05        Directory  misc
10/12/98 12:00        Directory  test
02/06/97 12:00        Directory  unix
03/04/98 12:00        Directory  whistle
08/31/98 12:00        Directory  windows
```

◼Internet Relay Chat

Internet Relay Chat (IRC) enables you to communicate with many different people simultaneously, regardless of where they are in the world, by simply typing back and forth. When you type text, it immediately appears on the screen of each person involved in the conversation. Every person in the group chooses a nickname. This lets the others know who is speaking and preserves the identity of that person.

A chat group, also known as a channel, focuses on particular topics for discussion. There are thousands of chat channels on topics as diverse as politics, hostess catering, English Premiership soccer and yoga.

The IRC channels are controlled by special computers on the Internet called IRC servers. To join an IRC, you will need an IRC client program installed on your computer. This program can be downloaded from a site on the Web.

◼Multimedia Conferencing

A range of software products is available that allows the Internet to be used to hold on-line conferences. The people 'attending' the conference can be located anywhere in the world. The services that these products provide include some or all of the following:

- A standard telephone service over the Internet
- Video capabilities
- Shared Whiteboard — this allows the participants to show drawings, plans or sketches to each other. A whiteboard is visible in a window of each participant's screen. An item inserted on the whiteboard, by one participant, is visible to the others.

Popular multimedia conferencing products include:
- CU-SeeMe
- Microsoft Net Meeting
- Netscape Conference

◼On-Line Games

There are many sites on the Internet providing games that you can download and install on your computer. You can also play on-line games with other games enthusiasts anywhere in the world. For example, you can have an on-line game of chess with a person in Los Angeles or Singapore. Games, known as Multi-User Dungeons (MUDs), are very popular; these take place in imaginary kingdoms. Many MUDs are text-based but some do include pictures. To play an on-line game, you will need to download and install a client program. This software will allow you to communicate with the server on the Internet on which a particular game is taking place.

◼Electronic Commerce (E-Commerce)

Electronic commerce (e-commerce) is the conducting of business on the Internet. Many companies and shops have websites where products or services are described and where purchase can be made on-line. A diverse range of products or services is available e.g. airline tickets, books, clothing, computers, flower delivery and food.

A growing number of shopping malls are a feature of the Internet. Each mall has a set of hyperlinks to all the different shopping pages. You can browse through products or services and make a purchase on-line.

The method of ordering a product or service can vary. You may be required to either:

- complete an on-line order form
- simply tick the product or service on a data entry form
- select an 'Add to the shopping basket' button.

There are two methods of paying for your on-line purchases:

- *Credit Card* — this is the most widely used method. You are asked to enter your credit card details using an on-line form before completing the purchase. Most reputable companies that are conducting business on the Internet have security measures in place to prevent unauthorised access to credit card details.
- *Digital Cash* — before you make a purchase on-line, you withdraw money from your bank in digital form using special software. The digital cash is stored on your hard disk. When you wish to complete a purchase, you send the digital money over the Internet to the seller of the product or service.

Security and Confidentiality

Security and confidentiality, on the Internet, are issues that are important for both the individual user and organisations. We will now examine some of the main security and confidentiality matters concerning the Internet and the World Wide Web.

◼Virus Protection

In connecting to the Internet, your computer may become infected by computer viruses in either of two ways:

- An infected file downloaded from the Internet to your computer.
- An infected file sent, as an e-mail attachment, to you.

Some common symptoms that could indicate your computer has been infected are:

- Unusual messages or displays on your monitor.
- Unusual sounds or music played at random times.
- Your system has less available memory than it should.
- A disk or volume name has been changed.

- Programs or files are suddenly missing.
- Unknown programs or files have been created.
- Some of your files become corrupted or suddenly don't work properly.

There are several programs (called virus protection software, anti-virus software, or virus checks) that will check your system for known viruses, scan incoming files, and warn you before any infected files are let in. An important fact about these programs is that they are only as good as their database of known viruses.

Since new and different viruses are being introduced all the time, anti-virus databases need to be updated often. When you buy anti-virus software, monthly or quarterly updates of the software are sent to you for a period of time (usually one year). The fee for these updates is usually included in the initial price. Two of the most popular anti-virus software products available are *McAfee Anti-Virus* and *Norton Anti-Virus*. Anti-virus software is also available as shareware on the World Wide Web. The quality of these shareware products can vary greatly.

If you have a computer that is not currently running virus protection software, the first thing you should do is install one of these programs and have it scan your hard drive. It will identify any files that have been infected by any virus it recognises and offer you the option to repair the file if it can. In most cases infected files can be 'cleaned' by your virus protection software; in some, however, the files may have to be discarded. Once you have determined that all the files in your system are virus-free, this would be a good time to do a complete backup of your system. If your computer gets infected in the future, you will really appreciate having clean copies of your files.

Filtering Software

The World Wide Web is a wonderful source of information. There are, however, sites on the World Wide Web that contain material unsuitable for children and vulnerable groups of people. For example, websites dedicated to gambling, pornography or subversive activities can be accessed quite easily using any of the popular search tools. Programs, which prevent access to objectionable information on the Internet, are available. These programs, known as *filtering software* products, monitor and search for keywords. The software can prevent the user from downloading or sending information containing certain words, address details, credit card details as well as audio, picture or video files. These programs can also prevent users from accessing specific sites by maintaining a list of forbidden URLs, newsgroups and addresses.

Popular filtering software products include:
- Cyber Patrol (www.cyberpatrol.com)
- Net Nanny (www.netnanny.com)
- Smart Parent (www.smartparent.com)
- Surf Watch (www.surfwatch.com)
- Xstop (www.xstop.com)

◪Firewalls

A *firewall* is a combination hardware and software buffer that many companies or organisations have in place between their internal networks and any outside network including the Internet. A firewall allows only specific kinds of messages from the Internet to flow in and out of the internal network. This protects the internal network from intruders or hackers who might try to use the Internet to gain access to those systems.

In general, firewalls are configured to protect against unapproved interactive logins from the 'outside' world. Some firewalls permit only e-mail traffic through them, thereby protecting the network against any attacks other than attacks against the e-mail service. Other firewalls provide less strict protections, and only block services that are known to be problems. Some elaborate firewalls block all traffic from the outside to the inside, but permit users on the inside to communicate freely with the outside.

Encryption

Encryption is a way of coding the information in a file or e-mail message. If a third party intercepts the encrypted file or message as it travels over a network it cannot be read. Only the person or persons who have the appropriate decoding software can decode or unscramble the message.

Some of the encryption methods available are:

- *PGP* — Pretty Good Privacy (PGP) is used to make e-mail messages private.
- *ROT13* — Rotate 13 (ROT13) is used to make newsgroup messages private.
- *SHTTP* — Secure HyperText Protocol (SHTTP) is used for security on the World Wide Web.
- *SSL* — Secure Sockets Layer (SSL) is used for security on the Internet and the World Wide Web.

Digital Signatures

A digital signature is a code that can be attached to an electronically transmitted message that uniquely identifies the sender. Like a written signature, the purpose of a digital signature is to guarantee that the individual sending the message really is who he or she claims to be. Digital signatures are especially important for electronic commerce and are a key component of most authentication schemes. Encryption techniques are used to guarantee the security of digital signatures.

When you use digital signature software, you create a matched pair of keys. One is the private key, which is typically installed on your computer. The *private* key is used only by you and is required during the signing process.

The second key is the public key. The *public* key is available for use by anyone wishing to authenticate documents you sign. The public key will 'read' the digital signature created by the private key and verify the authenticity of documents created with it. It would be similar to the process of accessing a safety deposit box. Your key must work with the bank's key before opening the box.

Cookies

A *cookie* is a message sent by a web *server* to a web *browser*. The browser software usually saves the cookie, as a text file, to the hard disk of the user's computer. The cookie can be sent back to the server whenever the browser makes additional requests. The main purpose of cookies is to identify visitors to a website and possibly prepare customised web pages for them e.g. personalised greetings.

Other reasons for using cookies include:

- Helping with on-line sales/services e.g. *Amazon Books* or *Microsoft*
- Tracking popular links or demographics e.g. *DoubleClick*.

As a cookie is a simple text file, it *cannot* be used to:

- Transmit viruses to your computer
- Access your hard drive
- Ascertain your e-mail address.

Cookies are very small files. Both Netscape and Microsoft, however, have measures in place that limits the number of cookies that will be saved on your hard disk at one time. These measures make it impossible for cookies to fill the hard disk of your computer. Netscape limits your total cookie count to 300. If you exceed this, the browser will discard your least-used cookies to make room for the new ones. Microsoft saves cookies into the *Temporary Internet Files* folder. The default size of this system folder is set to 2 per cent of your hard disk.

A negative aspect of the use of cookies is that they can be used in conjunction with web servers, as a 'tracking device', to build a profile of an individual's surfing and buying habits. Many people consider this as an invasion of privacy.

Chapter 10
Electronic Mail and Web Publishing

▦ Electronic Mail

Electronic Mail, or e-mail, is the most widely used feature of the Internet. E-mail is similar to conventional mail except that the letters are delivered over the Internet. A number of e-mail messages can by typed off-line. When you are ready to send your e-mail, a telephone connection to your ISP can be established and all of the messages can be sent together.

E-mail has a number of advantages over standard mail:
- Speed — a message can travel around the world in seconds.
- Cost — there is no charge for sending or receiving e-mail other than the cost of the phone call to connect you to your ISP's server.
- Content — full working computer files can be attached to the e-mail message e.g. spreadsheets and databases.
- Multiple copies — any number of copies of the same message can be sent to different destinations for less than the cost of a local telephone call.

E-mail also has a number of disadvantages when compared with standard mail:
- Security — e-mail messages can be intercepted. However, with the increasing use of encryption, it is likely that this problem will disappear in the future.
- Reading files — when you receive a file as an e-mail attachment, it is necessary to have the appropriate software to access it e.g. if you receive a *Microsoft Excel* spreadsheet as an attachment, it is necessary to have *Microsoft Excel* installed on your computer to work with the spreadsheet.
- E-mail documents are not legally binding (as of going to print).

◪ How does E-mail work?

You send your message using an e-mail program; it travels via your ISP over the Internet to a destination server computer. It is stored on that computer in a special folder called a *mailbox*. Most people have a mailbox provided to them by their ISP. If you send an e-mail message to somebody, it will go to his or her mailbox, which is located on his or her ISP's mail server computer. It will stay there until they access the mailbox to collect their messages. In order to send the e-mail message, however, you must have the *e-mail address* of the would-be recipient.

◼What is an E-mail Address?

An e-mail address defines the location of an individual's mailbox on the Internet. Examples of typical e-mail addresses would be:

Jdoe@iol.ie

or

glineker@bbc.co.uk

The address consists of two parts separated by the '@' symbol. The part before the '@' symbol is called *the user name*, this can be a real name or an alias. The part after the '@' symbol is called the *domain name* and gives the location of that person's account. In the first example the user name is 'jdoe' while the domain name tells us that John Doe's mailbox is located on a server belonging to the Ireland-Online company (iol) which is based in Ireland (.ie).

An e-mail address cannot contain spaces. The last few characters in an individual's e-mail address usually indicate the type of organisation and/or country the person belongs to. For example:

ORGANISATION	COUNTRY
.com — commercial	.ie — Ireland
.gov — American government	.uk — United Kingdom
.org — non-profit organisation	.au — Australia
.net — network	.ca — Canada
.mil — American military	.it — Italy

Characteristics of an E-mail Program

An e-mail program lets you send, receive and manage your e-mail messages. Currently, the most popular e-mail programs are *Outlook Express, Netscape Communicator* and *Eudora Mail*. All e-mail programs have similar characteristics:

- *Compose* — you can compose a message, this is similar to writing a letter using a word processor.
- *Reply* — you can reply to a message that you have received.
- *Forward* — you can send a copy of a message you have received to another person with an e-mail address.
- *Store* — you can store important messages so you can review them later. E-mail programs let you create folders to organise all of your stored messages.
- *Delete* — you can delete messages you no longer need.
- *Print* — you can produce a hard copy of a message.
- *Attachments* — the sender of an e-mail message can attach files created by other programs. You can open an attached file provided that you have the program, in which the file was created, installed on your computer.

Component Parts of an E-mail Message

The e-mail message below was created using *Outlook Express*. However, the component parts of any e-mail message are very similar regardless of the e-mail program used to create it.

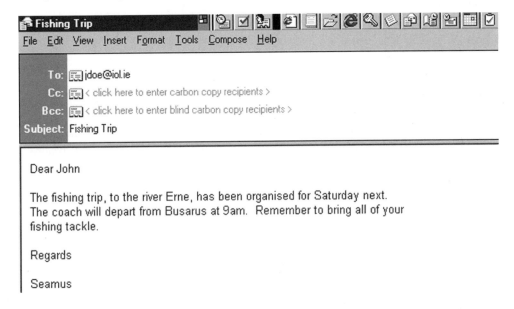

- *To*: This line holds the e-mail address of the person who will receive the message. In this case, it is jdoe@iol.ie.
- *Cc*: This stands for carbon copy. If you wish to send the e-mail to more than one person, you can enter a number of other e-mail addresses on this line (separated by commas or semi-colons). In our example, this line is blank meaning that we are only sending the message to John Doe.
- *Bcc*: This stands for blind carbon copy. This is similar to carbon copy except that each recipient of the message does not know that others have received the message. Again, in our example, this line is left blank.
- *Subject*: This identifies the content of the message. It is important to enter a short title or reference for your message, indicating what it is about. Appropriate subject titles makes it easier for the recipient to organise incoming mail. In our example, we have entered 'Fishing Trip' in our subject line.
- *Body of the Message*: This area holds the text of the message. In our case, it is notification of a forthcoming fishing trip to the river Erne. Most e-mail programs have an in-built spellchecker facility. We recommend that you use it before mailing the message.

◤Managing Mailboxes

The e-mail program uses a number of mailboxes or folders to help you manage the mail on your computer. These mailboxes must not be confused with the mailbox that the ISP provides for you on their server.

The five mailboxes common to most e-mail programs are:

- *Inbox*: When you download a new e-mail message from your mailbox on the server, it is stored in the inbox on your computer.
- *Outbox*: A message that you have composed, but not yet sent, is stored in an outbox.
- *Sent Items Box*: Copies of e-mail messages that have been mailed are automatically placed in the sent items box.
- *Drafts Box*: Copies of unfinished e-mail messages are usually held in the drafts box.
- *Deleted Items Box*: E-mail messages that you have deleted from the other boxes are moved to the delete box. You can retrieve messages from the delete box and restore them to the inbox or outbox. However, once you empty the delete box, any e-mail messages that were previously held in it cannot be retrieved.

The e-mail program allows you to create your own mailboxes or folders. This is useful in that you can move e-mail messages from your inbox or sent items box to appropriately named folders e.g. business, personal, family.

◤Emoticons and Acronyms

It is often hard to convey emotions in written communication. The task of conveying emotion is even more difficult if we are corresponding with people whom we have never met, who have different cultural values to our own, or whose native language may not be English.

Fortunately, a useful set of symbols has evolved to help us in conveying emotions in our e-mail messages. This set of symbols is continually growing. These symbols are called emoticons ('emotional icons') or 'smilies'. Some common examples and their meanings are shown below:

EMOTION	MEANING
Smile	:-)
Frown	:-(
Laugh	:-D
Cry	:'-(
Surprise	:-O
Wink	;-)

Try looking at the symbols in the table with your head tilted to the left.

Acronyms are frequently used in e-mail messages to save time typing and to convey emotion. Again the number of e-mail acronyms is growing all the time.

Some of the more commonly used acronyms are shown below:

ACRONYM	MEANING
BTW	By the way
FAQ	Frequently asked question
FOAF	Friend of a friend
IMHO	In my humble opinion
FYI	For your information
L8R	Later
LOL	Laughing out loud
ROTFL	Rolling on the floor laughing
SO	Significant other
WRT	With respect to

You may be sending an e-mail message to your cousin in Chicago informing her of your forthcoming visit there. You could include the following sentence, which includes an acronym and an emoticon, in the e-mail message:
'BTW, we have just booked our flight tickets and we are really looking forward to the holiday in Chicago :-)'

◪Good E-mail Etiquette
E-mail has evolved a much less formal style than traditional business writing. We advise, however, that you take a little care in composing e-mail messages. It is always a good idea to read through the message again before clicking the 'send' button. The message may contain spelling mistakes and poorly constructed sentences. This will convey an unfavourable impression of you to the recipient of the e-mail.

We recommend that you follow the guidelines set out below when using e-mail:
• E-mail messages should be relatively short and unambiguous.
• Check for incorrect spellings and poor grammar.
• Take care to enter the correct e-mail address of the would-be recipient.
• Never include anything in the e-mail message that you may later regret.
• Always enter a title for the message on the subject line.
• A message should not be written entirely in capital letters, this is known as *shouting*.
• Do not overuse acronyms and emoticons.
• Do not engage in *flaming*. A flame is an angry or insulting message directed at one person.
• Reply to e-mail promptly.
• Do not engage in *spamming*. This is the unsolicited mass distribution of e-mail messages.

◪Web Based E-mail Accounts
Some companies, with websites on the World Wide Web, offer a free web-based e-mail service. The most widely used service of this type is *Hotmail*. To register for a free web-based

e-mail account, you simply call up Hotmail's website and fill the on-line form. Hotmail's site can be found at www.hotmail.com. To access or send mail, all a person has to do is:

• Connect to the Internet through any server
• Call up Hotmail's website
• Enter his/her user name and password
• Download any new messages from their mailbox at Hotmail
• Compose and send new messages if he/she wishes.

This facility is of tremendous benefit to people who are travelling. No matter where they are, once they can connect to the Internet they can download their e-mail messages from their mailbox at Hotmail.

Mailing Lists

A *mailing list* is a discussion group that uses e-mail to communicate. There are thousands of mailing lists on the Internet. They cover a very wide range of interests from Andrew Lloyd Webber to zoo animals. When you send a message to a mailing list, a copy of the message is sent to the mailbox of each person on the list. You must subscribe to the mailing list to join the discussion group. You can unsubscribe from a mailing list at any time.

Each mailing list has two e-mail addresses. One address receives messages for the entire group while the other address is for administration. When you subscribe initially to a mailing list, make sure that you send your request to the administration address. If you are on one or more mailing lists, make sure that you check your e-mail frequently as the e-mail messages can mount up in a very short time.

Some mailing lists are *moderated*. This means that one member of the group reads each message. If the message is suitable, it is sent to the other members on the list. A moderated mailing list keeps discussion on-topic by screening out irrelevant messages. In an unmoderated mailing list, all messages are sent to everyone in the group. If you receive many messages from a mailing list, check if the list is available as a *digest*. A digest is a set of messages that have been grouped together and sent as one message.

Mailing lists can be *manually maintained* or *automated*. An administrator manages a manually maintained mailing list while a computer program manages an automated mailing list. Either one is charged with the duty of keeping track of the members.

A posting of available mailing lists is available at: http://www.neosoft.com/internet/paml/

Usenet Newsgroups

Let us digress for a moment to examine how a public notice board, say in a shopping centre, works. Anybody can pin notices to the notice board. The notices can be read by anyone who looks at the board. A person might place a notice advertising a computer for sale. An interested party could pin a reply notice with an offer or a request that the advertiser make contact with him or her. A shopping centre employee may take charge of organising the notice board. The different notices could be arranged under different category headings:

- Items for sale
- Accommodation offered
- Childminders
- Work available
- Miscellaneous

Usenet works in a similar way. It allows people with common interests to communicate with one another. Usenet consists of thousands of newsgroups (like our categories on the notice board). A newsgroup is an electronic discussion group consisting of collections of related postings (also called articles) on a particular topic. Making a posting to a newsgroup is similar to placing a notice on the notice board.

There are newsgroups on a diverse range of topics. For example, there are newsgroups on African music, artificial intelligence, comics, equestrian sports, Japanese culture, pharmacy and wines. The name of a newsgroup describes the type of information it discusses. A name consists of two or more words separated by periods:

rec.sport.soccer

The first word describes the main topic area (rec for recreation). Each of the following words narrows the topic area.

Some of the main newsgroup topic areas are:

NAME	TOPIC AREA
Alt	Alternative newsgroups covering a variety of topics
Biz	Business-oriented newsgroups
Comp	Computer-related newsgroups
Misc	Miscellaneous newsgroups
News	Newsgroups covering Usenet itself
Rec	Recreational and hobby newsgroups
Sci	Science-oriented newsgroups
Soc	Newsgroups for discussion of social issues
Talk	Newsgroups for discussing often controversial issues

You *subscribe* to newsgroups that you want to read on a regular basis. This is similar to subscribing to a magazine but in this case there is no charge. You can reply to an article or supply additional information. A program called a *newsreader* allows you to read and send articles to newsgroups. Both *Internet Explorer* and *Netscape Navigator* have built-in newsreader programs.

Newsgroup articles are stored on *news server* computers around the world. An ISP will operate at least one news server computer. It is very unlikely that the ISP will carry all of the newsgroups. For each newsgroup that it supports, the ISP will hold all the postings to that newsgroup for a period of time. The length of time will vary from newsgroup to newsgroup and range from as little as one day to several months. When a message has been on a server for longer than the specified time, the server deletes it. When you post an article to a newsgroup on a certain server, it is automatically passed on to all the other news servers around the world that carry the same newsgroup.

One way to start a subscription to a newsgroup is to review a complete list of newsgroups available to you from your own ISP.

▦ Web Publishing

Website Evaluation

In evaluating any website, we advise that you examine a number of different aspects.

1. Appearance and Layout

- *Consistency*: The web pages that go to make up the website should look as if they belong together. They should have common:
  - ■ Text colours and fonts
  - ■ Backgrounds
  - ■ Illustrations (if applicable).

  The website should have a consistent and easy-to-use navigation system i.e. anyone should be able to move around the website with ease using the hyperlinks. A navigation bar is often used for this purpose. This is a bar of icons or buttons with hyperlinks to other pages on the website.
- *Readability*: As it is more difficult to read on-screen as opposed to printed text, short paragraphs are better for web pages (no longer than 5 sentences).
- *Placement:* Text and graphic elements must not appear as if they were thrown onto the page. They should have a common alignment; it is not a good idea to centre, left-align and right-align different elements on the same page. A common alignment does not mean that all of the elements must be placed along the same invisible vertical line in the margin of the page. Indenting of elements, using the same alignment, may suit a particular web page.
- *Closeness*: Headings, subheadings, body text or graphic elements that belong to each other should be placed close together. A subheading separated by blank lines from the text to which it belongs, does not look right.
- *Contrast*: Most students know the importance of colour contrast on websites. A bright colour on a dark background (or vice versa) is much easier to read. Contrasting elements also show priorities. Text that is in a different colour, point size or font can indicate that it is a heading or subheading.

- *Page Size*: The entire website home page should fit in the browser window. Wherever possible, horizontal scrolling should be eliminated on every web page in the site.
- *Site Map*: On larger websites, one web page should include a site map or index. A site map shows how the various pages, in the site, are linked.

2. Appropriate Use of Graphics

- *Overuse of Graphics*: Some websites can have too many images or animations, which can detract greatly from the message of the website.
- *Large Images*: Some websites contain graphics that do not fit on the screen. They have not been scaled to suit the particular pages.
- *File Size*: A large graphics file can take a considerable length of time to download. Thumbnails, smaller versions of the same file, are recommended. If the user wishes to see a larger version of the image, he or she may click on the thumbnail that should have a hyperlink to a file containing a larger version of the image.
- *Alt Labels*: Graphic images, without alt labels, are not advisable. An alt label is a text alternative for an image. If an individual has disabled the graphics mode in his or her browser, he or she will be at a loss if there is no alt label displayed instead of the image.

3. Technical Considerations

- *Working Links*: It is of the utmost importance that all of the hyperlinks in the website work properly. Sometimes when you click on a hyperlink, you can get the message: 'URL not known'. This is evidence of a 'broken' link or a missing web page.
- *Browser Compatibility*: A website should be tested using at least two different browsers. For example, a site may appear fine when viewed using Internet Explorer but may not look right in Netscape Navigator or vice versa. Versions of web browsers should also be given consideration; some websites may not appear, as they should when viewed using an older version of a browser.
- *Necessity of Plug-ins*: Some websites require the use of at least one plug-in program in order to be viewed successfully. For example, in order to view a video clip, you will probably need to install a plug-in called *QuickTime*.
- *Meta Tags*: These are used to document web pages and/or provide information that can be used by search engines to classify or index the page. There are several Meta tags, but the most important for search engine indexing are the description and keywords tags. The description tag summarises the contents of a web page. The keywords tag provides a selection of words that the search engine can associate with the web page.
- *Frames*: The browser window can be divided into a number of panes known as frames. Different web pages in the site can appear in each of the frames. Too many frames in the browser window make it look cluttered and can convey an unfavourable impression.
- *Image Map*: Image maps are used for navigation purposes on a website. An image map is a graphic with a number of hyperlinks on it. For example, a photograph of a group of people could have a hyperlink from each person's face to a web page for that individual.

- *Interactivity*: Some sites are interactive. The user can enters details onto a web page and these are then processed. For example, you can order a book from the Amazon Bookstore's website by simply completing an on-line form; the order will then be processed and the book dispatched to you. The interactivity, of a website, normally depends on programs written in programming languages such as *Java, JavaScript* or *Perl*.

4. Linguistic Considerations

- *Spellings and Grammar:* Poor grammar and spelling can convey an unfavourable impression of the person who created the website. Great care should be taken to eliminate grammatical and spelling errors.
- *Vocabulary Range*: The range of words used, in the website, should be appropriate to the target audience. A website for children should contain words appropriate to their level of development.
- *Humour/Sarcasm*: A person from a different cultural or ethical background may access a website and not understand attempts at humour or sarcasm.
- *Colloquialisms or Slang*: These have no place on a website.

Creating a Web Page

There are two main ways of creating a web page.

1. Use a web editor program. This is also known as a web authoring program.
2. Enter the page details and relevant HTML tags using a text editor program. HyperText Mark up Language (HTML) instructs the browser how to display a page.

Web Editor Program

A web editor program has many features that are similar to those of a word processor. For example, the user is allowed to enter text, apply text formatting and insert graphics. The web editor facilitates the establishment of hyperlinks between pages. When you create a web page using a web editor program, the HTML tags are applied automatically. Popular web editor programs include *Microsoft FrontPage, Adobe Go-Live, Netscape Composer* and *Macromedia Dreamweaver*.

Text Editor and HyperText Mark-up Language (HTML)

Any program that allows the user to enter and save text as a text-only document can be used as a text editor e.g. *Microsoft Word, WordPad* or *NotePad*. To specify that the document is a web page, the file extension '.htm' must be added to the file name.

Each HTML tag is surrounded by angle brackets. For example: <B>Irish Tourism</B> gives the instruction — 'Make the text Irish Tourism appear in bold type' — to the Web browser. It is a good idea to capitalise the HTML tags so they stand out from the document text.

Many HTML tags work in pairs — *opening* and *closing* tags — that affect the text between them. The following table shows twenty frequently used HTML tags:

OPENING TAG	CLOSING TAG	PURPOSE
<A HREF>	</A>	Specifying the URL of the page where the link goes
<B>	</B>	Displaying text in bold face
<BODY>	</BODY>	Enclosing the main section of a web page
<BGSOUND>		Inserting background sound for a web page
 		Creating a line break
<CENTER>	</CENTER>	Centring text, images or other elements
<FONT>	</FONT>	Changing the font face, size and colour of text
<HEAD>	</HEAD>	Creating the head section of a web page
<Hn>		Creating headings of different sizes
<HR>		Inserting a horizontal rule
<HTML>	</HTML>	Identifying a text document as a web page
<I>	</I>	Displaying text in italics
<IMG>		Inserting images on a web page
<LI>		Creating a list item
<OL>	</OL>	Creating an ordered list
<P>		Creating a new paragraph
<PRE>	</PRE>	Displaying text exactly as it appears in the editor
<TITLE>	</TITLE>	Creating a caption in the title bar area
<U>	</U>	Underlining text
<UL>	</UL>	Creating an unordered list

◼ Sample Travel Agent Website

We will now examine how to construct a very basic website, consisting of only two web pages, using a text editor and HTML. The pages below appear as they would in the browser window:

Page 1

Going Places

Going Places, a travel agency founded by Mary O'Connor in 1996, is going from strength to strength. It has offices in Dublin, Cork and Galway. The company offers a variety of holiday types:

- European City Breaks
- Sun Holidays
- Skiing Packages
- Long haul tours
- Customised holidays

The company's policy is to provide quality low-cost holiday packages to its customers. On examining the phenomenal growth in its turnover over the years, it would appear that *Going Places* is living up to its name.

Page 2

European City Breaks

Going Places offers wonderful short holiday packages to a host of European destinations:

- London
- Paris
- Brussels
- Munich
- Florence

The 'two-night special' is popular with customers. This holiday break includes flights, two nights Bed & Breakfast with dinner on one evening in one of the cities listed above. The package also includes insurance, tax and transfer costs.

There is a hypertext link from European City Breaks on page 1 which, when clicked, calls up page 2.

The following shows the two pages, complete with text and the appropriate HTML tags, as each would appear in the text editor window.

Page 1

```
<HTML>
<HEAD>
<TITLE>Going Places</TITLE>
</HEAD>
<BODY BGCOLOR = WHITE TEXT = BLACK>
<H1>Going Places</H1>
<P>
<I>Going Places</I>, a travel agency founded by Mary O'Connor in 1996, is going from
strength to strength. It has offices in Dublin, Cork and Galway. The company offers a
variety of holiday types:
<UL>
<LI><A HREF = "holiday2.htm">European City Breaks</A>
<LI>Sun Holidays
<LI>Skiing Packages
<LI>Long haul tours
<LI>Customised holidays
</UL>
<P>The company's policy is to provide quality low-cost holiday packages to its customers.
On examining the phenomenal growth in its turnover over the years, it would appear
that <I>Going Places</I> is living up to its name.
</BODY>
</HTML>
```

This file is saved as *holiday1.htm*.

```
<HTML>
<HEAD>
<TITLE>Going Places</TITLE>
</HEAD>
<BODY BGCOLOR = White TEXT = Black>
<H1>European City Breaks</H1>
<I>Going Places</I> offers wonderful short holiday packages to a host of European
destinations:
<OL>
<LI>London
<LI>Paris
<LI>Brussels
<LI>Munich
<LI>Florence
</OL>
The 'two-night special' is popular with customers. This holiday break includes flights, two
nights Bed & Breakfast with dinner on one evening in one of the cities listed above. The
package also includes insurance, tax and transfer costs.
</BODY>
</HTML>
```

This file is saved as *holiday2.htm.*

How the HTML tags work

1. Each web page starts and finishes with the opening and closing 'HTML' tags — <HTML> and </HTML>. These tags tell the browser that whatever appears between them should be treated as a web page.
2. The <HEAD> and </HEAD> tags create a head section for the page.
3. The text between the <TITLE> and </TITLE> tags gives a brief title or description of the page. This text is displayed in the title bar of the browser program.
4. The contents of the web page appear between the <BODY> and </BODY> tags. This tag is used, in our website, with attributes; we have specified in the <BODY> tag the background and text colour attributes for each page. Notice the American spellings.
5. The header tags, <H1> and </H1>, specify that enclosed text will appear as a major heading on a text page.
6. The <P> tag indicates the start of a new paragraph.

7. The italics tags, <I> and </I>, specify that enclosed text will be shown in italics.
8. The unordered list tags, <UL> and </UL>, specify that enclosed text will be shown in a bulleted list.
9. The ordered list tags, <OL> and </OL>, specify that enclosed text will be shown in a numbered list.
10. The <LI> tag specifies items that should be bulleted or numbered.
11. The line, <A HREF = "holiday2.htm">European City Breaks</A>, specifies a hypertext link from 'European City Breaks' to the file saved as 'holiday2.htm'.

◼Inserting a Graphic

A graphic image may be placed on a Web page using the IMG tag. For example, let us replace the line: *<H1>Going Places</H1>* with the line *<IMG SRC = "logo.gif">* in the 'holiday1.htm' file. The newly updated 'holiday1.htm' appears in the browser window as follows:

Going Places, a travel agency founded by Mary O'Connor in 1996 is going from strength to strength. It has offices in Dublin, Cork and Galway. The company offers a variety of holiday types:
• <u>European City Breaks</u>
• Sun Holidays
• Skiing Packages
• Long haul tours
• Customised Holidays
The company's policy is to provide quality low-cost holiday packages to its customers. On examining the phenomenal growth in its turnover over the years, it would appear that *Going Places* is living up to its name.

The IMG tag has an SRC (source) attribute that inserts the file containing the logo graphic, *logo.gif*, onto the Web page. IMG has another attribute that can be used to align the graphic on the web page. For example, the instruction *<IMG SRC = "logo.gif" ALIGN = RIGHT>* would insert the logo onto the web page but align it along the right margin of the browser window.

We advise that you save all files, making up a website, in the same folder or on the same 3.5" disk.

Changing colours

Our web pages have black text on a white background. If we replace the tag *<BODY BGCOLOR = White TEXT = Black>* with *<BODY BGCOLOR = Green TEXT = Yellow>*, we will get yellow text on a green background. We can use choose combinations from the following 16 predefined colours:

THE SIXTEEN PREDEFINED COLOURS			
Silver	Maroon	Navy	Olive
Grey	Red	Blue	Yellow
White	Green	Purple	Teal
Black	Lime	Magenta	Cyan

You can choose from a greater range of colours by using the hexadecimal code for the colour. A discussion on hexadecimal colour codes is beyond the scope of this book. However, we can use the codes to give our web pages a greater burst of colour. For example if we substitute *<BODY BGCOLOR = white TEXT = black>* with *<BODY BGCOLOR = "#C6EFF7" TEXT = "#AD0000">*, we get bright blue text on a burgundy background. When using a hexadecimal colour code, you should always place the # symbol before the code and enclose it in quotation marks. A selection of colours and their hexadecimal equivalents can be found on the next page.

Using Backgrounds

A graphic can be used as a background instead of a specific colour. The *background* attribute is used instead of *bgcolor* for the body tag. Let us assume that we have a photograph of a partially clouded sky stored in a file called 'sky.gif'. We could get black text on a sky background by using the following:
<BODY BACKGROUND = "sky.gif" TEXT = black>

File Formats

The most common file formats on the World Wide Web are shown below:

FILE TYPE	FILE EXTENSION	MEANING
Web Page	HTM	HyperText Mark-up Language
Graphics	GIF	Graphics Interchange Format
Graphics	JPG	Joint Photographics Expert Group
Sound	AU	Audio Player
Sound	RA	Real Audio
Sound	WAV	Wave
Sound	MID	Midi
Animation and Video	AVI	Audio Video Interleaved
Animation and Video	MPG	Motion Picture Experts Group
Animation and Video	MOV	QuickTime

Hexadecimal Colour Codes

Alice Blue F0F8FF	Antique White FAEBD7	Aqua 00FFFF
Aqua Marine 7FFFD4	Azure F0FFFF	Beige F5F5DC
Bisque FFE4C4	Blanched Almond FFEBCD	Blue 0000EE
Blue Secondary 0000FF	Blue Violet 8A2BE2	Brown A52A2A
Burly Wood DEB887	Cadet Blue 5F9EA0	Chartreuse 7FFF00
Chocolate D2691E	Coral FF7F50	Cornflower Blue 6495ED
Corn Silk FFF8DC	Crimson DC143C	Cyan 00FFFF
Dark Blue 00008B	Dark Cyan 008B8B	Dark Golden Rod B8860B
Dark Grey A9A9A9	Dark Green 006400	Dark Khaki BDB76B
Dark Magenta 8B008B	Dark Olive Green 556B2F	Dark Orange FF8C00
Dark Orchid 9932CC	Dark Red 8B0000	Dark Salmon E9967A
Dark Sea Green 8FBC8F	Dark Slate Blue 483D8B	Dark Slate Grey 2F4F4F
Dark Turquoise 00CED1	Dark Violet 9400D3	Deep Pink FF1493
Deep Sky Blue 00BFFF	Dim Grey 696969	Dodger Blue 1E90FF
Fire Brick B22222	Floral White FFFAF0	Forest Green 228B22
Fuchsia FF00FF	Gainsboro DCDCDC	Ghost White F8F8FF
Gold FFD700	Golden Rod DAA520	Grey 808080
Green 008000	Green Yellow ADFF2F	Honey Dew F0FFF0
Hot Pink FF69B4	Indian Red CD5C5C	Indigo 4B0082
Ivory FFFFF0	Khaki F0E68C	Lavender E6E6FA
Lavender Blush FFF0F5	Lawn Green 7CFC00	Lemon Chiffon FFFACD
Light Blue ADD8E6	Light Coral F08080	Light Cyan E0FFFF
Light Golden Yellow FAFAD2	Light Green 90EE90	Light Grey D3D3D3
Light Pink FFB6C1	Light Salmon FFA07A	Light Sea Green 20B2AA
Light Sky Blue 87CEFA	Light Slate Grey 778899	Light Steel Blue B0C4DE
Light Yellow FFFFE0	Lime 00FF00	Lime Green 32CD32
Linen FAF0E6	Magenta FF00FF	Maroon 800000
Medium Aquamarine 66CDAA	Medium Blue 0000CD	Medium Orchid BA55D3
Medium Purple 9370D8	Medium Sea Green 3CB371	Medium Slate Blue 7B68EE
Medium Spring Green 00FA9A	Medium Turquoise 48D1CC	Medium Violet Red C71585
Midnight Blue 191970	Mint Cream F5FFFA	Misty Rose FFE4E1
Moccasin FFE4B5	Navajo White FFDEAD	Navy 000080
Old Lace FDF5E6	Olive 808000	Olive Drab 688E23
Orange FFA500	Orange Red FF4500	Orchid DA70D6
Pale Golden Rod EEE8AA	Pale Green 98FB98	Pale Turquoise AFEEEE
Pale Violet Red D87093	Papaya Whip FFEFD5	Peach Puff FFDAB9
Peru CD853F	Pink FFC0CB	Plum DDA0DD
Powder Blue B0E0E6	Purple 800080	Red FF0000
Rosy Brown BC8F8F	Royal Blue 4169E1	Saddle Brown 8B4513
Salmon FA8072	Sandy Brown F4A460	Sea Green 2E8B57
Seashell FFF5EE	Sienna A0522D	Silver C0C0C0
Sky Blue 87CEEB	Slate Blue 6A5ACD	Slate Grey 708090
Snow FFFAFA	Spring Green 00FF7F	Steel Blue 4682B4
Tan D2B48C	Teal 008080	Thistle D8BFD8
Tomato FF6347	Turquoise 40E0D0	Violet EE82EE
Wheat F5DEB3	White FFFFFF	White Smoke F5F5F5
Yellow FFFF00	Yellow Green 9ACD32	

Note: use the '#' symbol before the colour code.

Written Questions

1. Distinguish between the terms *Internet* and *World Wide Web*.
2. Who owns and pays for the Internet?
3. How would you evaluate an *Internet Service Provider*?
4. List the basic hardware and software necessary in order to use the Internet.
5. Examine briefly the factors that affect the speed of access to the Internet.
6. Distinguish between *IP addresses* and *domain names*.
7. What are *plug-ins* and give examples of how they are used.
8. Examine briefly the different software tools available for searching the Web.
9. How does *multimedia conferencing* work?
10. Outline the chief methods of paying for goods or services over the Internet.
11. Describe how viruses may spread from the Internet to your computer. How can this be prevented?
12. What is *filtering software* and how does it work?
13. Define the term *firewall*. What is its purpose?
14. In the context of the Internet, what are *cookies*? Outline their positive and negative aspects.
15. What are the advantages of *e-mail* over standard or *snail* mail?
16. Describe the components of an *e-mail address*.
17. Outline the chief characteristics of an e-mail program.
18. Outline the various parts of an e-mail message.
19. List some elements of what you consider as good e-mail etiquette.
20. Describe how a web-based e-mail account works.
21. Distinguish between *mailing lists* and *newsgroups*.
22. What elements do you look out for when evaluating a website?
23. What are the two main ways of creating a web page?
24. Choose any five HTML tags and explain the purpose of each one.
25. List the most common graphic, sound and video file formats on the Web.

▦ Glossary of Internet Terms

Advance Research Projects Network (ARPANET): an early US network that forms the basis of the Internet.

bandwidth: the rate of data transmission measured in bits per second.

browser: a program to help users view and search for information on the WWW.

cookie: a piece of information sent by a web server to a web browser that the browser software is expected to save and to send back to the server whenever the browser makes additional requests from the server.

digital signature: a code that can be attached to an electronically transmitted message that uniquely identifies the sender.

domain name: a unique word that acts like a nickname for the IP address of a server computer.

Domain Name System (DNS): regulates the naming of computers on the Internet.

download: the act of copying a file from a server computer on the Internet to your own computer.

electronic commerce (e-commerce): the buying and selling of products and services by businesses and consumers over the Internet.

electronic mail (e-mail): messages sent from one computer to another on a network.

e-mail address: defines the location of an individual's mailbox on the Internet.

emoticon: symbol composed of punctuation marks designed to express some form of emotion.

encryption: a way of coding information in a file or e-mail message so only the intended recipient can read it.

File Transfer Protocol (FTP): a set of rules for transferring files from one computer to another via the Internet.

filtering software: programs that prevent access to objectionable information on the World Wide Web.

firewall: a combination hardware and software buffer that many companies or organisations have in place, between their internal networks and any outside network including the Internet, to prevent unauthorised access.

flame: an angry or insulting e-mail message.

hyperlink: a link from one web page to another or within the same web page. Clicking on the link with a mouse activates it.

hypertext: a word or group of words that are hyperlinks.

HyperText Mark-up Language (HTML): the coding language used to create web pages.

Integrated Services Digital Network (ISDN): internationally developed telecommunications system for sending signals in digital format.

Internet: global computer network connecting millions of computers.

Internet Protocol (IP) Address: a unique code number assigned to each server computer on the Internet.

Internet Relay Chat (IRC): a service that allows users connected to the Internet to chat with each other over many channels.

Internet Service Provider (ISP): a company that provides access to the Internet usually for a fee.

intranet: the use of technologies and software developed for the Internet on an organisation's internal network.

mailbox: special folder on a computer for holding e-mail messages.

mailing list: a discussion group that uses e-mail to communicate.

netiquette: behaviour guidelines evolved by users of the Internet.

newsgroup: a discussion group on the Internet.

off-line: not connected to the Internet.

on-line: connected to the Internet.

plug-in: a program that works with your web browser to give it an extra capability.

portal: large website with hyperlinks to a wide range of topics and issues.

router: special computer that regulates traffic on the Internet.

search engine: remotely accessible program to help users find information on the Internet.

search tool: a computer program that helps us to find information on the Web.

site map: shows how the various pages, in a website, are linked.

spamming: the unsolicited mass distribution of e-mail messages or postings to multiple Internet newsgroups.

spider: a program that combs the Internet for new documents such as web pages and FTP files. All the references found are supplied to a database that can be used by a search engine.

streaming: sending data, for example radio broadcasts or video frames, in a steady flow over the Internet

Uniform Resource Locator (URL): the unique address of each web page on the World Wide Web.

USENET: a global collection of newsgroups with comments passed among hundreds of thousands of computers.

website: a collection of related web pages.

World Wide Web (WWW or Web): consists of millions of pages of information stored on thousands of server computers all over the world.

Chapter 11
Practical Internet
Assignments

Practical Assignments

◥E-Mail

The class tutor is advised to create a web-based e-mail account. The students can then direct e-mail messages, given in the following assignments, to the address of this account.

Assignment 1

1. Find a free web-based e-mail service on the Web.
2. Use this service to create your own web-based e-mail account.

Assignment 2

Use your new e-mail account to send the following e-mail message to the e-mail address provided to you by your tutor:

> Subject: Fishing Trip
>
> Dear Conor,
> The fishing trip to the river Boyne will take place on Saturday next. The coach to Trim will leave from the Ambassador cinema at 10a.m. Don't forget your fishing tackle :-)
>
> Regards,
>
> Sarah

Assignment 3

1. Enter the following text in a new word-processing document:

Agenda
1. Chairperson's address
2. Minutes of the last meeting
3. Secretary's Report
4. Treasurer's Report
5. Competitions for the forthcoming year
6. Election of club officials
7. Any other business

2. Save the file as *Agenda* to your disk.
3. Use the e-mail program to compose the following e-mail message:

Subject: Annual General Meeting

The Annual General Meeting of Carrigallen GAA club will take place in the Community Centre on Sunday next at 3 p.m. Please find the agenda for the meeting attached to this e-mail.

Yours faithfully,

Sean Cooke
Club Secretary

4. Attach the *Agenda* file to the e-mail message.
5. Send the e-mail message and attachment to the e-mail address provided for you by your tutor.

Assignment 4

1. Use your e-mail program to create a new mailbox or folder called *Hobbies*. Copies of the two messages, composed and sent in the previous two tasks, are now stored in the *Outbox* mailbox.
2. Move both messages from the *Outbox* mailbox to your new *Hobbies* mailbox.

Assignment 5

<u>Tutor Instruction</u>

The **tutor** is advised to e-mail the following message to the web-based e-mail accounts of all students in the class:

Subject: Printing

Dear Class Member,
Remember to check for misspellings before printing your document. It is also a good idea to use the print preview option if this is available. This latter option allows you to see the layout of your page before you decide to print.

Orla O'Brien
Class Tutor

<u>Student Instruction</u>

Check for any new mail. The message above should be downloaded to your *Inbox* folder.

▦ Searching the World Wide Web

Using a search engine of your choice to complete the following assignments:

Assignment 6

a) Find a recipe for apple pie.

b) Save the page as *pie* to your disk.

Assignment 7

a) Find a web page that contains the poem *The Road Not Taken* by Robert Frost.

b) Save the web page as *road* to your disk.

Assignment 8

a) Find a web page containing the lyrics of the song *The Sound of Silence* by Simon and Garfunkel.

b) Copy the lyrics of the song to a word-processing document.

c) Save the document as *silence* to your disk.

Assignment 9

I wish to buy a book, on the software product *Adobe Photoshop*, from an on-line bookstore. Find three different books, on *Adobe Photoshop*, together with their respective prices. You must:

a) Enter the details found into a word processing document.

b) Include the addresses (URLs) of the pages where you found the relevant information.

c) Save the file as *adobe* to your disk.

Assignment 10

Assume that you are a qualified Web Master or Web Designer. Find suitable positions in this field that are currently available in Ireland.

a) Copy the specifications of three positions found to a word-processing document.

b) Save this document as *Webjobs* to your disk.

Assignment 11

Assume that you wish to buy a house in either counties Cavan or Leitrim. You do not wish to spend more than £150,000.

a) Find five houses on the market that meet these criteria.

b) Use your browser software to save the details on each house as *house1* to *house5* respectively.

Assignment 12

A close family relative is travelling to the West Coast of America and has asked you to use the WWW to find:

a) The cost of a return flight from Dublin to San Francisco.

b) The name of a good hotel in San Francisco.

c) The nightly rate at this hotel.

- You can quote prices in the local currency i.e. USD (US dollars)
- You must enter the details found as follows into a word processor file:
  - → Flight Cost = £XXX or $XXX
  - → Airline(s) = AAAA
  - → Hotel Name = HHHH
  - → Nightly Hotel Cost = £NNNN or $NNNN
- You must also include the addresses (URLs) of the pages where you found the relevant information.
- Save the file as *travel* to your disk.

Assignment 13

a) Find a website that has free web page backgrounds available.

b) Download the background of your choice, saving it as *backgrnd*, to your disk.

Assignment 14

a) Find a web page that has a picture of a Claddagh ring

b) Save the picture only, under the file name *Claddagh*, to your disk.

Assignment 15

a) Find a midi sound file of the Irish National Anthem.

b) Save this file as *anthem* to your disk.

▦ Web Publishing

Assignment 16

1. Using a text editor, enter the *holiday1* and *holiday2* files as shown in the web publishing section. Save both files in htm format to your disk.
2. Load your browser program and view both files.
3. Using the text editor and appropriate HTML tags, create the following web page on the Italian city of Florence.

Florence — the capital of Tuscany

Florence, set in the heart of the Italian province of Tuscany, is a wonderful old city. The sights and smells of this city will live long in the memory of the traveller.

A browse in the antique shops on the Ponte Vecchio, a visit to the Sante Croche church and a pasta meal in one of the old Trattorias is a beautiful way to spend a day.

---

4. Save the web page as *Holiday3*, in htm format, to your disk.
5. Create a hyperlink from the word 'Florence' in the holiday2 file to the holiday3 file. Re-save the holiday2.htm file.
6. View the three-page website — holiday1, holiday2 and holiday3 — and ensure that hyperlinks are working properly.

In the following tasks, you may use a web editor program or a text editor and appropriate HTML tags.

Assignment 17

1. Produce the following web page:

> **Helen Keller (1880–1968)**
>
> Helen Adams Keller was born in the southern US State of Alabama. When 19 months old, she was stricken with an acute illness that left her *deaf* and *blind*. No method could be found to educate her until the age of seven, when she began her special education in reading and writing with Anne Sullivan. Helen quickly learned to read by the Braille system and to write by means of a specially constructed typewriter. In 1890 she learned to speak after only one month of study. Ten years later, she was able to enter Radcliffe College, from which she graduated with honours in 1904.
>
> Throughout her life Helen worked and raised funds for the *American Foundation for the Blind*, and she travelled and lectured in many countries, including England, France, Italy, Egypt, South Africa, Australia and Japan. Helen's life is the subject of a film, *The Unconquered* (1954).

2. Download a suitable background from the Internet.
3. Use the background for this web page.
4. Choose an appropriate text colour to contrast with the background.
5. Save the web page as *Keller.htm* to your disk.
6. Use your web browser to view the page.

Assignment 18

1. Produce the following web page:

The Titanic

One of the worst maritime disasters in history was the sinking of the *Titanic*. The British liner, on its maiden voyage from Southampton to New York City, struck an iceberg about 100 miles south of Newfoundland just before midnight on April 14, 1912. The mighty ship sank in less than three hours. Of the 2200 people aboard, over 1500 lost their lives.

Subsequent investigations found that:
- The ship had been steaming too fast in icy waters.
- Lifeboat space had been provided for less than half of the passengers and crew.
- The *Californian*, a ship close to the scene, had not come to the rescue because its radio operator was off duty and asleep.

In 1985, the wreck of the *Titanic* was located by a joint French-American expedition. They found that the ship had broken into two parts; these are lying over a half a mile apart on the ocean floor. A year later, an American research team explored the *Titanic* and took photographs of the wreck site.

2. Use appropriate background and text colours for the page.
3. Use a search engine to find a picture of the *Titanic* on the Web.
4. Save this picture to your disk.
5. Insert the picture, beneath the final paragraph, on the web page.
6. Use a search engine to find a midi sound file of the theme music — *My Heart Will Go On* — from the 1998 film *Titanic* on the Web.
7. Download the midi file to your disk.
8. Insert the midi file as background sound on your web page.
9. Save the file as *Titanic.htm*.
10. Use your web browser to view the page.

Assignment 19

Produce your own personal web page. You may include information on some or all of the following:

- Family and friends
- Interests and hobbies
- Achievements in the past
- Hopes and plans for the future.

Include a photograph of yourself on the web page.

Assignment 20

Produce a web page for a business or organisation in your local area. Include a logo, if one is available, on the web page.

Chapter 12
Integrated Assignments

▦Integrated packages

Microcomputer programs can be divided into three types according to the way in which they can be used in conjunction with other programs.

A 'standalone' program can be used for one application only — for example, word processing — and cannot incorporate files from other programs.

A 'non-standalone' program can also be used for only one application but has an 'import facility', which allows the user to include files from certain other applications: for example, to import a spreadsheet from a spreadsheet program into a word processor program in compiling a report.

An 'integrated package', on the other hand, contains a number of different applications, all within the same main program. Typical combinations include a word processor, a database, and a spreadsheet, and sometimes a communications program and a graphics program. These packages allow the user to import or export data files between applications; and — unlike the non-standalone programs — if data is changed in one application, the data change will be reflected in all related applications, so that, for example, a graph made up from spreadsheet data would change automatically to reflect recalculations on the spreadsheet.

Advantages of integrated packages

Integrated packages have a number of advantages over other types of program.

◪One program for most essential applications

An integrated package allows the user to produce all the usual business documents using only one program.

◪Easy to learn and use

Instead of having to become familiar with the conventions and commands of four or five different programs, the user has the advantage of a common method of entering commands; for example, the command to save data to a disk would be the same for all the applications in the program. Once the commands and conventions of the program are mastered the user will only have to learn the underlying concepts of the different applications to use the program.

◤Cost

There can be a large cost saving with an integrated package compared with the cost of purchasing four or five standalone application programs.

◤Disadvantages of integrated package use

Integrated packages also have a number of significant disadvantages, however.

◤Less advanced features

Applications in an integrated package contain less advanced features than standalone programs. Integrated packages never have enough memory to contain all the advanced features of standalone programs.

◤Limited space for data files

The packages occupy a large amount of RAM, limiting the size of data files that can be used.

Assignment

In this book so far, one particular application has been used to carry out each assignment: a database, spreadsheet or word processor program. There are, however, many situations where the computer user may use a combination of all three to carry out a particular task.

The following assignment is an example, where all three applications are used to generate a useful report. You may use standalone programs, non-standalone programs or an integrated package to complete the assignment.

Comfort Footwear PLC was established in Cork in 1979 by Peter Casey. The company manufactures a mid-range sports training shoe: the Marathon Marvel. Market research shows that it is bought mainly by people under the age of 25. The sales price is £25.50.

The company has its head office in Cork, but it supplies its product to retail shops throughout the country. The following market information is available to the marketing director of the company.

1. Competitors' sales

There are five competitor companies importing a similar type of sports shoe. Table 1 outlines the number of pairs of mid-range sports training shoes sold by Comfort Footwear and each of the competitor companies during the past year.

TABLE 1				
Company	Connacht	Leinster	Munster	Ulster
Comfort Footwear	4,400	32,200	21,200	3,500
Allweather Shoes	4,400	38,000	8,200	8,400
John Martin	8,700	46,000	17,800	18,600
Easyfeet Now	1,700	9,400	12,100	6,900
J.K. Williams and Son	5,500	24,000	4,800	44,500
Footwear Supplies	700	5,600	4,200	2,450

2. Market population structure

Table 2 shows a percentage breakdown of the population of Ireland by province and age group for 1995.

TABLE 2				
Age group	Connacht	Leinster	Munster	Ulster
Under 15	2	12	4	3
16 to 25	2	20	3	7
26 to 60	4	13	7	10
Over 60	1	6	3	

3. Company sales trends

Table 3 shows the total number of units sold by each of the six companies in four consecutive years.

TABLE 3				
Company	1992	1993	1994	1995
Comfort Footwear	33,000	34,550	47,800	61,300
Allweather Shoes	45,000	38,700	47,400	58,600
John Martin	30,000	80,500	62,000	49,700
Easyfeet Now	20,000	29,600	31,800	30,100
J.K. Williams and Son	45,000	92,500	83,600	78,800
Footwear Supplies	13,400	12,300	12,950	

4. The sales team

The company's sales team consists of the following twelve members:

Seán McCarthy has been with the company since its foundation. He is based in Cork. His sales for the past year were 8,300 units. The total distance covered by Seán to achieve these sales was 93,000 km, and he incurred £6,200 in expenses.

Ronan Byrne joined the company at the beginning of the year after completing his Sales and Management Diploma at the College of Commerce in Rathmines, Dublin. Ronan is based in the Carlow-Kilkenny region. The total distance covered in the course of his work was 45,000 km, and his expenses amounted to £3,400. For the past year Ronan's total sales amounted to 3,600 units.

Catherine Stephens joined the company in 1993 after gaining three years' experience in sales with John Martin Ltd. She is attached to the company's Dublin office, and her sales for the past year amounted to 7,500 units. Catherine's total travelling amounted to 35,000 km, and she had £2,400 of expenses.

Linda O'Connor has been with the company since 1990, and is responsible for sales in north Leinster. She was ill for three months during the year but still managed to sell 4,800 units. She had £3,900 of expenses and she travelled 29,000 km in the course of her work.

Brian Ward, a native of Castlebar, is the sole sales representative in Connacht. He joined the company in 1987 after three years as a member of the Garda Síochána. His sales for the past year were 4,400 units. During the year Brian travelled 75,000 km to achieve his sales, and had expenses of £35,100.

Claire Conroy joined the company in 1991 after returning from the United states, where she gained two years' valuable experience in selling and sales management with a large pharmaceutical company in San Francisco. She is attached to the company's Dublin office, and her sales for the past year were 6,800 units. She covered 50,000 km in making her sales, and her expenses were £5,800.

Liam Dolan, a native of Co. Kerry but now living in Waterford, has been with the company since 1993. His sales for the past year in Munster were 5,700 units. Liam travelled 145,000 km to make his sales, and he had expenses of £5,900.

Kevin Molloy is the sole sales representative in Ulster. He joined the company in 1986 after resigning his teaching position at a secondary school in Omagh. He was a successful member of the Leinster sales team, and this year he has been redeployed to the Ulster region. This is the first year that the company is selling the product in Ulster. Kevin's sales in Ulster amounted to 3,500 units for the past year. Kevin had expenses of £2,700, and he covered 38,000 km in the course of his work.

Peter McNicholl is another member of the Leinster sales team. He has been with the company since 1984, and his sales for the past year were 5,300 units. Peter had £4,100 expenses during the year and covered 50,000 km to achieve his sales.

Rachel Doyle, a native of Dublin but now living in Co. Tipperary, is responsible for sales in north Munster. She joined the company in 1990 on her return from Glasgow, where she worked for one year as a member of the sales team of a cosmetics company. She was attached to Comfort Footwear's Dublin office until 1994. Her sales amounted to 4,000 units for the past year. Rachel's travelling for the company during the year was 42,000 km, and her expenses amounted to £3,300.

Jim Ellis joined the company in 1992 after spending three years with Allweather Shoes as a member of their sales team. His sales in Munster for the past year were 3,200 units. Jim had to travel 37,000 km for the company during the year, and his expenses were £3,600.

Brenda Scott joined the company in 1989 as a secretary to the managing director, and in 1987 she joined the sales team, of which she is now an effective member. She operates in Kildare, Wicklow and Wexford, and her sales for the past year were 4,200 units. Brenda's travelling for the company during the year totalled 35,000 km, and she had expenses of £2,400.

◪Carry out the following tasks:

You are required to generate a report for the managing director of Comfort Footwear, using the following applications programs: database, spreadsheet, graphics (if available) and word processor.

Outputs from the database, spreadsheet and graphics programs are to be included in the appendices of the report (if you are using standalone programs). Comments and explanations marked with an asterisk (*) are to be produced using the word processor program, making reference to the appendices. (If you are using an integrated package, the word 'output' will refer to output files that will be integrated into the report. If you are using standalone programs, 'output' will refer to print-outs obtained.)

The report must be divided into two sections:

◪Section A: general sales report

In compiling the general sales report you must take the following steps:

1. Enter the data from Table 3 into a spreadsheet; you should then use this spreadsheet to show:
   (a) the overall sales in Ireland of mid-range sports training shoes for each year, and
   (b) the percentage market share for each company for each year, using the overall sales calculated above.
2. Produce two line graphs, one showing the number of units sold for each company and the other showing the percentage market share for each company for the four-year period. These graphs can be obtained by using the graphics capability of your spreadsheet program, or otherwise.
3. Include this spreadsheet and these graphs as Appendix A in the report.
*4. Comment on the percentage market share for each company and the changing trend in units sold.
5. Enter the data from Table 1 into a spreadsheet, showing total units sold in each province, and show the percentage market share in each province for each company during the past year.
6. Include this spreadsheet as Appendix B in the report
*7. With reference to Appendix B:
   (a) indicate the company with the highest market share in each province, and
   (b) show how the companies have spread their sales across the provinces, and which seems the most successful policy.

Section B: Sales team report

In compiling the sales team report you must take the following steps:

1. Enter the information on Comfort Footwear's sales team into a database file. Each record in the file should contain the following fields for each salesperson as given in the sales personnel data above:

   (a) name (surname first);

   (b) province;

   (c) sales (units) during 1995;

   (d) expenses incurred during 1995;

   (e) distance travelled for 1995;

   (f) number of years' sales experience (including experience with other companies) to the end of 1995.

2. Extract from this database file an output list of the sales personnel, sorted in descending order of the number of units sold by each salesperson in 1995, together with their respective province and number of years' experience.

3. Include this output list as Appendix C in the report.

*4. Comment on the relationship between unit sales achieved and the number of years' sales experience of the members of the sales team.

5. Extract from the database file an output list showing name, sales and province of all sales staff who did not reach the company's sales quota of 5,000 units during 1995, sorted into alphabetical order of name. Include this list as Appendix D in the report.

*6. In each case where the sales quota was not reached, comment on possible reasons, other than sales experience, with particular reference to population structure (Table 2) and competition in each region (Table 1 and Appendices A and B).

7. Extract from the database file an output list showing the name, distance travelled, sales and province of the entire sales team, sorted in descending order of distance travelled. Include this list as Appendix E in the report.

*8. After you have examined Appendix E, consider whether there is a stronger relationship between distance travelled and sales in certain provinces.

9. Extract from the database file an output list showing the name and distance travelled, in descending order of distance covered during 1995, of those sales personnel who are exempt from 'benefit in kind' tax (see question 12 below). Include this list as Appendix F in the report. *Explain that the sales personnel in Appendix F are exempt from benefit-in-kind tax, and explain why.

10. Produce an output list in alphabetical order of surname for each member of the sales team showing name, sales experience, distance travelled and unit sales (Appendix G).

11. Using the output list from Appendix G above, enter on a spreadsheet the name, sales experience, distance travelled and unit sales for each member of the sales team for 1995.

12. Sales representatives using company cars can be liable for 'benefit in kind' tax. The aim of

this tax is to discourage people from registering cars for business purposes and then using them largely for private purposes.

The tax is calculated as a percentage of the value of the car. Those who travel more than 40,234 km (25,000 miles) in one year are exempt from this tax. For those whose annual travelling was less than 40,234 km the tax is calculated as follows:

For each successive 1,609 km (1,000 miles) less than 40,234 an extra 2 per cent of the car's value is charged as tax; for example, a salesperson who has a car valued at £10,000 and a total travelling distance in one year of 37,000 km would pay £400 tax:

Rate of tax = ((40,234 — 37,000) ÷ 1,609) x 0.02 = 0.04

Amount of tax = 0.04 X 10,000 = £400

The following general formulae can be used:

Tax rate = ((40234 — distance)/1609)*0.02

Tax amount = tax rate*value of car

Set up a new column showing the 'benefit in kind' tax for each member of Comfort Footwear's sales team. (Assume each salesperson drives a car valued £12,500.)

13. Set up a SALES VALUE column in the spreadsheet, showing the total sales value for each salesperson by multiplying the number of units sold by the unit retail price.

14. Set up a VARIANCE column, to contain the difference in unit sales and the company's 1995 sales quota (5,000 units) for each of the sales personnel.

15. As an incentive to its sales team the company operates the following bonus scheme: those who sell more than the sales quota will receive 5 per cent of the unit price as a bonus for each unit sold over the quota. Set up a BONUS column to display the total bonus, if any, paid to each member of the sales team.

16. Each member of the sales team receives a basic salary of £10,000 and a further £500 for each year's sales experience. Set up a SALARY column to include these salary details.

17. Commission is calculated on the basis of 1 per cent of sales value. Set up a COMMISSION column to show the commission paid to each of the sales personnel.

18. The total income of each salesperson is calculated by adding the salary, commission and any bonus earned. Include an INCOME column to show the total income of each member of the sales team in the past year.

19. Include this spreadsheet as appendix H in the report.

*20. Outline in the report the method of calculating the bonus, salary and commission, and give a full explanation of 'benefit in kind' tax.